THE MEDIEVAL WORLD OF NATURE

A Book of Essays

Edited by
JOYCE E. SALISBURY

Routledge
Taylor & Francis Group

LONDON AND NEW YORK

First published in 1993 by Garland Publishing, Inc.

This edition first published in 2020
by Routledge
2 Park Square, Milton Park, Abingdon, Oxon OX14 4RN

and by Routledge
52 Vanderbilt Avenue, New York, NY 10017

Routledge is an imprint of the Taylor & Francis Group, an informa business

British Library Cataloguing in Publication Data
A catalogue record for this book is available from the British Library

ISBN: 978-0-367-22090-7 (Set)
ISBN: 978-0-429-27322-3 (Set) (ebk)
ISBN: 978-0-367-18791-0 (Volume 46) (hbk)
ISBN: 978-0-367-18792-7 (Volume 46) (pbk)
ISBN: 978-0-429-19825-0 (Volume 46) (ebk)

Publisher's Note
The publisher has gone to great lengths to ensure the quality of this reprint but points out that some imperfections in the original copies may be apparent.

Disclaimer
The publisher has made every effort to trace copyright holders and would welcome correspondence from those they have been unable to trace.

GARLAND MEDIEVAL CASEBOOKS
Joyce E. Salisbury and Christopher Kleinhenz
Series Editors

1. *Sagas of the Icelanders: A Book of Essays*
   edited by John Tucker

2. *Discovering New Worlds: Essays on Medieval
   Exploration and Imagination*
   edited by Scott D. Westrem

3. *Sex in the Middle Ages: A Book of Essays*
   edited by Joyce E. Salisbury

4. *Margery Kempe: A Book of Essays*
   edited by Sandra J. McEntire

5. *The Medieval World of Nature: A Book of Essays*
   edited by Joyce E. Salisbury

THE MEDIEVAL WORLD
OF NATURE
A Book of Essays

edited by
Joyce E. Salisbury

GARLAND PUBLISHING, INC. • NEW YORK & LONDON
1993

Library of Congress Cataloging-in-Publication Data

The medieval world of nature: a book of essays / edited by Joyce E.
Salisbury.
      p. cm. — (Garland reference library of the humanities ; v.
1550. Garland medieval casebooks ; v. 5)
     ISBN 0-8153-0752-7
     1. Literature, medieval—History and criticism. 2. Nature in
literature. 3. Allegory. 4. Man—Influence on nature—History.
I. Salisbury, Joyce E. II. Series: Garland reference library of the
humanities ; vol. 1550. III. Series: Garland reference library of the
humanities. Garland medieval casebooks ; vol. 5.
PN682.N3M43 1993
809'.9336'0902—dc20   92-27492

Printed on acid-free, 250-year-life paper
Manufactured in the United States of America

To Ashley Marie

CONTENTS

PEOPLE AND THE LAND

ACKNOWLEDGMENTS

For all collections such as this, the greatest thanks must go to the authors of the essays, who generously contributed the fruits of their research. It is always a pleasure to work with such contributors. In addition to working with authors, of course, editors must work with a publisher. I would like to thank Gary Kuris of Garland for making the task of an editor almost painless.

For all the benefits and convenience of the computer age, putting together volumes like this requires a good deal of patient computer work. I'd like to thank Eowyn Bates for her careful formatting work, which helped me get the articles in standardized form.

Finally, the dedication is for my niece, Ashley, in thanks for many good walks and talks and in anticipation of many more.

INTRODUCTION

This book is not about "nature" as abstract ideal so praised in the nineteenth century (and beyond). That sort of nature was supposed, at least, to inspire awe and, at most, to enhance one's spiritual feelings. Keith Thomas in *Man and the Natural World* (New York: Pantheon Books, 1983) brilliantly traced the origins of this view of nature to a changing sensibility that took place between 1500 and 1800. But change from what? That question has led me to compile this volume, which is intended to begin to explore medieval perceptions not of "nature" but of the natural world of which we have always been a part.

The main question underlying the essays in this volume is how did medieval people view the natural world around them? Not surprisingly, the answer is complex. Some people at some times viewed the natural world simply as the sum total of the plants and animals, all created to be of service to humans. Animals were food, labor, and sport. Any thought of saving wolves simply because they were wolves (and useless to humans) would have been incomprehensible. Medieval people took seriously the biblical charge of assuming dominion over animals. This dominion applied to plants as well as animals. Gardens represented "cultured" nature (a positive thing), to be distinguished from wild nature (a negative thing). The goal of a human's relation to the natural world was control.

However, this pragmatic approach to the natural world was not the whole medieval story. Plants and animals, individually and collectively, could serve humans as allegories of larger truths. Bestiaries, highly popular descriptions of animals through the late Middle Ages, listed the moral to be drawn from animals on the same level of importance as any scientific information included. A reader learns that a monkey has no tail, and that its "excessively disgraceful bottom" reminds one that the devil will perish in the end (T.H. White, *The Bestiary: A Book of Beasts* [New York: G.P. Putnam's Sons, 1960], 35). The twentieth-century mind reels at such associations. Yet, medieval thinkers moved rapidly and comfortably from the practical to the allegoric and back again. Thus, the world of nature was a means of exploring the truths hidden within the created world.

The essays in this volume, then, begin to look at the medieval world of nature. In some ways, most of the articles take a medieval approach that we can see in the bestiary. They look at one element of nature but yield much larger truths that reveal the medieval mind. I have organized the articles thematically to highlight some of the differing ways people interacted with nature. Sometimes people stood a bit apart to look at the animals that shared their world. Sometimes people interacted so closely with animals that they began to wonder what it was that set human apart from animal. Sometimes people looked closely at the land itself, which always formed the foundation of their world.

Animals

Of course, many things inhabit the medieval world of nature, and a large and diverse volume could be compiled discussing many of these various inhabitants. Here I have limited myself to three examples drawn from land, sea, and air. From these studies, we can learn much, not only about the animals but also about the humans who were thinking about them.

The volume begins with Nona Flores's essay, "The Mirror of Nature Distorted: The Medieval Artist's Dilemma in Depicting Animals," which focuses mainly on elephants. Flores shows that in the Middle Ages people's views of animals were dominated by two different attitudes. Animals were portrayed allegorically or scientifically, and while both attitudes prevailed throughout the Middle Ages, over time one can see a gradual shift in dominance from the former to the latter. Illustrating her article with portrayals of elephants in art, Flores shows us this shift in ideas, demonstrating that "The elephant's knees may be considered a kind of dividing point between the medieval and modern attitudes toward nature." This article highlights one of the questions about the natural world that shaped the medieval imagination. Were animals simply there to reveal higher truths of allegory, or were they valuable in themselves?

As Flores can demonstrate a move to modernity in the treatment of elephants' knees, Robin Oggins in "Falconry and Medieval Views of

Nature" also reveals a great deal about medieval views of nature by looking at one animal. Oggins shows how studies of the sport of falconry can serve as a revealing indicator of the diverse views of nature. Beyond the two large categories of allegory and science that Flores outlined, Oggins shows that in the Middle Ages (as now) nature could also represent something to control, a source of recreation, a source of beauty, as well as something to study scientifically. Medieval tracts on falconry depict all these approaches to the natural world.

Richard Hoffmann closes this look at a few individual animals with his detailed "Protohistory of Pike." Like Flores, Hoffmann demonstrates a shift in people's treatment of pike from allegoric to scientific. Early medieval tracts focused on the mythic and allegoric significance of a fish that seemed to have the implements of Christ's passion marked on its head. Some of the late medieval scientific works begin to look at the fish for other purposes. However, Hoffmann shows that when it comes to the practical desire for a fish dinner, allegory and theory take a backseat. In practical manuals on pisciculture, medieval approaches to nature included highly sophisticated applications that showed medieval abilities of observation that were not fully expressed in the "scientific" works. Hoffmann's essay reveals much about medieval notions about the natural world, and at the same time it offers more detailed information than I would have thought possible about one kind of fish.

This section on animals closes with a consideration of the use of animals in a purely literary work. In her essay on animal images in Gottfried's *Tristan*, Margaret Schleissner looks at references to falcons, boars, dogs, and stags. She shows that the author's use of these animals was laden with symbolism, and the metaphoric associations drawn from several sources (for example, Germanic and Christian) are sometimes competing. Gottfried accepts and uses these conflicting symbols to forward his narrative and enrich his tale. Schleissner shows that even when medieval writers approach animals at the literary and allegorical level, that level is complex indeed.

Animals and People

In all the previous essays, people were of course present. Their views of the natural world shaped their views of animals of the land, air, and sea. This section looks more closely, and self-consciously, at a particularly medieval puzzle of the relationship between humans and animals. Even in the Middle Ages, when at least churchmen took pride in humans' privileged position of distinction from and superiority to animals, people realized the obvious fact that people and their animals interacted. These interactions sometimes led to reflections on what actually was the difference between humans and animals.

Maureen Tilley, in "Martyrs, Monks, Insects, and Animals," studies the interactions between humans and animals in extraordinary circumstances. Extraordinary humans (holy people) interacted with remarkable animals that had been influenced by holiness into acting not like animals at all. Like Schleissner, Tilley shows that the Christian West drew from several traditions as it tried to make sense of the relative place of humans and animals within the natural world. These traditions included Greco-Roman, Judaic, Stoic, and Platonic ideas, and Tilley shows how the miraculous interactions were influenced by these intellectual traditions. Tilley further suggests that our modern disagreements about how humans and animals ought to interact have a long history.

Peter Sobol in his essay "The Shadow of Reason" looks more closely at the distinctions between humans and animals. He considers the question of what is "animal" behavior by looking at the thirteenth-century philosophical tracts that contrasted human and animal intelligence. The greatest medieval intellects thought about the way humans and animals think and respond while they tried to "uphold rigid distinctions between mental powers of animals and humans," and they found that preserving such distinctions was very difficult to do. Sobol explains the subtle reasoning of Avicenna, Albertus Magnus, Roger Bacon, Thomas Aquinas, and others in a way that makes their arguments clear, and reveals the profound medieval question of what was animal, and what was human.

Veronica Fraser's article, "The Goddess Natura in the Occitan Lyric," gives the question of what is human and what is animal a different look. Fraser traces the continuation through the Middle Ages of classical characteristics of the goddess Nature. The goddess's traditional functions were "healing, abundance, fertility and renewal, harmony and unity." Fraser shows that all these characteristics traditionally ascribed to nature were attributed to human women in the medieval vernacular lyrics of southern France. Thus, by their association with nature, women are more associated with the animal world, perhaps leaving men as definitively human.

The lines between humans and animals blur completely in David Sprunger's article "Wild Folk and Lunatics in Medieval Romance." Sprunger discusses the medieval tradition of wild folk, beings that existed along the border of human and animal worlds. In these wild folk we can glimpse medieval perceptions of humanity and bestiality. Sprunger shows us (in both text and illustrations) that among the things that separate the species from humans are body hair, posture, diet, language, and fingers with broad nails. His analysis goes futher to show that in medieval romances, wild folk had a dual potential. By descending to the depths of their animal nature, aspiring heroes could rise to greater heights than the average human. By exploring the borders of humanity, we can see that the relationship between humans and animals was complex indeed.

People and the Land

Of course, the natural world was not all (or even predominately) animal. The overwhelming relationship people had with nature was with the land itself and the plants that people associated so intimately with the land.

From the earliest medieval period, the main relationship between people and the natural world was one of ownership. Animals, plants, and the land itself belonged to humans. John Hilary Martin in "The Land, Who Owns It?" studies the concept of land ownership as it appeared in religious and, particularly, scholastic writings. He observes that while Thomas Aquinas said that possession was among the vices that could get in the way of the practice of justice, possession was nevertheless central to people's relationship with nature.

Perhaps the most visible expression of land as property may be seen in gardens. These cultivated corners of the world of nature were self-consciously created to contrast with the wild nature that surrounded them. Laura L. Howes, in "Cultured Nature in Chaucer's Early Dream-Poems," shows that the gardens that appear in Chaucer's poems were very real; he described actual gardens that served as tranquil retreats for aristocrats. However, just as we have seen animals serving both actual and allegoric functions, Chaucer's gardens do, too. Howes demonstrates that the narrative structure of the poems grows organically from the gardens they feature.

Howes showed us that although Chaucer's gardens were full of symbolic meaning, the descriptions of them were nevertheless full of the details that brought such corners of cultivated nature alive. Brenda Deen Schildgen, in "Dante's Utopian Landscape: The Garden of God," reveals a different medieval use of gardens. Schildgen shows that Dante's gardens are not often described concretely; they are "metaphorical topography." In this treatment of the natural world, allegory takes over. Gardens for Dante were Church, Empire, Paradise, and Utopia, all outside time and history. There is no leisure and lovemaking in these groves. Further, Schildgen traces the medieval intellectual traditions for such a heavily allegoric treatment of gardens, and shows that Dante was building upon images that had been available throughout the medieval world.

This section, and the volume, concludes with Karen Jolly's essay "Father God and Mother Earth." In this article, we move to the most abstract questions in the relationship between humans and the natural world in which they live and of which they are a part. Jolly argues that prior to the twelfth century people had a "mystical world view" in which everything was linked through God, and that modern perceptions of nature derive from the post–twelfth-century view that isolated nature as a "rationally understood phenomenon." Jolly looks at the older view in which elaborate fertility charms make total sense to a Christian world.

I close with Professor Jolly's article because perhaps even more obviously than the others, it points to modern concerns with human beings' place in the natural world and contributes to ongoing discussions of how our perceptions shape our stewardship of the world. In fact, many of the issues raised in all these articles are still echoed today. Animal rights' movements, anti–fur-wearing activists, environmentalists, and many others insist that we reconsider our relationship with the natural world. I hope these essays contribute not only a fuller understanding of medieval perspectives, but also a different perspective on modern concerns.

Animals

THE MIRROR OF NATURE DISTORTED: THE MEDIEVAL ARTIST'S DILEMMA IN DEPICTING ANIMALS

Nona C. Flores

How the Middle Ages viewed nature is one of the mysteries of cultural history, for during this period the influence of authority often outweighed the importance of direct observation. Because such creatures as the unicorn and the siren had been discussed by the Church Fathers and in works like the *Physiologus* and the bestiary, these creatures commanded as much physical reality for the medieval audience as the dog or the horse. Under such circumstances, strange pictures of unfamiliar (or even nonexistent) animals were inevitable. Hence we still enjoy medieval representations of such beasts as the fabulous unicorn and the equally mythical griffin, not to mention wonderfully untrue-to-life pictures of what were to western Europe exotic animals such as lions, elephants, and crocodiles. But what of odd depictions of creatures perfectly familiar to the artist? Modern scholars have waxed witty at blue squirrels and pigs with forefeet folded in prayer. Yet medieval artists were capable of observing nature and depicting it with photographic realism. One thinks of the birds, insects, and flowers in the borders of certain fifteenth-century northern European books of hours. In the *Hastings Hours*, for example, it appears that two butterflies have alighted on the flowers depicted on the wide gold border of the Annunciation miniature, deceived by the very lifelike blooms. This illusion of realism is furthered by the fact that the artist has so positioned the insects to violate the boundary of the page as defined by the border, in order to emphasize their independence from the framed design (Figure 1).

3

Figure 1. The Annunciation. Hastings Hours (Flanders, ca. 1480), London, British Library, Additional MS. 54782, folio 73v (photo: by permission of the British Library).

In examining depictions of animals during the Middle Ages, it becomes apparent that an artist's ability to reproduce nature is not necessarily the overriding consideration in his creation of a work of art. How artists see animals and how that vision is tempered by contemporary intellectual attitudes and interests is the subject of this essay. Two principal attitudes toward animals existed during the Middle Ages: one that we will call allegorical, and the other scientific. Writers using the allegorical treatment—which is best seen in the medieval handbooks we call the *Physiologus* and the bestiary—were primarily interested in showing that the real value in actual or purported animal behavior was to point a spiritual moral to the reader. The actual physical animal was of little or no importance to these writers. Scientific writers, on the other hand, focused on the physical animal itself, and were often desirous of actually seeing individual animals and reporting their impressions of their anatomy and behavior. These two attitudes exist simultaneously, although we will find a gradual chronological shift in dominance from the allegorical toward the scientific.

In studying the bestiaries, medievalists have generally been preoccupied with tracing their sources in the Bible, in the Fathers, in classical writers such as Pliny, and so on, or with showing how the text—particularly the allegorical interpretations of animal traits and behavior—has influenced other literary or artistic works. Little interest has been devoted to the natural history described in the text or reflected in the illustrations, since it is generally felt that much of it is imaginary and thus not valuable to the interpretation. Florence McCulloch, for example, writes: "One would never study the illustrations in French bestiaries, any more than in the Latin versions, for evidence of the artist's awareness of the world of nature."[1] Yet the zoologist Wilma George has found that the bestiary is fairly accurate in describing and illustrating the natural history of animals from both the Near East and western Europe. She concludes that "the mockery that has been made of the bestiary illustrations is the result of our ignorance, not [that of medieval artists]."[2] Brunsdon Yapp has similarly found that some of the bestiary artists knew and observed birds carefully and almost certainly drew them from life or at least from recently dead bodies. His assessment of others' efforts at evaluating these illustrations is quite blunt: "Art historians have naturally concentrated their attention on the more expensive productions, and say that the pictures are 'fine' because they are brightly colored or gilded, when from the point of view of a zoologist they are useless."[3]

The two extremes of animal depiction—the fabulous beast created by an artist's imaginative rendering of a bestiary description versus the photographic exactness of the *Horae* butterfly—reflect two ways people looked at nature in the Middle Ages. These, as we have said, can be conveniently if facilely referred to as the allegorical and the scientific, respectively. The principal purpose of the allegorical method derived from the Pauline doctrine expressed in Romans 1:20: "For the things of [God] are clearly seen from the creation of the world, even His eternal power and Godhead are understood by the things that are made." The second half of Origen's *Commentary on the Song of Songs* also examines this anagogical interpretation of nature. He explains how "the book of nature" corresponds to divine archetypes: "And perhaps just as God made man in his own image and likeness, so also did he make the remaining creatures after certain other heavenly images as a likeness. And perhaps every single thing on earth has something of an image and likeness in heavenly things."[4] Hence the *Physiologus* and the bestiaries interpreted the creatures of the natural world on moral and metaphysical levels. For example, the pelican, an animal symbol much used by Christian writers, was thought to nourish its young from its own blood, and thus was understood as symbolic of Christ giving life to mankind through His blood. As Lynn White, Jr. points out, "In such a world there was no thought of hiding behind a clump of reeds actually to observe the habits of a pelican. There would have been no point in it. Once one had grasped the spiritual meaning of the pelican, one lost interest in individual pelicans."[5] Inevitably such a view of the world produced art that distorted natural forms to better emphasize their supernatural meaning.

How then does this intellectual attitude influence an artist's portrayal of nature? Let us consider an animal that must certainly have been well known to many medieval artists: the lamb. In Figure 2, which comes from a missal completed in southeastern Italy during the first half of the eleventh century, the lamb appears as The Lamb of God, a symbol of Christ, at the beginning of the section of the mass in which the eucharistic bread and wine are consecrated. This lamb looks very much like a stylized greyhound with greatly exaggerated clawed feet, and it supports on its head a cross that is akin to the banner with a cross, or patibulum, carried by the Lamb of God in other represen-

Figure 2. The Lamb of God atop the letter *T*. Missal, Baltimore, Walters Art Gallery, MS. W. 6, folio 68 (photo: Walters Art Gallery).

tations. Its unrealistic portrayal as an animal is immaterial, because along with the tau-cross–shaped *T* of "Te igitur," the invocation to God, the lamb's purpose is to serve as a visual representation of Christ's sacrifice, which is celebrated in the portion of the mass that follows.

The scientific view, on the other hand, can be said to derive from Aristotle's studies of animals—the *History of Animals, Parts of Animals,* and *Generation of Animals*—though his works were not available in the Middle Ages until Michael Scot's translations from Arabic texts in the early thirteenth century. In the scientific view— perhaps more accurately described as the anatomical or veterinary view of nature—the animal is examined for its own sake, not used to point a moral or to illustrate some aspect of Christian dogma. This view of nature is characterized by a reliance on accurate first-hand observation, hands-on research, an ability to draw reasonable conclusions from data, and use of reliable, experienced witnesses. This is the methodology we associate with the modern naturalist. Probably the medieval work that best exemplifies the scientific tradition is the Emperor Frederick II's *De Arte Venandi cum Avibus,* written shortly before 1250 and often regarded as the first zoological treatise written in the critical spirit of modern science.[6] Like Aristotle before him and the modern zoologists who were to follow, the emperor sought to group and classify the birds used for hunting and those that were their prey, as well as describe their anatomical characteristics, habits, methods of training, and diseases, all in considerable and orderly detail. "Our purpose," says Frederick, "is to present the facts as we find them,"[7] and his observations and experiments led him to dismiss many of the conclusions in his written sources, particularly Aristotle, whose works he knew through the translations of Michael Scot. "In his work, the *Liber Animalium,*" writes the emperor, "we find many quotations from authors whose statements he did not verify, and who in their turn were not speaking from experience. Entire conviction of the truth never follows mere hearsay."[8]

Frederick's preoccupation with first-hand observation is seen, for example, in his discussion of the barnacle goose, which was thought to be generated spontaneously from dead trees or rotting wood. Gerald of Wales first reported on "barnacles" around 1188 in his *History and Topography of Ireland* as birds "which nature, acting against her own laws, produces in a wonderful way."[9] He described them as appearing first as excrescences on water-logged treetrunks. These developed into small birds which hung from the trunk by their beaks while their developing bodies were enclosed in mussel-shaped shells. Gerald's emphasis is on the fact that these birds "are not born of flesh"—no eggs are laid as a result of mating, no nests are built, no breeding of any kind takes place. He then uses this spontaneous generation of barnacle geese to point a moral, much in the manner of the *Physiologus* or bestiary: he rebukes the Jews for denying the possibility of Christ's immaculate conception, when nature "daily produces and brings forth new creatures without the cooperation of any male or female for our instruction and in confirmation of the Faith." Significantly, no illustration by Gerald accompanies this text (many of the other natural history stories in the work are accompanied by the author's sketches), although Gerald swears he saw many thousands of these birds "many times with my own eyes."[10]

How different is the thrust of the eyewitness examination of the barnacle goose in the scientific manner as reported by the Emperor Frederick II:

> We have made prolonged research into the origin and truth of this legend and even sent special envoys to the North with orders to bring back specimens for our investigation. When we examined them we did observe shell-like formations clinging to the rotten wood, but these bore no resemblance to any avian body. We therefore doubt the truth of this legend in the absence of corroborating evidence. In our opinion this superstition arose from the fact that barnacle geese breed in such remote latitutes that men, in ignorance of their real nesting places, invented this explanation.[11]

In addition to observation and ratiocination, the emperor performed experiments to test his conclusions. He determined, for example, that vultures are not attracted to carrion by its scent, as some writers maintained, but by what they see. As he explains, "We have ourselves many times experimented and observed that an assemblage of seeled vultures [i.e., birds whose eyelids have been sewn shut], whose noses are not stopped up, did not scent the meat cast before them."[12] Fredrick's son, King Manfred, followed the methods of his father's scientific discourse when emending the text of *De Art Venandi cum Avibus*. He explains in the following way why waterfowl are ill adapted to walking: since their survival depends on their swimming ability,

such birds have short, crooked tibiae rather than long legs, which allow
them greater force to propel themselves in the water. It is similar, he
says, to the case of galley rowers who do not immerse their oars deeply
in the water when they wish to make speed, but dip them on the
surface. "Nature," he concludes, "has therefore provided this class of
aquatic birds with short legs to facilitate swimming; but since such
limbs render walking more difficult, as one sees in the case of dwarfs, it
follows that these waterfowl are poor pedestrians."[13] The course of his
reasoning is especially interesting in this case, since it employs
comparative anatomy (dwarves' legs) and the mechanics of motion (the
galley rowers) in order to support his conclusions.

By the mid-thirteenth century, artists were also looking more
critically at nature and using it more often as a model for their
creations. The zoological accuracy of bird illustrations in the bestiaries
has already been mentioned.[14] Gothic floral sculpture mirrors the
accuracy of contemporary botanical manuscript illustrations,[15] while a
comparison of illustrations in scholarly medical works of the late
Middle Ages and Renaissance with contemporary statues and paintings
shows that the artists were well ahead of scientists in the acuity with
which they observed human anatomy.[16] Indeed, Erwin Panofsky
suggests that "the rise of those particular branches of natural science
which may be called observational or descriptive—zoology, botany,
paleontology, several aspects of physics and, first and foremost,
anatomy—was . . . directly predicated upon the rise of the represen-
tational techniques."[17]

The new aesthetic principle is well summarized in the words of
St. Thomas Aquinas: "Art is the imitation of nature. Works of art are
successful to the extent that they achieve a likeness of nature."[18] In a
late fourteenth-century handbook for artists, the Tuscan painter
Cennino di Drea Cennini recommends that beginners make use of only
the very best masters to copy, but beyond that to draw from nature:
"Mind you, the most perfect steersman that you can have, and the best
helm, lie in the trimphant gateway of copying from nature. And this
outdoes all other models."[19]

However, the passion for drawing from nature is tempered by the
influence of preexisting artistic conceptions. A much studied case in
point are the drawings of lions in the *Sketchbook* of Villard de
Honnecourt, which he compiled over a period of years during the first
half of the thirteenth century. Of the several animal drawings included

in the collection, only those of the lion (shown facing the viewer and in profile with its trainer) are identified as being drawn from the life ("sacies bien qu'il fu contrefait al vif"), remarkable in that they are both clearly based on some artistic model. Various sources have been suggested although no one prototype has been identified. Certainly Villard's three-toed front-facing lion (Figure 3) has a rather human face and undeniably human teeth, as well as a somewhat flabby and overly wide chest. William Hecksher gives Villard the award for "intended realism," explaining that the caption merely indicates that the artist did use a living model.[20] (Villard may have seen lions and their trainers in one of the menageries of the Emperor Frederick II.)[21] But clearly the image of that living model was conditioned by, and even subordinated to, some authoritative and preexisting version of what a lion ought to look like. According to Julius Schlosser, "without doubt Villard did not intend to dissemble when quite clearly he did not draw from nature, for to him 'nature' meant something different from what it means to us; for a man of the Middle Ages it was impossible to consider as meaningful anything but the idea, the concept behind the appearance of things. The natural form was like soft wax which had to yield to the artistic intention."[22] Depictions of the lion are especially open to the influence of established authority (textual and pictorial) because of the animal's preeminence as a symbol in both religious and heraldic iconography.

The previous examples served to define and differentiate the allegorical and scientific attitudes toward animals, and to provide examples of how particular artists have reflected these influences in their portrayal of nature. The remainder of this essay will focus on the literary and artistic treatment of a single animal throughout the Middle Ages. This will allow us to look at some of the major texts, and will also illustrate the gradual shift in dominance from the allegorical toward the scientific interest in animals. I have chosen the elephant because it is a real animal but one that was rarely seen in western Europe during the Middle Ages.[23] Thus, artists were largely dependent on descriptions from literary sources that we will therefore examine in some detail.

The elephant has been used in Christian allegory from a very early period. Practically every aspect of its behavior has been moralized

Figure 3. Lion and porcupine. Villard de Honnecourt, *Sketchbook*,
Paris, Bibliothèque Nationale, MS. fr. 19093, folio 24v
(photo: Giraudon/Art Resource, New York).

by exegetes, including as bizarre an activity as the elephant's talents at tightrope dancing, reported by classical writers such as Pliny.[24] The early Christian Fathers (notably Basil, Ambrose, and Eustathius) wrote at length on the elephant in their commentaries on the Hexaemeron. Like classical writers of natural history, these Christian authors regarded animals in terms of their service to man, but they also added a moral aspect to this relationship. Comparison is made between animal and human characteristics in order to provide exempla urging men to recognize God and repent of their sins. There is, however, little of the elaborate allegorization of animal lore characteristic of the *Physiologus* or bestiaries. As Basil explains:

> I know the laws of allegory, though less from my own work than from the work of others. There are those who do not concede the ordinary sense of the Scriptures. They will not call water "water" but something else. They see in a plant or fish what their fancy wishes. They change the nature of reptiles and wild beasts to fit their allegories, like those who explain . . . dreams to suit their own ends. When I hear the word "grass," I understand that grass is meant. Plant, fish, wild beast, domestic animal, I take all in the literal sense.[25]

For these writers, the elephant illustrated God's graciousness to man. As Ambrose explains, "God ordained the elephant, so vast in size, to be subject to man . . . showing clearly by this that all things have been subjected to us, because we have been made in the likeness of God and may observe His incalculable wisdom in the biggest of animals."[26]

It is the *Physiologus*, or *The Naturalist*, which serves as the major source for the medieval allegorization of elephant lore. (The *Physiologus*, in fact, is ultimately responsible for many familiar symbols of Christianity, including the pelican, the phoenix, the unicorn, the lion, and the whale.) The *Physiologus*, às Michael Curley has pointed out, was never meant to be read as a work of natural history; its author, Physiologus, was not simply "the naturalist," but one who interpreted the natural world in terms of its divine significances.[27] This Greek text, originating in Alexandria perhaps as early as the second century A.D., is a compilation of the supposed characteristics of some forty animals, birds, and mystic stones interpreted in terms of Christian dogma. The *Physiologus* interpreted the world in a moral and metaphysical sense in order to introduce its readers to the Christian mysteries. Its author drew on the compilations and descriptions of classical naturalists such as Aristotle, Pliny, Oppian, Aelian, and Solinus and on folklore and oral tradition, rather than on direct observation of living creatures, and reshaped his materials to conform with preconceived allegories related to specific biblical texts. Although these allegories were not accepted as canonical by later writers, its popularity as a handbook persisted. The text was widely disseminated in many forms as attested by its translation into such diverse vernaculars as Syriac, Ethiopian, Russian, Flemish, Provençal, Old English, and Icelandic. "Perhaps no book except the Bible," according to E.P. Evans, "has ever been so widely distributed among so many people and for so many centuries as the *Physiologus.*"[28] In Michael Curley's words, the *Physiologus* ranks among the "books which have made a difference in the way we think."[29] Even today, when we refer to "licking someone into shape" or something "rising like a phoenix from the ashes," we refer to allegories that originated in the *Physiologus.*

A chapter on the elephant appears in some form in all major versions of the text.[30] From the Latin *Physiologus* we learn that the elephant is naturally chaste and has no innate desire to copulate. When he and his mate wish to have children, the female seduces the male into joining with her to eat the root of the mandrake tree which grows near Paradise. This stimulates them to mate, and from this coupling the female conceives instantly. She gives birth to the calf while standing in a lake; the male elephant guards her and the calf from the shore, and is prepared to trample any serpents that may try to steal the calf, for the two animals are natural enemies.

In addition, we learn that the elephant has no knee joints, and therefore is unable to get up if it falls down. Thus it must sleep standing up and is accustomed to do so by resting its weight against a large tree. Hunters who want to capture an elephant saw partially through the trunk of these trees, which then collapse and break when an elephant leans against them. The downed and helpless beast trumpets in his distress, and a great elephant answers his call for help but cannot raise the fallen animal, nor can a group of twelve additional elephants; but a single tiny elephant appears that puts his trunk beneath the fallen animals and lifts him up.

What does this all signify for readers of the *Physiologus*? In the moralization we learn that the elephant couple represent Adam and Eve who lived in chaste innocence until they ate the fruit of the forbidden tree and grew great with evil. Eve conceived and bore Cain. Sinful man is overthrown by the dragon, which makes them strangers to God, and neither the Old Law—the single great elephant—nor the twelve prophets can save him. Only the single tiny elephant, Christ, who humbled Himself by taking on mortal flesh, can raise man up.

How did artists interpret this material? Illustrations were an important part of these manuscripts, giving graphic emphasis to key points of the text. Since the text was divided into two parts—a natural history and a moralization—the artist could choose which half he wished to picture. In the earliest surviving illustrated Latin *Physiologus*, a ninth-century Carolingian manuscript now in the Municiple Library in Bern, the illustration for this chapter shows that the artist has decided to treat the subject as natural history.[31] The elephant is easily recognized as such, despite its small ear and equine hooves, because of its trunk, tusks, and general shape. It hooks its trunk around a tall branched stalk, presumably the mandrake, and seems to keep its large roguish eye fixed warily on the serpent, which twines in the grass near its feet. A trickle of water winds along the bottom of the picture, suggesting the baby elephant's water-nativity, which is shown on the reverse of the folio. The artist has arranged the elements from the first part of the *Physiologus* chapter in a veristic landscape, so that even without reading the text, someone browsing through the text would recognize this as a picture of animal life in a foreign land.[32]

By the tenth century, however, artists were increasingly bound by the allegorical interpretation of the text and tended to abandon such naturalistic depictions. A crude sketch was acceptable as long as it emphasized those animal characteristics that the text associated with the necessary morally didactic meaning.[33] Sometimes the artist's rendition is recognizable as an elephant only by virtue of what one imagines to be a trunk, tusks, and a castle attached to a creature placed in the correct allegorical context. Thus, this same scene is rendered much differently in a mid-thirteenth-century manuscript from northern France of the Latin version of the *Physiologus* known as the *Dicta Chrysostomi* (Figure 4). Four elephants are shown with a serpent to the left and a mandrake root to the right. The elephants have a somewhat bovine shape, though they have rounded ears. The male elephants bear tusks, and this depiction reflects the common medieval error of showing the tusks thrusting upwards from the lower jaw, influenced possibly by the defensive positioning of the unicorn's horn. Trunks are long, pipelike extensions of the nose. Both serpent and mandrake are highly stylized—the one shown with wings, feet, and a canine head and the other represented in human form. Without familiarity with the text, however, the relationship of these elements as arranged within their frame is meaningless. The viewer needs to know the story in order to recognize that the male elephant confronts the serpent at the left, thus protecting the female and the calf at the right, and that the tusked elephant next to the mandrake root represents another part of the story. The picture's importance lies entirely in its value as a shorthand reminder of the Christian moralization of the story.

Along with the *Physiologus*, the bestiary or "Book of Beasts" served as the principal source of animal lore during the Middle Ages.[34] "Bestiary" was the generic title for a popular nature book that developed around the end of the twelfth century and flourished through the fourteenth century; some of the finest extant versions are Latin manuscripts produced in England, many of them beautifully illustrated. Like the *Physiologus*, the bestiary was a compilation of accumulated folklore, legend, pseudoscience, and rudimentary scientific observation of an assortment of real and imaginary animals. The bestiary included the *Physiologus*, but was greatly expanded by the incorporation of many additional sources, the original 40 chapters increasing to as many as 150 in some versions. These chapters were often divided into neat zoological categories: mammals, fish, birds, and serpents. There was less emphasis on allegory, and many animals that had not originally appeared in the *Physiologus* were given no moral interpretation at all.

The bestiary provides readers with new information about the elephant especially in the chapter on *draco*, in which the enmity between the elephant and dragon is discussed.[35] The dragon is venomless and kills by winding itself around other animals. Even the elephant is not safe despite its great size, for the dragon lies in wait near paths frequented by elephants. It lassoes the elephant's legs with its tail and suffocates it by plugging the elephant's trunk with its head. The dragon—clearly originating from a huge python or boa constrictor—signifies the Devil, whose strength is not in his teeth but in his tail because he beguiles man through deceit. The Devil lies hidden around the paths men follow, encumbering their way to heaven by the knots of their sins, so that he strangles them to death. Some medieval artists took great delight in portraying these knots, as can be seen in an early

Figure 4. Elephants, mandrake, and serpent. *Dicta Chrysostomi*, London, British Library, Sloane MS. 278, folio 48v (photo: by permission of the British Library).

thirteenth-century bestiary illustration (Figure 5). Here the elephant—distinguished as such by its cobralike trunk and upthrust tusks—looks somewhat puzzled by the coils of serpentine tail in which it finds itself enmeshed. The anatomically incorrect rounded feet, cow's tail, and small draped ears are all characteristic of medieval elephant representations, and none of these features are described in the text of the *Physiologus* or the bestiary. The dragon is stylized as a raptorial bird with a long serpentine tail.

If we again turn to the miniatures of the *Dicta Chrysostomi* manuscript in the Sloan collection, we see a further simplification and distortion of natural forms in order to emphasize their supernatural meaning (Figure 6). Here the elephant (rather chihuahua-like except for its awkwardly bent pipelike trunk and cloven feet) is greatly dwarfed by the dragon, possibly because *draco* rather then *elephas* is the subject of the chapter, or possibly to emphasize man's helplessness before Satan. The serpent has an almost human face, and its ears are pointed as though the figure is designed to link it pictorially with popular representations of the devil. However, the actual physical entrapment of the elephant by the dragon is only suggested by the tip of the serpent's tail, which lies loosely around one of the elephant's legs. Again, the reader must be familiar with the moralization of the text in order to understand the relationship between the elephant and the serpent.

Eventually the ending of the elephant-dragon battle was modified so that the dying elephant crushes the serpent to death as it falls. Accordingly, Hugh of Folieto explains that the dragon that lies in wait for a chaste animal like the elephant is the Devil: "thus he persecuted to the death Christ the guardian of chastity being born of a chaste virgin; but he was overcome, having been crushed by Him and His death."[36]

The elephant that perishes in its triumph over the serpent derives from a well-known *topos* of classical antiquity. In addition to using this theme in the bestiary, Christianity found and moralized a closely parallel story of mutually inflicted death in the first Book of Maccabees, the only place in the Bible in which the elephant is specifically mentioned.[37] King Antiochus goes to battle against the rebellious Jews with a squadron of war elephants bearing on their backs castles full of soldiers. The warrior hero Eleazar boldly attacks the elephant wearing royal armor, going underneath to its unprotected belly

Figure 5. Elephant and dragon. Bestiary, London, British Library, Royal MS. 12 C xix, folio 62 (photo: by permission of the British Library).

Figure 6. Elephant and dragon. *Dicta Chrysostomi*, London, British Library, Sloane MS. 278, folio 57 (photo: by permission of the British Library).

and thrusting at it from below. But as the elephant dies, it also crushes Eleazar to death. Thus, says the author, Eleazar gave his life to save his people and win eternal renown for himself. This story was widely circulated by its inclusion in the popular *Speculum Humanae Salvationis*, where it was used as a prefiguration of Christ's crucifixion. In the Middle English version of the text, the moralization is expressed in this way:

> The stronge assaylled the stronge and both felle in the stede,
> And thus Eleazare and the beest in this wise ware both dede.
> Thus stronge Crist the stronge deth assailled chyvalerously,
> And with his deth slewe oures, blissid be he eendelesly.[38]

> [Strength fought against strength, and both fell in this place, and thus Eleazar and the beast both died in this way. Thus strong Christ fought strong death chivalrously, and with His death slew ours, blessed be He forever.]

The fifteenth-century wall painting illustrating this battle (from the cathedral cloisters at Bressanone, Italy) shows a relatively large-scale Eleazar lying beneath a relatively small-scale elephant, which bears an elaborate castle full of armored men on its back (Figure 7). The artist has emphasized Eleazar by his size, since he is not only the hero in the historical sense, but also the Christ figure in the moralization. Again, realistic portrayal is subordinated to another purpose, this time typological interpretation. In other portrayals of Eleazar and the elephant, the artist sometimes emphasizes the satanic interpretation of the elephant by adding especially ferocious if false attributes to the beast. A miniature in a *Speculum Humanae Salvationis* manuscript in the Benedictine convent in Kremsmünster, Austria,[39] for example, shows a shaggy elephant as fabulous in design as a griffin or manticore, with taloned lion's feet and vicious teeth, as well as prominent tusks, a red-ringed (bloodied?) mouth, and a trunk ending with a sharp fleur-de-lis shape at its tip. Even its ear is positioned and drawn to resemble an armored helmet. Clearly the artist has no idea what an actual elephant looks like, but this wholly imaginative representation succeeds extremely well in conveying the moral stance of the animal in its typological setting.

We note as an aside here that the Bressanone artist (Figure 7) uses a compositional technique common in the depiction of an

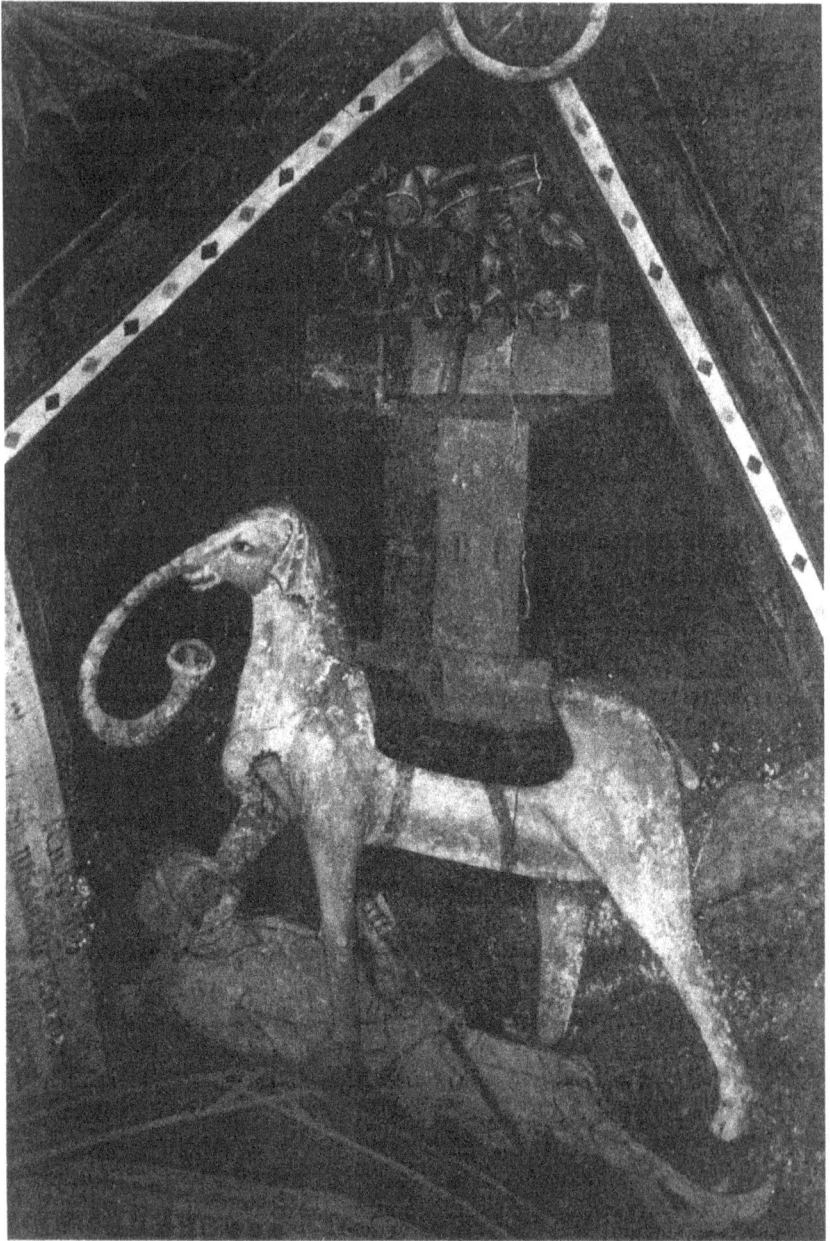

Figure 7. Eleazar and the elephant. Wall painting, cathedral cloisters, Bressanone, Italy (photo: N. Flores).

unfamiliar animal like the elephant: basically, he has attached elephant
accoutrements (a trunk, tusks, a castle) to a familiar animal, in this case,
a horse with a bobbed tail. The horse was often used as the basis for
elephant representations, possibly because the elephant functioned as
cavalry in ancient warfare. Artists used not only domesticated but also
wild animals in this way: Figure 8 shows an elephant as seen in an
eleventh-century Anglo-Saxon manuscript, *The Wonders of the East*.
This elephant is based on one of the "big cats," possibly a leopard, to
which boarlike tusks and a very long, curling tongue representing the
trunk have been added.[40]
   Of course, a chapter on the elephant itself appears in the many
different extant versions of the bestiary. Though it retains the
information and moralizations found in the *Physiologus*, this chapter is
considerably longer, providing additional information about the
elephant's physical attributes and behavior.[41] For example, see how the
incorporation of Isidore of Seville's *Etymologiae* influences the
description of some of the elephant's most salient features: "People say
that it is called an Elephant by the Greeks on account of its size, for it
approaches the form of a mountain: you see, a mountain is called
eliphio in Greek. In the Indies, however, it is known by the name
barrus because of its voice—whence both the voice is called "baritone"
and tusks are called "ivory." Its nose is called a proboscis (for the
bushes), because it carries leaf food to its mouth with it, and it looks
like a snake."[42]
   New information is jumbled together without any sense of
organization. We learn that elephants protect themselves with ivory
tusks, that no larger animals can be found, that they possess great
intelligence and memory, that they march about in herds, that they
copulate back-to-back, and that bulls fear them but they themselves are
afraid of mice. Another addition to the bestiary text is the description of
the elephant in battle, a legacy of Alexander's conquest of the East:
"The Persians and the Indians, collected into wooden towers on them,
sometimes fight each other with javelins as if from a castle."[43]
   What is significant is that although the bestiary retains the stories
of the elephant's sexuality and its ill-fated sleeping habit, along with
the Christian moralizations of those tales, the text does not moralize the
new details. The elephant's "castle," as well as its trunk and tusks, is
simply presented as natural history. This trend away from the
allegorical toward a secularized presentation of natural history is one

Figure 8. Elephant. *The Wonders of the East*, London, British Library, Cotton MS. Tiberius B v, folio 81 (photo: by permission of the British Library).

that we will follow in subsequent medieval texts. We must also remember, however, that secular does not imply scientific—this additional information is rarely derived from first-hand observation of a living elephant. Religious allegory and moralization gradually disappear, to be replaced by descriptions of the elephant's habits and its use in war. A miniature from the Rochester Bestiary (Figure 9) reflects this transition, for its upper register depicts an elephant wearing a castle in battle against mounted knights while the lower register is an unusual portrayal of the religious allegory of the little elephant who represents Christ raising fallen man after the unavailing efforts of those elephants who signify the law and prophets of the Old Dispensation.

By the thirteenth and fourteenth centuries, the elephant with a castle on its back was the preferred representation of the beast, particularly in English manuscript illumination. The castle is the Western elaboration of the fairly simple howdah familiar to us today in pictures of Indian elephants. There is an increasing interest in depicting not the animal itself but the tower on its back in elaborate detail, emphasizing its architectural structure as a castle, its armory, and the number of soldiers it could contain. This can be seen in the upper register of the Rochester Bestiary illustration (Figure 9): the elephant is drawn on a much smaller scale than the other figures, so that the knights mounted on horses are on the same level with the men in the castle on the elephant's back. There are several reasons for this development. We have already mentioned the popularity of the story of Eleazar and King Antiochus's elephant; similarly, the popular Alexander romances included the story of Alexander's victory over the Indian King Porus, who had a corps of 400 elephants, "each with the same wooden castle bound to its back, / With thirty men in each tower wearing plate armor."[44] Furthermore, artists catered to the secular interests of the nobility, the audience who purchased luxurious illustrated manuscripts. The textual reference in the bestiary to the use of the elephant in battle by the Indians and Persians provided an opportunity for vivid if entirely imaginary representations of medieval warfare. Moreover, the "marvels of the East" literary tradition, which included exotic animals and fabulous monstrous races, encouraged a certain fantastic element in the portrayal of the elephant in such contexts as the Alexander romances. In one battle scene from a fifteenth-century luxury manuscript, the elephants are portrayed as fiercely bellicose beasts, with trumpeting trunks, upthrust tusks similar

Figure 9. Elephant and castle with soldiers; raising the fallen elephant. Rochester Bestiary, London, British Library, Royal MS. 12 F xiii, folio 11v (photo: by permission of the British Library).

to the tusks of the wild pigs fighting them,[45] hooves apparently ready to trample their opposition, and thick, elongated, muscular necks (Figure 10). Again we see that realistic portrayal of the elephant is subordinated to a contemporary interest, this one secular chivalry and exoticism rather than religious or moral allegory.[46]

We have discussed the allegorical treatment of the elephant, although we have interpreted allegorical somewhat loosely to include portrayals of the elephant directed by secular as well as moral/didactic interests. There were, however, works in the Middle Ages that looked at animals for their own sakes, and some that even observed and described the nature of living beasts.

Such works did not include the great natural history encyclopedias of the twelfth and thirteenth centuries—Alexander Neckam's *De naturis rerum*, Thomas of Cantimpré's *De natura rerum*, Bartholomaeus Anglicus's *De proprietatibus rerum*, and the *Speculum naturale* of Vincent of Beauvais—which have a closer relationship to the bestiaries than to modern zoological studies. Actual observation of any of the creatures described, even if they were familiar domestic animals, is irrelevant. Like the *Physiologus* and the bestiary, these works are compendia of natural history encompassing all their literary predecessors, both classical and medieval. Authority rather than reality directs their composition. Organization is by source rather than by material, so the presentation of information often seems disordered or repetitive. Furthermore, the authors often do not even attempt to reconcile conflicting statements between different sources. Vincent of Beauvais, for example, tells his readers outright in the prologue that as a mere compiler he is not responsible for inconsistencies. What sets these works apart from the *Physiologus* and bestiary, however, is the elimination of the point-by-point allegorization of animal lore that had characterized the earlier works, although the encyclopedias maintain an overall theological interest in natural phenomena. The *De proprietatibus rerum*, for example, written around the middle of the thirteenth century by the English Franciscan Batholomaeus, who was famed for his teaching at the University of Paris, was intended originally as a simplified analysis of patristic exegesis on the nature of the universe and designed as an aid to theology students. It became one of the most popular reference books of the Middle Ages and Renaissance, used in both the original Latin and in many vernacular translations, and only went out of print after the Scientific Revolution

Figure 10. Battle scene with elephants and pigs. *Romance of Alexander*, London, British Library, Royal MS. 20 B xx, folio 57 (photo: by permission of the British Library).

of the seventeenth century. If Bartholomaeus sees a *moralitas* in the behavior of animals, it is as a direct model for human behavior rather then as an allegory.

Bartholomaeus devotes several chapters in his eighteenth book *De Animalibus* to elephants,[47] and names Pliny, Solinus, Aristotle, Avicenna, and the *Physiologus* as his sources, although there are additional uncredited sources, such as Isidore of Seville. Although the account is long and provides much information that we have not discussed earlier, I am going to focus on only one point of elephant anatomy that we are going to examine at greater length: the elephant's knees. Bartholomaeus's treatment of this subject illustrates the encyclopedists' lack of interest in evaluating conflicting sources, as well as their disregard for the traditional *significatio* of the *Physiologus*. Quoting from Pliny, Bartholomaeus says that elephants are intelligent and learn quickly; they can be taught to recognize a king and show respect, which they do by bending their knees in worship of him.[48] In his next chapter, he cites Aristotle, saying that elephants can bend their hind legs as a man does.[49] When excerpting from the *Physiologus*, Bartholomaeus repeats the story of the hazards that elephants face when they try to sleep leaning against a sabotaged treetrunk, but without mentioning explicitly that the elephant has no knee joints. The result, nevertheless, is the same: the elephant falls and is unable to get up.[50] However, the allegorical interpretation of this—as well as all other moral and metaphysical interpretations of the characteristics of individual animals—has been ruthlessly eliminated in *De proprietatibus rerum*. Instead, the very ending of the story is revised to violate the entire point of the original allegory; in answer to the frantic calls for help from the fallen animal, *many* young elephants come to his aid and raise him up with affection and love through their might and strength.

More in the scientific tradition of recording observations of living animals are the last five books of the Dominican Albertus Magnus's *De animalibus*. The first nineteen books of this work are a paraphrase, with extensive additional commentary, of Aristotle's treatises on animals, and the following two are appendixes on biological issues raised by Aristotle. In the final five books,[51] however, Albertus turns from his role as scholastic philosopher to that of zoologist, demonstrating an abundance of information especially regarding European fauna, much of it personal observations collected since childhood. These are supplemented by the work of various

authorities. Written around 1260, these books are an alphabetically
arranged description of animals, which are divided into five groups by
their means of locomotion: walking animals, swimming animals, flying
animals, crawling animals, and "vermes" (insects). The orderliness of
the text's organization is in striking contrast to the source-driven
organization of Bartholmaeus. Each section is organized according to
the following categories: a physical description, including a delineation
of the differences between male and female; humoral makeup; habits
and behavior; method of reproduction; diseases the animal is prone to,
and their treatments; and the use made of the animal's parts in human
and veterinary medicine. Unlike the rather haphazard melange of the
encyclopedists, Albertus presents a "systematic inventory" intended as
a guide for beginning students and as a handy reference for those more
advanced.

When Albertus discusses animals with which he is familiar, his
descriptions are accurate, often sharply detailed with an accumulation
of information, and vivid in style. He draws conclusions from his
evidence, which is occasionally erroneous, but his conclusions are
always logically reasoned. He tempers his use of experts, dependable
observers, and workers in the field with common sense. He is as
dependent for information about animals and as unable to observe as
his near contemporaries the encyclopedists. However, unlike them he
evaluates the information he receives, critizing that which he deems
fantastic or contrary to common sense, even if his source is Aristotle. In
the case of the elephant, for example, he writes that some authors
"assert that there are large-bodied dragons which grapple with
elephants and, after besting them, drink their blood to cool and
moderate the raging heat of their own bodies. In my estimation, this is
merely a fabulous tale."[52]

Again, Albertus distinguishes himself from his contemporaries
in his discussion of the elephant's knees. The anatomical description is
extensive:

> Their legs are massive and uniform in diameter from top to
> bottom, much like the columns of a building. Though each foot
> is divided into multiple digits, nature has conjoined the toes to
> give added strength for weight bearing. For the same reason,
> they are believed to have no flexible joints above their knees;
> more likely, these joints are stiff rather than freely movable, but
> to the superficial observer appear to have no fulcrum points of

flexure. In actuality, if the elephant had no flexibility, it would be unable to walk with a coordinated gait.[53]

Whether this description derives wholly from Aristotle, or whether Albertus has observed an elephant, possibly in the menageries of Frederick II, is not known. What is apparent, however, is that the interest and attitude that he has toward this issue is very different from that of Bartholomaeus Anglicus.

Although works like the great medieval encyclopedias and Albertus Magnus's *De animalibus* were usually not illustrated, it is useful to examine them at length because their treatment of animals, one that distances itself from the allegorization of earlier works, is indicative of the general attitude toward animals by artists in the late Middle Ages. As in the case of Albertus Magnus, when artists were able to study an animal first-hand, the portrayal was increasingly true to life.

There were some opportunities for medieval artists to see real elephants, primarily in royal menageries like those of Frederick II. Exotic animals were regularly exchanged as gifts by medieval monarchs. As early as 801, Harun al-Rashid had presented Charlemagne with the famous elephant Abul-Abbas; although its presence is vividly recorded in contemporary chronicles, Carolingian art does not seem to have preserved any records of this royal favorite. Perhaps the most famous medieval depictions of elephants are the drawings by the historian and artist Matthew Paris of the African elephant given to Henry III by Louis IX of France upon the latter's return from the Crusades. The beast arrived in England in February 1255 and lived for four years in a special elephant house built in the Tower of London. Matthew Paris gives this event only a brief entry in his annal for 1255 ("everyone hastened [there] on account of the rareness of the sight")[54] but he also made two large sketches of the animal, both accompanied by short descriptive tracts. In the *Chronica Majora* manuscript in Corpus Christi College (Figure 11), the elephant is shown with its keeper, and the caption makes Matthew's intent clear: "by the size of the man drawn here, the size of the beast . . . can be estimated."[55] Proportional relationships are thus rendered pictorially. From this simple statement we can see the great contrast between the allegorical and scientific attitudes: here man and beast are depicted in realistic

Figure 11. Elephant and keeper. Matthew Paris, *Chronica Majora*, Cambridge, Corpus Christi College, MS. 16, folio iv (photo: Conway Library by permission of the Master and Fellows of Corpus Christi College, Cambridge).

proportion to one another, whereas in the illustration of Eleazar's death beneath the elephant (Figure 7), the dying Eleazar, who represents Christ's sacrifice for mankind, is drawn on a much larger scale than the elephant because he is the more important figure in the moralization. Moreover, like his contemporary Villard de Honnecourt, Matthew proudly points out that this drawing is made from life: "ipso elephante exemplariter assistente." In the tract accompanying the drawing, he describes the elephant as ten years old and ten feet high, and observes that it has a very hard, rough hide—grayish-black in color—rather than fur. Its eyes are small and located in the upper part of the head, and it uses its trunk ("promiscuida") to obtain food and drink in the manner shown in the illustration.

Note the shape of the head and trunk, the placement of the tusks, the concave depression on its back, and the relatively small eye and large ear. Even the legs and feet, notorious stumbling blocks for medieval artists, closely approximate those of an African elephant. Observation from nature has clearly made a difference in Matthew's artistic conception of an elephant, as we can see by comparing this drawing with one he did fourteen years earlier to illustrate the triumphal entry of Richard of Cornwall into Cremona in 1241 (Figure 12).[56] The earlier elephant is apparently copied from a pictorial model. With its piglike body, vacuum hose trunk, triangular flap ears, and saucerlike hooves, it is strikingly similar to the beast (Figure 13) in a thirteenth-century English bestiary, even to the man goading it with a pointed stick at the rear of the castle.[57]

Matthew Paris is often cited by historians for his unusually good ability to describe his world and its events, for his visual sense, and for his interest in "realistic observations" as Antonia Gransden has called them.[58] Indeed, his two large elephant drawings are often used as examples of the newly awakened "realism of the thirteenth century," Kenneth Clark going so far as to describe Figure 11 as "almost the first realistic animal in post-Classical Western art."[59]

This realism is also evident in Matthew's other portrait of the Tower elephant, found in the *Liber Additamentorum* manuscript now in the British Library (Figure 14). As in the Corpus Christi College drawing, the animal is shown in profile, drawn in heavy brown line, and tinted with dark gray and ocher washes. The details of the skin folds on the trunk and rear flank, as well as the flap covering the upper

Figure 12. Cremona's processional elephant. Matthew Paris, *Chronica Majora*, Cambridge, Corpus Christi College, MS. 16, folio 151v (photo: Conway Library by permission of the Master and Fellows of Corpus Christi College, Cambridge).

Figure 13. Elephant and castle with revelers. Bestiary, London, British Library, Harley MS. 3244, folio 39 (photo: by permission of the British Library).

part of the tusk, are less stylized, so this probably represents the earlier of the two drawings. Especially interesting here is the wonderfully pliant detail drawing of the trunk, which was incorporated into the more finished illustration of the Corpus Christi College manuscript. The tactile grace with which this is rendered certainly illustrates Cennino di Drea Cennini's contention, mentioned earlier, that nature is the best of all models for artists. Finally, as Suzanne Lewis suggests in her study of Matthew Paris's art, the most remarkable aspect of both these drawings may be the "pronounced articulation of the knee joints, accurately placed very low, just above the massive feet. Based on the chronicler's observation of a living specimen, these drawings may constitute the earliest contradiction of the familiar physiological myth of the 'jointless' elephant which had prevailed in the Middle Ages since Ambrose."[60]

This is where the case of Matthew's elephant becomes curious indeed, for the artist apparently accomodates for at least one discrepancy between empirically acquired knowledge and traditionally accepted information. The short tracts that were added after the illustrations were done are incomplete in both cases and the two versions differ from one another, but both include descriptive material from Matthew's observations, as well as material from such accepted authorities as the Bible, Bernardus Sylvestris, Virgil, Horace, and the bestiary. In the Corpus Christi College manuscript, Matthew includes a brief version of the *Physiologus* story that the elephant cannot bend its legs because it has no joints, and how hunters use this anatomical deficit to trap them. Here, however, Matthew does not give the traditional explanation for the elephant's inability to rise or its allegorical interpretation as representating the Fall of Man, but only remarks that it is difficult for them to get up once they are down.[61]

Matthew Paris's elephant drawings are an appropriate conclusion to a discussion of how medieval man regarded animals, and how that vision was shaped by prevailing intellectual attitudes. These sketches exemplify the new realism in art, which began around the mid-thirteenth century and culminated in Italian trecento art. They also appeared at a time when Aristotle's studies of natural science were again being studied in the universities after their prohibition in 1210 from the University of Paris. Despite all of this, and although these drawing have been characterized as "a decisive step in the medieval evolution of seeing and thinking," according to William Heckscher,[62] we

Figure 14. Elephant and detail of trunk. Matthew Paris, *Liber Additamentorum*, London, British Library, Cotton MS. Nero D i, folio 169v (photo: by permission of the British Library).

have seen that Matthew falls back on traditional authorities when he discusses the elephant in the text accompanying the drawings. In his ready use of both accepted authority and personally observed detail that contradicts authority, Matthew, like the encyclopedists, is very much a man of his time. The elephant's knees may, in fact, be considered a kind of dividing point between the medieval and the modern attitudes toward nature, what I have been calling the allegorical and the scientific views in this essay. Even though Aristotle himself had expressly refuted the tale of the jointless elephant,[63] as we have seen it reappears in many medieval texts, and the strength of its persistence was such that Sir Thomas Brown was still discussing it in 1645 as the first of the "common and vulgar errors" regarding animals.[64] This fascination with the jointless elephant (first circulated in antiquity by Ctesias) was such an enduring animal myth that many elephant observers of the Renaissance made a point of refuting it. In 1514, for example, Pope Leo X was presented with an elephant which was made to kneel before him, not only as a mark of respect but also to demonstrate the existence of its flexible joints. Let us end here with the testimony of the traveler André Thevet, who included an illustration of an elephant kneeling at the command of its keeper (Figure 15). Elephants can do this, Thevet explains, because they have joints in their knees, "which is contrary to the opinion of many who have described the elephant." Not only had he himself seen elephants kneeling many times in Cairo, but he also reports that an elephant flayed in Aleppo was found to have joints in its legs.[65] Thevet's reliance on repeatable observation and anatomical dissection point the way toward the modern basis of natural history, which today has completely superseded the medieval view of nature as spiritual allegory.

Figure 15. Elephant kneeling on command from its keeper. André Thevet, *Cosmographie de Levant*, 1554 (photo: by permission of the British Library).

NOTES

An earlier version of this essay was presented at the 25th International Congress on Medieval Studies, Kalamazoo, Michigan, in May 1990. I am indebted to Professors Janetta Rebold Benton and Julia Meyer for their critical comments on both the preliminary and final versions of this paper.

1. Florence McCulloch, Medieval Latin and French Bestiaries (Chapel Hill, N.C.: University of North Carolina Press, 1960), 77.
2. Wilma George, "The Bestiary: A Handbook of Local Fauna," *Archives of Natural History* 10 (1981), 187–203.
3. Brunsdon Yapp, "Birds in Bestiaries: Medieval Knowledge of Nature," *The Cambridge Review* (20 Nov. 1984), 186. See also his "A New Look at English Bestiaries," *Medium Aevum* 54 (1985), 1–19. Wilma George and Brunsdon Yapp have recently collaborated on a book that evaluates how much of the information in bestiaries was based on real natural history: *The Naming of the Beasts: Natural History in the Medieval Bestiary* (London: Duckworth, 1991).
4. As quoted by Michael J. Curley, *Physiologus* (Austin: University of Texas Press, 1979), xiii–xiv.
5. Lynn S. White, Jr., "Natural Science and Naturalistic Art in the Middle Ages," *AHR* 52 (1947), 424–5.
6. See, for example, Thomas van Cleve, *The Emperor Frederick II of Hohenstaufen* (Oxford: The Clarendon Press, 1972), 314–15.
7. *The Art of Falconry, being the De Arte Venandi cum Avibus of Frederick II of Hohenstauffen*, translated and edited by Casey A. Wood and F. Marjorie Fyfe (Stanford, Calif.: Stanford University Press, 1943), 4. The most recent edition of *De Arte Venandi* is by C.A. Willemsen (Leipzig, 1942).
8. *The Art of Falconry*, 4
9. Gerald of Wales, *The History and Topography of Ireland*, translated by John J. O'Meara (New York: Penguin Books, 1982), 41–2.
10. For Gerald's generally "superior talents" as a zoological observer, see Urban T. Holmes, "Gerald the Naturalist," *Speculum* 47 (1972), 110–21.
11. *The Art of Falconry*, 51–2.
12. Ibid., 22.
13. Ibid., 15.
14. See note 3.
15. D. Jalabert, "La flore gothique: ses origines, son évolution du XIIe au XVe siècle," *Bulletin Monumental* 91 (1932), 181–246. See also L. White, 426–27.
16. L. White, 427.

17. Erwin Panofsky, "Artist, Scientist, Genius: Notes on the Renaissance-Dämmerung,'" in *The Renaissance: Six Essays* (New York: Harper and Row, 1962), 140.

18. "Ea quae sunt secundum artem imitantur ea quae sunt secundam naturam, et tanto magis opus artis est melius quanto magis assequitur similitudinem ejus quod est in natura," *De regimine principum*, lib. I, c. 2, in *Opuscula omnia*, ed. P. Mandonnet (Paris, 1927), I, 317. Quoted and translated by L. White, 428.

19. Cennino d'Andrea Cennini, *The Craftsmen's Handbook. The Italian "Il Libro dell'Arte*, translated by Daniel V. Thompson (New York: Dover, n.d.), as excerpted in Teresa G. Frisch, *Gothic Art 1140–c. 1450: Sources and Documents* (Toronto: University of Toronto Press, 1987), 161.

20. William S. Heckscher, "Bernini's Elephant and Obelisk," *Art Bulletin* 29 (1947), 164. See also R. Recht, "Sur le dessin d'architecture gothique," in *Etudes d'art médiéval offertes a Louis Grodecki*, ed. S. Crosby et al. (Paris, 1981), 235. The primary critical study of the *Sketchbook* remains *Villard de Honnecourt: Kritische Gesamtausgabe des Bauhüttenbuches MS. fr. 19093 der Pariser Nationalbibliothek*, ed. Hans R. Hanloser (Vienna: Verlag von Anton Schroll, 1935), who discusses this drawing on pages 147–48 in relation to possible models.

21. Hahnloser, 145.

22. Julius von Schlosser, "Materialien zur Quellenkunde der Kunstgeschicte," *Sitzungsberichte der Kaiserlichen Akademie der Wissenschaften in Wien* 177/I, "Mittelalter" (Vienna: Alfred Holder, 1914), 93, as quoted in Frisch, 47. See also Hahnloser, 268–72, on Villard's animal drawings.

23. For medieval interest in the elephant see Heckscher, 158ff, and G.C. Druce, "The Elephant in Medieval Legend and Art," *Archeological Journal* 76, 2nd series 26 (1919), 1–73.

24. Pliny, *Natural History*, Book VIII, ii–iii. In 1610 the Milanese celebration of the canonization of St. Carlo Borromeo included a representation of a tightrope-dancing elephant. This was interpreted as an illustration of "how San Carlo had arrived at perfection and saintliness by walking on the steep path and by subduing to his discipline the oppressive weight of the body that had been a load to the soul." Filippo Picinelli, *Mondo Simbolico*, 2nd ed. (Venice, 1678), sec. 309, quoted by Heckscher, 173.

25. *Hexaemeron.*, IX, 1, as quoted by Beryl Rowland, "The Relationship of St. Basil's *Hexaemeron* to the *Physiologus*," in *Epopée Animale, Fable, Fabliau*, ed. Gabriel Bianciotto and Michel Salvat (Paris: Publications de l'Université de Rouen, 1984), 491.

26. *Hex.* IX, 5; *PL* 14, 225.

27. Curley, xv. Curley's translation, based on Latin versions of the *Physiologus* as established by Francis Carmody, includes an excellent

introduction which places the work in its historical and intellectual context, as well as a very useful selected bibliography divided between editions, modern translations, and general studies.

28. E.P. Evans, *Animal Symbolism in Ecclesiastical Art* (New York: Harry Holt, 1896), 62.

29. Curley, xxviii.

30. Curley, 29–32.

31. Bern, Municipal Library, MS. 318, folio 19. Reproduced in Francis Klingender, *Animals in Art and Thought to the End of the Middle Ages*, ed. Evelyn Antal and John Harthan (Cambridge, Mass.: M.I.T. Press, 1971), 383, fig. 214. A facsimile of the manuscript has also been reproduced: *Physiologus Bernensis . . . wissenschaftlichen Kommentar con Chr. Steiger und Otto Homberger* (Basle, 1964).

32. Helen Woodruff suggests that the Bern *Physiologus* was illustrated at Fleury, and that the naturalism of the animals and landscapes point to a late Alexandrian model: "The *Physiologus* of Bern," *Art Bulletin* 12 (1930), 226–53. See also Xenia Muratova, "Problemes de l'origine et des sources des cycles d'illustrations des manuscrits des bestiares," in Bianciotti and Salvat, 383–408.

33. J.P. Harthan, "Medieval Bestiaries," *Geographical Magazine* 22 (1949), 185.

34. The most readily available edition of the bestiary remains that of T.H. White, *The Bestiary, A Book of Beasts* (New York: G.P. Putnam's Sons, 1960), a translation of Cambridge University Library MS. I i 4.26, a twelfth-century Latin prose manuscript. For studies and bibliography on the bestiary, see McCulloch and *Beasts and Birds of the Middle Ages: The Bestiary and Its Legacy*, ed. Willene B. Clark and Meredith T. McMunn (Philadelphia: University of Pennsylvania Press, 1989), which updates the bibliography of bestiary studies since 1962. Ann Payne, *Medieval Animals* (London: British Library, 1990), is a handsome compilation of texts and illustrations of medieval animal lore arranged in the order of a medieval bestiary and drawn from the bestiary manuscripts of the British Library.

35. T.H. White, 165–67.

36. Druce, 35, citing London, British Library, Sloane MS. 278, folio 57.

37. 1. Macc. 6:33–46. Also see Josephus, *The Jewish War*, I, 37.

38. *The Mirour of Mans Saluacioune*, ed. Avril Henry (Philadelphia: University of Pennsylvania Press, 1987), 137. The original Latin text of the moralization may be found in *Speculum humanae salvationis: texte critique, etc.*, ed. J. Lutz and P. Perdrizet (Mulhouse: 1907–1909), chap. xxiv, ll. 95–98.

39. MS. Kremsmünster, Stiftsbibliothek 243, fol. 30. Willibrod Neumüller has published a facsimile, *Speculum humanae salvationis: Vollst. Faks.-Aug. des Codex Cremifanensis 243 des Benediktinerstifts Kremsmünster* (Graz, 1972). I am indebted to Professor John B. Friedman for bringing this manuscript to my attention.

40. For his 1981 photograph entitled "Elephant," artist William Wegman used this technique of attaching elephant accoutrements to a domestic animal. His pet weimaraner Man Ray is shown wearing a pair of ivory-colored tusks along his jaw and an extremely long green sock on the end of his muzzle. The toe of the sock is attached to a large rubber tree, which serves as a "jungle" landscape. Reproduced on the front cover of William Wegman, *Man's Best Friend* (New York: Harry N. Abrams, 1982).

41. T.H. White, 24–28.

42. Ibid., 25.

43. Ibid., 25.

44. *The Wars of Alexander, An Alliterative Romance*, ed. W.W. Skeat, EETS e.s. 47 (London: Trubner, 1886; rpt. Millwood, N.Y.: Kraus, 1975), 211, ll. 3601–3:

Foure hundreth olyfants in-fere   folowid him enarmi[d]
With ilkane bunden on his bake   a borden castell
And thretty tulkis in ilk toure   tired in platis.

45. It was thought that elephants were frightened by the squealing of pigs; see, for example, Aelian, *De natura animalium* I, 31, and Seneca, *De ira* II, I, I.5.

46. For elephants in the Alexander romances, see A.T. Hatto, "The Elephants in the Strassburg *Alexander*," in *The Medieval Alexander Legend and Romance Epic: Essays in Honour of David J.A. Ross*, ed. Peter Noble, Lucie Polak, and Claire Isoz (Millwood, N.Y.: Kraus, 1982), 85–105.

47. *On the Properties of Things: John Trevisa's translation of Bartholomaeus Anglicus De Proprietatibus Rerum: A Critical Text*, ed. M.C. Seymour et al. (Oxford: Clarendon Press, 1975), Bk. XVIII, xlii–xlv; vol. 2, 1191–97.

48. Ibid., 1192.

49. Ibid., 1194.

50. Ibid., 1196.

51. Recently edited and translated as Albert the Great, *Man and the Beasts: De Animalibus (Books 22–26)*, translated by James J. Scanlan, M.D. (Binghamton, N.Y.: Medieval and Renaissance Texts and Studies, 1987). The standard edition of *De animalibus libri XXVI* is edited by Hermann Stadler in *Beitrage zur Geschicte der Philosophie des Mittelalters*, 15–16 (Munich, 1916–20).

52. Albert the Great, Tract 2, chap. 1, 37, 100.

53. Ibid., Tract 2, chap. 1, 37, 101.

54. "Nec credimus quod unquam aliquis elephas visus est in Anglia, immo nec etiam in partibus cisalpinis, practer illum; unde confluebant populi ad

tantae spectaculum novitatis." Matthew Paris, *Chronica majora*, ed. H.R. Luard (London: Rolls Series, 1872–1884, 7 vols.), V, 489.

55. "Per quantitatem hominis hic protracti considerari potest quantitas bestie hic figurate."

56. Matthew's account in the *Chronica majora* describes the elephant's entourage as told to him by Duke Richard himself: "On his approaching Cremona, the Cremonese came joyfully to meet him, with the emperor's elephant in advance of them, handsomely decorated, and bearing a wooden sort of tower, in which the masters of the elephant sat, playing on trumpets and exultingly clapping their hands together." *Matthew Paris's English History*, trans. J.A. Giles (London: Henry G. Bohn, 1852), I, 385–86. The elephant had been given to Cremona as a mark of imperial favor by Frederick II of Hohenstaufen.

57. Ann Payne (*Medieval Animals*, 15) says that recent scholarship dates British Library Harley MS. 3244 to about 1255, partially because of the "well-observed drawing of the elephant" on folio 39, which may derive its realism from observation of the Tower elephant itself or from one of Matthew's drawings of the Tower elephant. Given the congruity between Figures 12 and 13, it is more likely that Matthew's Cremonese elephant of 1241, rather than the Tower elephant, influenced the artist of Harley 3244.

58. Antonia Gransden, "Realistic Observation in Twelfth-Century England," *Speculum* 47 (1972), 32. See also Miriam Helene Marshall, "Thirteenth Century Culture as Illustrated by Matthew Paris," *Speculum* 14 (1939), 473–76.

59. Sir Kenneth Clark, *Men and Animals* (New York: William Morrow, 1977), 26, 104; Michael Evans, "An Illustrated Fragment of Peraldus's *Summa* of Vice: Harleian MS. 3244," *JWCI* 45 (1982), 41–42; and Madeline H. Caviness, "'The Simple Perception of Matter' and the Representation of Narrative, ca. 1180–1280," *Gesta* 30 (1991), 52–53.

60. Suzanne Lewis, *The Art of Matthew Paris in the Chronica Majora* (Berkeley: University of California Press, 1987), 215.

61. Richard Vaughn, *Matthew Paris* (Cambridge: Cambridge University Press, 1958), 256–57, finds Matthew's tract "a characteristic example of medieval natural history studies, and its significance lies in its demonstration of Matthew's interest in them rather than in any inherent merit."

62. Hecksher, 164.

63. *Historia Animalium* II.I; 498a 3f.

64. *Pseudodoxia Epidemica*, III, chap. 1.

65. André Thevet, *Cosmographie de Levant* (1554), 69–74, as quoted in Joan Barclay Lloyd, *African Animals in Renaissance Literature and Art* (Oxford: Clarendon Press, 1971), 116.

FALCONRY AND MEDIEVAL VIEWS OF NATURE

Robin S. Oggins

When one talks about nature in the Middle Ages, one should make clear whose nature one is talking about. In the Middle Ages there was no single conception of the natural world. "Nature," then as today, represented different things to different groups of people. For the great majority, nature was something to struggle against to produce a livelihood. For the upper classes, "nature" provided an important source of recreation; for poets and artists, nature was a convenient backdrop; and for intellectuals, nature was the visible portion of God's handiwork. Nature in the Middle Ages, then, can be considered from practical, artistic, or conceptual points of view.

The study of the sport of falconry provides a useful perspective on changes in these viewpoints over time. The practical need and desire to control nature can be seen in such phenomena as writings on hawk medicine and changes in falconry-training techniques (e.g., the introduction of the hood). A new, more "scientific" attitude toward nature is manifested in the increasing sophistication of treatises on hawks and falconry, and in the growing realism of depictions of birds of prey. Medieval development in both practical and scientific views of nature culminates in the *De arte venandi cum avibus* of Emperor Frederick II of Hohenstaufen—probably the most remarkable medieval work on natural history. In the period after Frederick's death a more popular literature on falconry is produced aimed at a wider range of social groups, and this literature reflects a broader intellectual approach towards nature. I propose in this paper, therefore, to trace developments in medieval writings about birds of prey, and shall try to place these developments in the general context of changing medieval views of the natural world.

The earliest record of falconry in Europe dates from the fifth century A.D. Around 459, Paulinus of Pella, at the age of eighty, wrote an autobiographical poem in which he recorded his youthful desire to own "a horse with fine trappings, a swift dog, and a splendid hawk."[1] From that time on there are a growing number of references to falconry: in letters, in the history of Gregory of Tours, in church legislation, and in barbarian law codes.[2] It is evident that from an early date falconry was primarily a sport of the well-to-do. In the laws of the Ripuarian Franks a trained hawk was equal to the value of a stallion; an untrained hawk equaled the value of a mare. Among the Burgundians, compensation for stealing a hawk was greater than that for stealing a slave, twice as much as for stealing a horse, and three times as much as for stealing the best kind of ox.[3] The fact that the first references to falconry in England are in royal letters would seem to be significant. Nevertheless there were also more humble practitioners—men like Ælfric's fowler, who tamed hawks in order to catch food and released the hawks in the spring because they ate too much once hunting season was over.[4]

For both king and fowler, the practical need and ability to control nature were manifested in falconry-training techniques—both in taming the hawks and, in some cases, training them to fly at prey larger than they would ordinarily attack in the wild, such as cranes and herons. A second area in which an attempt to control nature can be seen is that of hawk medicine: the attempt to treat the many afflictions that birds of prey are subject to.

The earliest surviving Western work on falconry comes from a tenth-century fragment dealing with remedies for various ailments of hawks.[5] While various works on falconry (now lost) are mentioned in the next century, the next surviving works (written in Latin) date from almost 200 years after the first fragment.[6] As Haskins notes of this literature:

> Severely practical throughout, it is concerned in the first instance with the animals which aid in the chase, horses, dogs, hawks, and falcons, and especially with the diseases of these and their remedies. It would be rash to deny any connexion between this and the veterinary medicine of antiquity, but for the most part it shows a humbler origin, its precepts drawn rather from the popular cures and leechdoms of current practice.[7]

Two things are particularly striking about these works. One is their attribution to, or purported connection with, royalty; the second is the strange nature of some of the remedies. Lost works on falconry were credited to King Harold and to Grimaldus, Count of the Sacred Palace, while Daude de Pradas mentioned using a "book of King Henry of England," also no longer extant. A surviving work is attributed to King Dancus, and other surviving works exist under such titles as "The Letter of Aquila and Symmachus and Theodotion to King Ptolemy" and the "Letter of Grisofus the Spaniard to the Emperor Theodosius." Guillelmus the Falconer, author of another work, described himself as nourished in the court of King Roger of Sicily.[8] The only early Latin treatise we have that can be attributed to a known individual is that by Adelard of Bath, who introduced the abacus to England and wrote a treatise on the astrolabe. But even so good a contemporary scientist as Adelard could become fanciful when writing about the care of hawks. He suggested feeding a hawk that did not want to fly a little tender cow's flesh dipped in urine in the evening, followed by a bit of pig's tongue on the next day, while a hawk that was not moulting properly might be fed pellets of grain cooked in the broth of a red serpent.[9] Daude de Pradas suggested feeding a weak hawk on the flesh of a blind puppy, sprinkling hawks with baked lizard dust to speed up moulting, and, to stop a hawk from shrieking, feeding it frequently with a bat stuffed with pepper.[10] Gerardus Falconarius favored the use of spells to keep the bird safe.[11] Even when the remedies seem fairly straightforward—herbs, spices, the flesh of various animals—their application was often determined by the then current philosophy of humours: Dancus Rex, for example, suggested different remedies for black falcons, which were melancholy, white falcons, which were phlegmatic and dry, and red falcons, which were sanguine.[12] At their worst, contemporary remedies have been described as "obviously nonsensical abracadabra methods of exquisite torture and blatant quackery."[13]

But along with the "abracadabra" there was sound advice. Hans Epstein, writing about Dancus Rex, Guillelmus, and Gerardus Falconarius, noted that their works

> were highly regarded—as a sort of concise, practical vademecum, the falconer's mews-equivalent of Dr. Spock—by the skilled austringer's brotherhood of the late Middle Ages. . . . The limited evidence of modern falconry likewise suggests that the three treatises . . . must be taken seriously. It will be noted

that Dancus, William, and Gerard alike rely heavily in their
preventives and cures on the efficacy of condiments, drugs,
herbs, and natural products: pepper, cinnamon, rue, rock-salt,
cardamom, cumin, olive-oil, honey, myrtle, cassia, lye-wash,
fresh pigeon's blood, and the flesh of hedgehog, lizard, and
chicken (natural food of various species of hawks) are all
mentioned. It is at least highly suggestive that many of these are
also recommended by a modern falconry authority.[14]

As a last resort, appeal for a sick bird might be made to still higher
authority. In the thirteenth century King Edward I of England bent
pennies over his falcons' heads and sent the pennies to shrines, sent
wax images of sick falcons to shrines, and even sent sick birds
themselves on pilgrimage.[15]

Along with such attempts to control nature, some of the twelfth-
century treatises, in an attempt at classification, described and rated
different "species" of falcon. Neither the descriptions nor the ratings
were particularly systematic. Dancus wrote about falcons with black,
red, and white feathers, provided a brief description of the "mountain
falcon," and characterized falcons as either "noble" or "rustic."[16]
Guillelmus stated that "red" and "white" falcons descended from the
"black," and he described all three—unfortunately, not so clearly that
the birds can be identified with modern species.[17] One can say that the
twelfth-century treatises were essentially practical works that dealt with
specific problems without attempting to relate these problems to a
wider view of nature. Thirteenth-century writers on falconry put aspects
of the sport in a broader perspective, but in doing so they used large
portions of the earlier works. The twelfth-century works are important,
therefore, because they helped to establish the directions taken by later
writers.

In the thirteenth century, treatises on falconry evolved in two
directions. In one group were works primarily concerned with birds of
prey rather than with the sport of falconry—works that viewed the birds
as one aspect of a larger synthesis, God's creation. The works of the
encyclopedists fall into this category. A second group consisted of
works that focused specifically on falconry, continuing the earlier
practical tradition.

A great deal has been written about the medieval encyclopedists
and their overall methods and purposes.[18] From our narrow perspective,
the fact that authors concerned with birds of prey were writing about

ornithology rather than merely about falconry is important and demonstrates an expanded conception of nature. On the other hand, the *methods* used by the encyclopedists were much less forward-looking. They tended to copy from one another, and, with a few significant exceptions, they produced little original work. For example, the section on falcons in the *Speculum naturale* of Vincent of Beauvais contains an almost verbatim transcript of the first part of "The Letter of Aquila and Symmachus and Theodotion to King Ptolemy," followed by an abridgement of Albertus Magnus's work on hawks and falcons. In the same way, Brunetto Latini based his section on falcons on Daude de Pradas's work and the book of Gandolfus Persianus. Alexander Neckam's account contains allusions to Isidore of Seville, Hector, Ajax, and Alexander the Great, and is of almost no value.[19]

The only completely original account produced by the encyclopedists was that of Bartholomeus Anglicus (fl. 1230–50), a Franciscan who was born in England and who lived in turn at Oxford, Paris, and Magdeburg. He described his *De proprietatibus rerum* as "a simple and rude compilation" written for "young scholars and the general reader."[20] While much of Bartholomeus's work is said to be out-of-date by thirteenth-century standards, some of it was based on his own observation and, according to Lynn Thorndike, "is manifestly actuated by a scientific interest in present facts and phenomena."[21] This is clearly the case in Bartholomeus's short chapter on the goshawk, part of a book on the creatures of the air. The chapter is concise, accurate, and contains information on the natural behavior and training of the goshawk. Bartholomeus commented on the social aspects of hawking, and concluded with a wry but undoubtedly accurate comment:

> And this hawk is of a disdainful kind. . . . And she must have ordinate diet, nother too scarce, ne too full. For by too much meat she waxeth . . . slow, and disdaineth to come to reclaim. And if the meat be too scarce then she faileth, and is feeble and unmighty to take her prey. Also the eyen of such birds should oft be seled and closed, or hid, that she bate not too oft from his hand that beareth her, when she seeth a bird that she desireth to take; and also her legs must be fastened with gesses, that she shall not fly freely to every bird. And they be borne on the left hand, that they may somewhat take of the right hand, and be fed therewith.

And so such tame hawks be kept in mews, that they may be
discharged of old feathers and hard, and so be renewed in
fairness of youth. Also men give them meat of some manner of
flesh, which is somedeal venomous, that they may the sooner
change their feathers. And smoke grieveth such hawks and doth
them harm. And therefore their mews must be far from smoky
places, that their bodies be not grieved with bitterness of smoke,
nor their feathers infect with blackness of smoke. They should
be fed with fresh flesh and bloody, and men should use to give
them to eat the hearts of fowls that they take. All the while they
are alive and are strong and mighty to take their prey, they are
beloved of their lords, and borne on hands, and set on perches,
and stroked on the breast and on the tail, and made plain and
smooth, and are nourished with great business and diligence. But
when they are dead, all men hold them unprofitable and nothing
worth, and be not eaten, but rather thrown out on dunghills.[22]

Bartholomeus's work combined the two types of falconry
literature: he was an encyclopedist writing in the practical tradition. His
contemporary Albertus Magnus also wrote in the encyclopedist
tradition, basing much of his work on earlier writers; but unlike most of
the other encyclopedists he supplemented the works he used with his
own observations. Among his written sources, Albertus specifically
acknowledged "The Letter of Aquila, Symmachus, and Theodotion to
Ptolemy," Guillelmus and Gerardus Falconarius, and the work of the
Emperor Frederick II—though it is doubtful that Albertus used
Frederick's written work. Albertus probably drew material without
acknowledgement from his student Thomas of Cantimpré's *Liber de
natura rerum*.[23] But Albertus supplemented his material with
information provided at first hand by falconers.[24] And even when he
relied for whole sections of his work on information provided by others,
he might add material from his own experience. As he wrote at one
point, "We have followed the expert knowledge of William the falconer
of King Roger, adding a few words of our own."[25]

Like the earlier practitioners, Albertus discussed the taming and
training of falcons and treatments for their diseases; but the most
significant part of his "De avibus" is the section in which he described
and ranked the birds. His main written source for this section was "The
Letter of Aquila, Symmachus, and Theodotion." From that work he
seems to have derived the basic idea of grouping falcons together and
ranking them, the idea of the "nobility" of different falcons, names for

some of the falcons he listed, and portions of some of the descriptions. Albertus took the earlier list, rearranged the birds in his own order of excellence, and added several kinds of falcon. He also created the formal categories of ignoble and mixed falcons, and expanded the descriptions of the birds.[26] In this work, unlike the bestiaries and other encyclopedists, Albertus did not follow the medieval approach that sought symbolic meanings in natural phenomena.[27] Rather, he came much closer to being scientific in the modern sense. He was concerned with telling the reader what the birds he was describing looked like, how they behaved, what their prey was. In consequence, many of the hawks he described can be identified from his descriptions of them, though he gave the birds names we do not recognize; and many of his incidental observations on the behavior of particular species are borne out by modern authorities. With respect to one important concept in natural science Albertus was ahead of his time: he noted that "since there are two things which we consider with respect to exterior appearance in living things, that is to say, shape and color, shape indicates conformity to or difference from a species more than does color."[28] Albertus's work on hawks and falcons was therefore not only important in itself but was still more important as an example for his time of how scientific enquiry into the natural world might be carried out.

Early in the fourteenth century Petrus Crescentius continued the encyclopedist tradition with his *Ruralium commodorum libri XII*. Written by a layman at the request of Charles II, King of Sicily, this work covered agriculture and field sports and included a chapter on falconry.[29]

The two main thirteenth-century works that focused specifically on falconry, in contrast to the encyclopedists, were Daude de Pradas's *Dels auzels cassadors* and the Emperor Frederick II's *De arte venandi cum avibus*. Daude de Pradas was a clergyman and a lyric poet. His *Dels auzels cassadors* was written in Provençal in the form of a long poem, and is the earliest surviving vernacular treatise on falconry. Daude's sources were the familiar ones: the letters to Ptolemy and to the Emperor Theodosius, and Guillelmus Falconarius. But included with his primarily derivative material were some observations based on Daude's own experience, as well as such practical advice as how to disguise another man's hawk so that the true owner would not recognize it.[30]

The second thirteenth-century treatise on falconry, Frederick II
of Hohenstaufen's *De arte venandi cum avibus,* is beyond doubt the
finest work based on actual observation of nature written in the Middle
Ages.[31] Frederick states that he had considered writing a work on
falconry for nearly thirty years,

> to correct the many errors made by our predecessors who, when
> writing on the subject, degraded the noble art of falconry by
> slavishly copying the misleading and often insufficient
> statements to be found in the works of certain hackneyed
> authors.[32]

In writing his work Frederick consulted the standard classical
authorities, had the works of several Arabic falconers translated for his
use, and (to quote his own words),

> at great expense, summoned from the four quarters of the earth
> masters in the practice of the art of falconry. We entertained
> these experts in our own domains, meantime seeking their
> opinions, weighing the importance of their knowledge, and
> endeavoring to retain in memory the more valuable of their
> words and deeds.[33]

But the *De arte venandi* was predominantly based on Frederick's own
observations and experiments, even when his findings ran counter to
the *dicta* of Aristotle. Frederick was explicit about this: "We discovered
by hard-won experience that the deductions of Aristotle . . . were not
entirely to be relied upon, more particularly in his descriptions of the
characters of certain birds."[34] Among the experiments Frederick made
was one in which he proved that vultures were attracted to carrion by
their sense of sight—not, as had been thought, by smell. He discovered
this by blindfolding a number of vultures and then putting meat before
them.[35] The Arab falconers Frederick invited to Sicily brought the
falcon's hood along with them. When Frederick saw its advantages, he
not only adopted it but improved it.[36] Other customs, such as the use of
live birds for luring, he did not adopt; but in the *De arte venandi* he
describes such customs and gives his reasons for not using them.[37] In
Haskins's words, his work "is a book of the open air, not of the
closet."[38]

The earliest surviving manuscript of the *De arte venandi*
contains many drawings of the various birds and stages of training

Frederick described.[39] Whether Frederick or his son Manfred planned the drawings is not certain. For a long time the drawings of birds were considered to be highly accurate representations, but this belief has recently been challenged.[40] The drawings of handling and training techniques, however, are full, detailed, and certainly the earliest of their kind so far as falconry is concerned. Their inclusion resulted not only in a beautiful volume, but also in one of the finest surviving examples of medieval scientific illumination. It has been said that Frederick's "Falcon Book marks a turning point in Western thought, the beginning of experimental science in the West."[41] However, Frederick's masterpiece had little direct influence in its period, while the less advanced and at times derivative work of Albertus Magnus was much more important in changing the views of contemporaries.[42]

In the fourteenth and fifteenth centuries a number of other treatises written by laymen appeared. Some of these works were limited to falconry, others dealt also with hunting, and one dealt with fishing as well. Many of these works are longer than the earlier treatises (with the exception of Frederick's), with more material on the training of birds; and they often contain social commentary—Juliana Berners's list of birds of prey appropriate to various ranks of society comes immediately to mind.[43] These works were almost all written in the vernacular, and they appear throughout Europe: in Spain in Juan Manuel's *Libro de la caza* and Pero López de Ayala's *Libro de la caça de las aves,* in the French *Livre du Roy Modus et de la Royne Ratio* and Gace de la Vigne's *Le Roman des déduis,* and in the English *Boke of St. Albans* attributed to Juliana Berners.[44] While there is some question as to the audience at which earlier works were aimed, the vernacular works were clearly directed at the upper levels of lay society. At the same time there were translations of earlier works into various languages, (Crescentius, for example, was translated into Italian, German, and French), and works on falconry appear among the earliest printed books.[45]

Where does this all leave us? First, one can conclude that the literature of falconry manifested the same trends exhibited in other kinds of scientific writing. The works move from citation of traditional authorities, or at least from "authority" established through attribution or rank and through antiquity, to works increasingly based on observation and, in Frederick's case, on experimentation. The treatment of hawking goes from the practical and particular to the more general, as authors seek and develop fuller and more realistic conceptions of the natural world. Writers on falconry put the sport in a wider perspective, and their interest shifts from the minutiae of the sport to consideration of the birds as part of the natural world. But while these trends are developing, there continues to be an interest in the sport itself, and this leads to more detailed works, written by a different class of author, for a wider—and perhaps a new—audience. For this audience—kings, nobles, and even rich bourgeois—falconry is transformed from a traditional sport whose maxims are passed down through a largely oral tradition, to a subject that can be studied systematically and analytically and can be developed and improved.

Nature at the end of the Middle Ages still represented different things to different groups of people. For the great majority, nature continued to be something to struggle against in the effort to produce a livelihood. But if works on falconry are an indicator, both upper classes and intellectuals experienced nature in new ways. As a by-product of this change, the upper classes, whose enthusiasm and money supported falconry, employed more effective techniques learned from the readily available treatises created by the theoreticians. And whether philosophers, theorists, and artists studied falconry as an aspect of God's universe or as a subject in itself, they no longer required authority to substantiate their view of the natural world; they were free to examine nature for themselves and to pass on the results of that experience.

NOTES

1. K. Lindner and H. Birkhan feel that falconry came to the West between 150 and 350 A.D. and cite as evidence several works earlier than that of Paulinus (*Reallexikon der Germanischen Altertumskunde,* 2d ed. [Berlin, 1968–], s.v. "Beizjagd"). I follow the analysis of Hans J. Epstein ("The Origin and Earliest History of Falconry," *Isis* 34, no. 6 [Autumn 1943]: 504), who believes that these earlier works refer to fowling as distinct from falconry. For Paulinus of Pella, see Epstein, p. 505, citing "Paulini Pellaei Eucharisticos," ed. W. Brandes, in *Corpus scriptorum ecclesiasticorum latinorum,* vol. 16, *Poetae Christiani minores: Pars I* (Vienna, 1888), 287, ll. 144–45.

2. For two letters of Sidonius Apollinaris in which hawking is mentioned see *Auctores antiquissimi,* vol. 8, *Gai Sollii Apollinaris Sidonii*

epistulae et carmina, ed. Christian Luetjohann, Monumenta Germaniae Historica (hereafter cited as MGH) (Berlin, 1887), 41, 61. For a reference by Gregory of Tours, see *Scriptores rerum Merovingicarum*, vol. 1, pt. 1, fasc. i, *Gregorii Episcopi Turonensis historiarum libri X*, ed. Bruno Krusch, MGH (Hanover, 1937), 211. For legislation at the councils of Agde (A.D. 506), Epaon (517), and Mâcon (585) against ownership of falcons by members of the clergy, see *Corpus Christianorum, Series Latina* (cited as *CCSL*), vol. 98, *Concilia Galliae, A. 314–A. 506*, ed. C. Munier (Turnhout, 1963), 226; and *CCSL*, vol. 98A, *Concilia Galliae, A. 511–A. 695*, ed. Charles de Clercq (Turnhout, 1963), 25, 245. For the relevant sections of the Salic, Burgundian, Alemannic, Ripuarian, Lombard, Bavarian, and Frisian laws, see *Legum sectio I: Leges nationum Germanicarum*, vol. 4, pt. 1, *Pactus Legis Salicae*, ed. Karl August Eckhardt, MGH (Hanover, 1962), 38–41; and *Leges*, 5 vols., MGH (Hanover, 1835–89), 3:39, 82, 117, 331, 572, 662; 4:73–74, 376; 5:231–32.

3. *Leges* 5:231–32; 3:571–72.

4. For letters from St. Boniface to King Ethelbald of Mercia and from King Ethelbald of Kent to St. Boniface, see *Epistolae*, vol. 3, *Epistolae Merowingici et Karolini Aevi*, MGH (Berlin, 1957), 337 (no. 69), 392 (no. 105). For Ælfric's fowler see *Ælfric's Colloquy*, ed. G.N. Garmonsway, 2d ed. (London, 1947), 30–32. On early English falconry in general, see Robin S. Oggins, "Falconry in Anglo-Saxon England," *Mediaevalia* 7 (1984 for 1981): 173–208.

5. Bernhard Bischoff, "Die älteste europäische Falkenmedizin (Mitte des zehnten Jahrhunderts)," in *Anecdota novissima: Texte des vierten bis sechzehnten Jahrhunderts*, Quellen und Untersuchungen zur Lateinischen Philologie des Mittelalters, 7 (Stuttgart, 1984), 171–82.

6. See Baudouin van den Abele, "Les traités de fauconnerie latins du XIIe siècle: Manuscrits et perspectives," *Scriptorium* 44 (1990): 276–86.

7. Charles Homer Haskins, "The Latin Literature of Sport," in *Studies in Medieval Culture* (Oxford, 1929; reprint, New York, n.d.), 110.

8. Haskins, *Studies in Medieval Culture*, 111; Daude de Pradas, *The Romance of Daude de Pradas, called Dels auzels cassadors*, ed. Alexander Herman Schutz (Columbus, Ohio, 1945), 136; "Guillelmus Falconarius," in Gunnar Tilander, ed., *Dancus Rex, Guillelmus Falconarius, Gerardus Falconarius: Les plus anciens traités de fauconnerie de l'occident publiés d'après tous les manuscrits connus*, Cynegetica, 9 (Lund, 1963), 134.

9. Adelard of Bath, *De cura accipitrum: A Mediaeval Latin Treatise by Adelard of Bath*, ed. A.E.H. Swaen (Groningen, 1937), 4; and see Dafydd Evans, "Adelard on Falconry," in Charles Burnett, ed., *Adelard of Bath: An English Scientist and Arabist of the Early Twelfth Century* (London, 1987), 25–27.

10. Daude de Pradas, 103, 122, 139.

11. "Gerardus Falconarius," ed. Tilander, 226–29.

58   Robin S. Oggins

12. "Dancus Rex," ed. Tilander, 86–88.

13. Hans J. Epstein, review of *Dancus Rex* . . . , ed. Gunnar Tilander, *Speculum* 40 (1965): 759–60.

14. Epstein, review of *Dancus Rex* . . . , 760.

15. Michael Prestwich, *Edward I* (Berkeley, 1988), 116–17; Great Britain, Public Record Office, E101/350/6, E101/351/20, E101/351/24, E101/351/30, E101/352/20, E101/352/56, E101/353/4/4, E101/364/14, E101/369/11. Sometimes pennies were bent over healthy birds, presumably to keep them in that condition. For Spanish presentations of wax images of hawks as ex-votos to regain three lost or stolen birds and to restore a sick goshawk to health, see D.P. Seniff, "Falconry, Venery, and Fishing in the *Cantigas de Santa Maria*," in Israel J. Katz and John E. Keller, eds., *Studies on the "Cantigas de Santa Maria": Art, Music, and Poetry* (Madison, 1987), 465–68.

16. "Dancus Rex," ed. Tilander, 12–16, 86–91.

17. "Guillelmus Falconarius," ed. Tilander, 158–61.

18. Recent works include Maurice de Gandillac, et al., *La Pensée encyclopédique au Moyen Age* (Neuchatel, 1966), and various articles in Annie Becq, *L'Encyclopédisme: Actes du Colloque de Caen, 12–16 janvier 1987* (Paris, 1991).

19. Vincent of Beauvais, *Speculum quadruplex sive speculum maius naturale / doctrinale / morale / historiale: Speculum naturale* (Graz, 1964), bk. 16, cols. 1196–99; Brunetto Latini, *Li livres dou tresor*, ed. Francis J. Carmody, University of California Publications in Modern Philology, 22 (Berkeley, 1948), 140–41; Alexander Neckam, *De naturis rerum, libri duo; with the Poem of the Same Author, De laudibus divinae sapientiae*, ed. Thomas Wright, Rolls Series [no. 34] (London, 1863), 77–78.

20. For Bartholomaeus Anglicus, see George Sarton, *Introduction to the History of Science*, vol. 2, *From Rabbi Ben Ezra to Roger Bacon* (Baltimore, 1931), pt. 2, 586–88; and Lynn Thorndike, *A History of Magic and Experimental Science During the First Thirteen Centuries of Our Era*, 2 vols. (New York, 1923), 2:401–35, and esp. quotation on p. 402.

21. Thorndike, 2:402.

22. Bartholomaeus Anglicus, *Medieval Lore from Bartholomew Anglicus*, ed. Robert Steele (London, 1924), 120–21.

23. Robin S. Oggins, "Albertus Magnus on Falcons and Hawks," in James A. Weisheipl, ed., *Albertus Magnus and the Sciences: Commemorative Essays, 1980* (Toronto, 1980), 443–44, 447–50, 453–60. Albertus's borrowing from Thomas may have been inadvertent: see Oggins, "Albertus Magnus on Falcons and Hawks," 443 n. 9 and 444 n. 17.

24. Albertus Magnus, "De avibus," in *De animalibus libri XXVI: nach der Cölner Urschrift*, ed. Hermann Stadler, 2 vols. (Münster in Westphalia, 1916–20), 2:1461, 1463–64. All references to Albertus's work will be to this edition.

25. Albertus Magnus, 2:1478.
26. Albertus Magnus, 2:1457–71, 1492–93.
27. For example, see *The Medieval Book of Birds: Hugh of Fouilloy's Aviarium*, ed. and trans. Willene B. Clark (Medieval & Renaissance Texts & Studies, vol. 80 [Binghamton, N.Y., 1992]), chap. 19, "That the Hawk is Carried on the Left Hand":

> It is customary to carry a hawk on the left hand, so that when released for hunting it may fly to the right. <Scripture> states, *His left hand is under my head, and his right hand shall embrace me* (Cant. 2:6). Worldly goods are on the left hand, but those to the right are eternal. Therefore, on the left sits the person who is concerned with worldly goods, but on the right soars the one who, with all his will, desires eternal things. There <on the right> the hawk will seize the dove, that is, anyone changed for the better will receive the grace of the Holy Spirit.

28. Albertus Magnus, 2:1464–65. For an analysis of Albertus's observations of nature in this work and of the accuracy of the observations, see Oggins, "Albertus Magnus on Falcons and Hawks," and see the identifications of the hawks proposed there. For other attempts to identify Albertus's hawks see Kurt Lindner, *Von Falken, Hunden und Pferden: Deutsche Albertus-Magnus-Übersetzungen aus der ersten Hälfte des 15. Jahrhunderts*, 2 vols., Quellen und Studien zur Geschichte der Jagd, 7 (Berlin, 1962), 1:44–54; Sebastian Killerman, *Die Vogelkunde des Albertus Magnus (1207–1280)* (Regensburg, 1910), 32–37; H. Stadler, ed., notes in Albertus Magnus, *De animalibus*; James J. Scanlan, ed. and trans., *Albert the Great, Man and the Beasts: De animalibus (Books 22–26)*, Medieval & Renaissance Texts & Studies, vol. 47 (Binghamton, N.Y., 1987), 222–88; and see additional references in Oggins, "Albertus Magnus on Falcons and Hawks," 445 n. 19. For an analysis of Albertus's material on the ailments of hawks and their treatment in the light of modern diagnoses, see Scanlan, Introduction, 41–44. It is characteristic of Albertus's outlook in his work on hawks that he notes, with respect to treatment, that "experience is the best master in such things" (Albertus Magnus, 2:1481).
29. Edmund Harting, *Bibliotheca accipitraria: A Catalogue of Books Ancient and Modern Relating to Falconry, with Notes, Glossary, and Vocabulary* (London, 1891), 161.
30. "Daude de Pradas," ed. Tilander, 8–9, 20–21, 69–71, 85ff., 110–11.
31. For bibliography on Frederick II see Carl A. Willemsen, *Bibliographie zur Geschichte Kaiser Friedrichs II. und der letzten Staufer*, MGH Hilfsmittel, 8 (Munich, 1986). For texts, see Friderici Romanorum Imperatoris Secundi, *De arte venandi cum avibus*, ed. Carl Arnold Willemsen,

2 vols. (Leipzig, 1942); and *The Art of Falconry, being the "De arte venandi cum avibus" of Frederick II of Hohenstaufen*, trans. and ed. by Casey A. Wood and F. Marjorie Fyfe (Stanford, Calif., 1943). The classic commentaries are still those of Charles Homer Haskins, "The *De Arte Venandi cum Avibus* of Frederick II" and "Science at the Court of the Emperor Frederick II," in *Studies in the History of Medieval Science* (Cambridge, Mass., 1924; reprint, New York, 1960): 299–326, 242–71; and Haskins, "The Latin Literature of Sport," in *Studies in Medieval Culture*, 105–23.

32. Frederick II, ed. Wood and Fyfe, 3. The references that follow will be to this edition.

33. Frederick II, 3.

34. Frederick II, 3–4.

35. Frederick II, 22.

36. Frederick II, 205–6.

37. Frederick II, 227–28.

38. Haskins, *Studies in Medieval Science*, 320.

39. For a facsimile of the Vatican manuscript of the *De arte venandi cum avibus* see Fredericus II, *De arte venandi cum avibus: Ms. Pal. Lat. 1071, Biblioteca Apostolica Vaticana*, with commentary by Carl Arnold Willemsen, Codices selecti 16 (text); codices e Vaticanis selecti 31 (commentary) (Graz, 1969). This has been reprinted in a smaller, much more affordable format as *Das Falkenbuch Kaiser Friedrichs II*, Die bibliophilen Taschenbücher, no. 152 (Dortmund, 1980).

40. W.B. Yapp, "The Illustrations of Birds in the Vatican Manuscript of *De arte venandi cum avibus* of Frederick II," in *Annals of Science* 40 (1983): 597–634. Elsewhere Yapp comments, "[The] birds [of *De arte venandi cum avibus*] . . . are remarkable for their time (mid-thirteenth century), even though they are not as good representations as has sometimes been claimed." *(Birds in Medieval Manuscripts* [London, 1981], 9).

41. Ernst Kantorowicz, *Frederick the Second, 1194–1250* (London, 1931; reprint, New York, 1957), 364.

42. On the survival of manuscripts of the *De arte venandi cum avibus*, see Frederick II, ed. Wood and Fyfe, lvii–lxxv.

43. Rachel Hands, *English Hawking and Hunting in "The Boke of St. Albans"* (London, 1975), 54–55.

44. Harting, 113–17, 61–66, 73–74, 1–2.

45. Harting, 138, 48–49, 71; Margaret Bingham Stillwell, *The Awakening Interest in Science During the First Century of Printing, 1450–1550* (New York, 1970), 186, 193, 206, 207, 212; and see Robin S. Oggins, "Falconry and Medieval Social Status," *Mediaevalia* 12 (1989 for 1986): 43–55.

THE PROTOHISTORY OF PIKE IN WESTERN CULTURE

Richard C. Hoffmann

The Entry of Pike into European Consciousnesses

The first, and most, humans who confronted *E. lucius* left no, or merely indirect, traces in the surviving record. In prehistoric and undocumented pasts, Europeans treated pike as a food. Pike remains from human occupation sites affirm this for all periods since the early Neolithic, but the evidence of bones and scales can carry only limited information. Early Europeans evidently brought pike to campsites, huts, halls, and castles generally across the native range of the species. At sites at which careful modern archaeologists have recovered many fish remains, those of pike are often well represented. We may infer that in the minds of the people who once lived there the creature we call pike was "food," perhaps even "preferred food," but all else can be but speculation. Did they distinguish by name this fish from others? Did they intentionally seek this fish rather than just accept the luck of the net, trap, hook, or spear? Did they have and use knowledge of its haunts and habits? Analogy with other hunting-and-gathering cultures suggests affirmative answers, but to confirm them requires products of human minds more conscious than a garbage heap where a few vertebrae landed after a meal. Perhaps because the native European range of *E. lucius* only slightly overlaps that of early literate civilizations in the Mediterranean basin, consciously produced evidence to give a sense of what at least some person or people *thought* about pike comes late.

When the fish identifiably enters the extant verbal record, it bears a less than flattering reputation. A late Roman poet and teacher of rhetoric, Decimus Magnus Ausonius (310–393), traveled from Bordeaux northeast to Trier to tutor the future emperor Gratian. The trip inspired

Ausonius to write the *Mosella*, a Latin poem on the Rhine tributary of the same name. When he there catalogued the fishes of the river, he introduced to the world of letters what he called *lucius*.[1] The first known written reference to pike deserves quotation in the original:

> Hic etiam latio risus praenomine cultor
> stagnorum, querulis vis infestissima ranis,
> lucius, obscuras ulva caenoque lacunas
> obsidet. Hic nullos mensarum lectus ad usus
> feruet fumosis olido nidore popinis.
>
> (*Mosella*, lines 120–124)

The precise sense and connotation of such typically stylized late classical poetry is hard to put into English. Something like this comes close:

> A dweller in backwaters does enjoy a proper Latin name,
> Lucius besieges the complaining frogs
> in obscure holes among sedges and mud.
> His meat is not for the dining table
> but sold at cheap shops smoky with its reeking stink.

At the very end of ancient civilization, then, Ausonius first articulated a perception of pike as fish and as resource. This creature lives in a swampy habitat and preys, from concealment, on other animals. Enmity between pike and frogs will be a regular theme of later literature. For late Roman consumers, however, Ausonius thought the pike poor fare (a status that some later writers will dispute).

Along the Wake of the "Water Wolf"

The two elements in Ausonius's introduction—object of nature and usefulness for humans—provide a frame for considering much of the subsequent record medieval Europeans left of the pike. Scattered references and allusions rank *lucius* with trout and carp among the freshwater fishes best known to humans, but this familiarity and knowledge long remained unsystematized.

Pike and other natural objects or phenomena belonged to what medieval Europeans long understood as a material veil that separated them from an ultimately spiritual reality. Some of them conceived the world of nature as actively hostile to humankind and to the divine plan for human salvation: for these, any concern for the material was but foolish sin. Others conceded a godly origin to this imperfect creation but thought it worth attention only insofar as it might thus dimly reflect the divine plan for ultimate perfection. In the latter context things of nature either served the mundane (and hence uninteresting) needs of life in this transient world or signified with their characteristics analogous powers and truths of the supernatural.

People who saw signs in nature focused on the fearsomeness and the predatory habits of pike. One early text asserts that the great Theodoric, king of the Ostrogoths, died in terror in 526 after seeing in the face of a pike brought to his dining table the visage of his recently executed enemy Symmachus. When Ruodlieb, hero of an eleventh-century Bavarian fairy tale, caught by quasi-magical means a whole list of fishes, pike were among the few given more than just a name: "Lucius . . . are the wolves among fishes, for they devour fish whenever they can catch them."[2]

Folktales and popular practices that perhaps originated in the assimilation of Christian notions by early medieval Europeans treated the pike and its attributes in mythic ways. In a widespread story the markings on the pike's head were seen as displaying the implements of Christ's passion: cross, ladder, hammer, nails, thorns, whip, and sponge. The tale explained that as Christ carried his cross through a brook where the pike lived, the fish looked out and was forever marked by what it saw. One variant of Scandinavian provenance listed the pike among the harmful things created by the devil to vex God. When angels captured these creatures and brought them before God, He saw on the pike's head a cross. So He blessed the fish and made it good and useful to humankind. A Latvian legend told how the pike grew very large and, forgetting in its pride God's command to eat only fish, caught and ate a fisherman. As a reminder, lest the pike again so err, the tale continued, God ordered the pike to carry in its head all the tools of the fisherman: the set net as jaws, the spear as teeth, the hooks as gills. What enters the set net is trapped; what the spear grasps is held firm; what reaches the hooks sticks tight. Of freshwater species only the pike appears as a protagonist in any of the family of stories about a competition (which collapsed in disorder) to be king among the fishes. Perhaps the idea of the pike as a fish of superior standing explains why in 1177 nobles in charge of a great knightly tournament held in Champagne offered a trophy pike to the champion.

Men of formal learning, who until the twelfth century came almost exclusively from a monastic environment, used natural history more formally to explicate moral or doctrinal points. A late exponent of this approach, the English canon and teacher Alexander Neckam, assembled in his *De naturis rerum* of the 1180s many such allegorical interpretations. For Alexander, *lucius* was the "aquatic wolf" and "tyrant of the waters" that fish could no more escape than humans could old age. When this greedy eater swallows fish too big for its stomach, it digests them by halves. In another passage, Neckam tells how, when the perch sees the pike, it raises its prickly fins in defence while the bream flees into the mud; so thwarted, the pike attacks other fishes. As wolfish as the pike, the writer continues, are the human despoilers of churches, but their subjects, being neither perch nor bream, must suffer their evil deeds. When shaped by a doctrine of signs, observations of nature gave understanding in ways alien to modern sensibilities.

Into (and, in some instances, beyond) the twelfth century, then, those literate Europeans who thought to write about the pike did so with emphasis on the predatory "water wolf." At the same time and for much longer, however, other Europeans, mostly illiterates, were perceiving in wild pike populations objects of use and value.

Human exploitation of pike drew in the Middle Ages only occasional literate attention, though the record grows from the twelfth century onwards. A tenth-century Anglo-Saxon schoolmaster, Ælfric of Eysham, taught his pupils Latin with made-up stories, including one about a fisherman who earned his living taking pike and other species with hooks and nets. Just about the same time Ælfric was composing his schoolbook, real fishermen in and around the estuary of the Odra (Oder) River on the south coast of the Baltic were angling for pike with iron and bronze spoons. (The shape of those lures found by archaeologists is familiar to any modern pike fisher.) Then, too, the Count of Anjou reserved the pike for his own use when he donated a fishery to the abbey of Marmoutier. Comparable passing references or incidental local evidence of pike fishing continue thereafter. The species was important in the yield of fisheries for which, in the late fourteenth century, the church of Troyes in Champagne kept income accounts. By that time pike were mentioned in contracts made between landowners and commercial fishermen near Arles and in records of disputes among the same kinds of people in Prussia. The earliest medieval sport fisher we can so far document, a late twelfth-century canon of Châlons-sur-Marne called Gui of Bazoches, listed pike among the fishes he enjoyed catching on a holiday at his uncle's country estate. Still, for long thereafter the techniques of fish capture remained unworthy of coherent and intentional written consideration by contemporaries.

The fishing, growth of human populations, clearance of land for farming, and development of the European economy during the tenth through thirteenth centuries brought wild pike populations under noticeable pressure. Expanding state authorities and literate administrations took measures to conserve valued fishery resources. In 1289 King Philip IV of France issued for all public waters a fisheries ordinance that established general gear restrictions and closed seasons and specified size limits for various fishes. No pike so small as to be worth 2 denier or less on the market could be legally taken. Comparable royal decrees went out regularly thereafter, though little is known of their enforcement or effect. In areas with less precocious central governments than France had, local and regional authorities took the lead. In the fifteenth century communities along the upper Rhine closed fishing for small pike from early spring until dates in late July or August to give the fish a chance to grow. In 1506 the Emperor Maximilian I, himself an enthusiastic and self-advertised devotee of field sports, decreed in his hereditary capacity as duke of Lower Austria minimum-size and season regulations for numerous species in that territory. To invalidate the excuse of misidentification, the copy of the decree used by the city government in Vienna included colored illustrations of each fish. The pike is unmistakable.

Maximilian and other authorities wanted to protect fish populations, including those of pike, because these were perceived as important sources of food. Medieval Europeans evidently thought pike far better meat than had Ausonius. In excavations of tenth-through fourteenth-century levels at Novgorod, remains of *E. lucius* ranked second in number only to those of zander (*Stizostedion lucioperca*). Popes at Avignon had purchasing agents obtain pike on buying trips to Burgundy. Inventories and account books kept by officials of Teutonic Order houses in late fourteenth-century Bohemia list pantry supplies of pike, both preserved (salted, pickled, dried) and fresh. Contemporaries in France paid 60 sous for a pike, while a carp went for 15. At Eger in western Bohemia the municipal price-fixing ordinance of 1465 set fresh pike at 36 heller per pound, below only salmon; salt pike at 30 heller per pound were the most expensive preserved fish. These price relationships probably explain why, when all prices in Europe rose during the sixteenth century, pike slowly gave way to carp in the extant menus of hospitals, convents, and orphanages, though they continued to grace the tables of the elite.

By then pike had also appeared in a developing but poorly studied genre of writing that offered readers a mix of medical, dietary, and culinary advice. Hildegard of Bingen was a mystic and abbess from the middle Rhine who in the 1150s carefully investigated the foods available for her nuns. She noted that what she called the *hecht* preferred pure water and ate fish rather than mud or weeds, and she concluded that it had good healthful flesh. She thus recommended pike meat for both the sick and the well and, to promote good digestion, the eating of pike livers. The housekeeping manual compiled in the 1390s by an elderly Parisian for his young wife advised male in preference to female pike except if she wished to make *rissoles* from the eggs. He offered particular recipes suited to pike in their ascending order of size: "lanterel, brochet, quarrel, lux et luceau."[3] In what is now recognized as the earliest known printed book on fishing, a manual done in Heidelberg in 1493 and many times reprinted in German, Flemish, and French (sometimes called *Dit Boecxken* after the Flemish title), the anonymous author also favored the milter (male) over the roe (female), but emphasized that any large pike was good eating all year round except when it was spawning. Gregor Mangolt of Zürich copied this advice on size and seasons—along with the traditional notion that pike was "like a wolf"—into his early sixteen-century handbook on the purchase and preparation of fish from the Bodensee (Lake Constance). The pirated edition of 1557 highly recommends a specimen taken in October and cooked whole either in its own juices, in a broth of sweet wine and salt, or "blue [*sic*]" in vinegar. If we better understood the history of such medieval cookbooks and medico-dietary thinking, we might detect therein early systematic knowledge about one aspect of the pike.

The Pike Enters Scholarship

The institutional and intellectual setting of the twelfth century, which yielded some of Hildergard's knowledge and in which Alexander Neckam worked, laid the foundations for modern scholarly and scientific traditions. New intellectual movements then justified the study of man and of nature without necessary reference to the supernatural, so that secular learning, though still subordinated to theology, could claim autonomous legitimacy. Scholastics at Paris and elsewhere recovered Aristotle's writings, including those on natural history, and compiled and updated what they learned from them. The great thirteenth-century natural philosophers like Thomas of Cantimpré, Vincent of Beauvais, and Albertus Magnus devoted to fish whole sections of their encyclopedias.[4] Perhaps more significantly, they organized their learning to distinguish between the general and the particular and to indicate the sources of their data. High medieval scholasticism thus took the necessary first step from mere incidental comment to the accumulation of knowledge that is one characteristic of scientific scholarship.

The authors of surviving thirteenth-century encyclopedias copied extensively from one another and from an earlier generation of writers (whose works they so effectively superseded as to cause their disappearance). As a result, much the same things were repeated in most scholastic discussions of pike. They point out that *lucius* is known as the "aquatic wolf" from its predatory habits. They describe it as a fish of fresh waters, with a wide mouth and many sharp teeth, that eats frogs and smaller fishes, preferably those without sharp spines and scales, but does not spare even its own kind or fish almost its own size. Their prey is taken in head first, for otherwise the scales and fins would prevent the pike from swallowing it. Albertus, who grew up in the vicinity of the Rhine, adds at this point in his treatment that he had seen that the pike first catches its prey crosswise to the body and, after carrying it a while and puncturing it with its teeth, releases it to turn it about and swallow it whole, head first. There is discussion of the shape of the pike's stomach and of a crystalline stone to be found in its head. Vincent alleges that Aristotle (who had not, in fact, written about *E. lucius*) is his source for the claim that female pike are made gravid by the south wind and ascend rivers to spawn where they do not live, so that their children will not be a burden to them. Other authorities, Vincent continues, see in the spawning movement a search for purer water. He

and his colleagues did not know that, a half century before, Hildegard of
Bingen had recorded direct observations of spawning behavior.

What the high medieval schoolmen had to say about pike must
be understood in terms of their principal intellectual concern: to
assemble statements from authoritative earlier writers into a coherent
body of learning, which could then be examined through the tools of
logic. The method had originated in the disciplines of law and
metaphysics and subsequently spread into theology, history, and natural
history. Because they achieved that purpose, the scholastic encyclopedists dominated learned European understandings of nature, of fish,
and of pike into the sixteenth century.

Towards Conscious Manipulation and Systematic Knowledge

Late twelfth- and thirteenth-century schoolmen were, therefore,
the first Europeans to write extensively and with broad intellectual
purpose about *lucius*, but rarely, however, did medieval intellectuals
connect their work directly with observed natural phenomena or see it as
affecting what people actually did in the world of nature. However,
during the later Middle Ages and the sixteenth century some Europeans
who encountered pike did come to link observation, thought, writing,
and action in three separate areas: pisciculture, fishing, and an emerging
science of ichthyology. Although these activities, or at least the
literatures of them, display occasional interconnections, they mainly
evolved, and can be examined, independently.

Artificial fish culture in medieval Europe differed from the
Roman emphasis on warm brackish-water coastal store ponds serving
the private needs of luxurious epicures. By processes not yet well
investigated, medieval Europeans established and spread a pisciculture
using regulated complexes of artificial freshwater ponds to segregate by
year-classes large numbers of cyprinids (mainly carp) for reproduction,
growth, fattening, and subsequent market sale. Incidental references in
documents transferring land or reporting court proceedings suggest that
the technical features of this system were available in northern and
central France around 1200. The evidence thereafter becomes
voluminous, first in western, then in east-central, Europe.

Intentional use of pike as a biological control agent in, and by-product of, carp culture by the thirteenth century in at least some regions of Europe is revealed in incidental and administrative records but, like fish culture in general, is not then the object of comprehensive, integrated, or synthetic discussion. A brief passage on fish ponds in the late thirteenth-century Anglo-French manual of property management called *Fleta* recommended against admission of "aquatic wolves" that would eat other fish. However, thirteenth-through fifteenth-century texts from regions as far apart as England, central France, and Bohemia do show pond owners purposely exploiting the pike's piscivorous habits by placing a few in their finishing ponds to keep down the numbers of small carp and thus encourage growth of the large. In 1258 Count Thibaut V of Champagne stocked six large pike along with 3520 carp and 10,000 bream and roach. Ponds belonging to the Duke of Burgundy a century later yielded at harvest numbers like 4,638 carp, 650 bream, and 533 pike from Sarée or 5,740 carp and 268 pike from l'Epervière. In late fourteenth-century England, where the exotic carp was still very rare or absent and the elaborated multipond technology likely not common, Chaucer described the well-to-do franklin of the *Canterbury Tales* as having "many a breme and luce" in his pond.

Conscious use of knowledge about the predatory pike and its effect on populations of other species for managing domesticated fish production thus long antedated codification of this knowledge into intentionally composed manuals of fish culture. A specialized technical literature on the operation of artificial fish ponds developed only with the late fifteenth-and early sixteenth-century proliferation of carp culture in east-central Europe—notably Bohemia, Moravia, Silesia, and parts of southern Poland and Germany. Handbooks like *De piscinis* ("On fishponds") by the Moravian prelate Jan Skaly z Dubravka (Dubravius), composed privately for the rich merchant Anton Fugger in 1525 and printed in Wroclaw in 1547, or *O sprawie, sypaniu, wynierzeniu, i rybnieniu stawów* (*On the Operation, Excavation, Surveying, and Stocking of Ponds*) by the veteran Polish pond master Olbrycht Strumieński, printed in Kraków in 1573, or others known only in manuscript or done somewhat later make explicit little about pike that cannot now be inferred as known earlier to late medieval operators of piscicultural enterprises. These manuals advise keeping the predator out of the spawning ponds but stocking it in the third pond to eat the superfluous offspring of precocious three-year-old carp, which would otherwise inhibit the growth of the market-destined parents. They point out as well that pike from these well-managed and clean waters will be delicious for the pond owner's dining or remunerative for sale. The sixteenth-century writers on artificial fish culture also affirmed more clearly than may be shown before that pike spawn in weeds and shallows like the other fishes of their ponds and earlier in the season than carp.

In the present context, however, the intellectual role of the writers on fish culture has greater importance than the particular data they offered. Their observational knowledge of pike was integrated and systematized in ways hitherto unknown. The whole empirical technology of rearing fish, which had developed outside the ambit of literate social groups, was brought by these authors into that cultural setting, organized for communication through the written word, and disseminated by the new means of handling information, the printed book. Their works were translated and adapted into other languages and used in the writings of other commentators. A cumulative literate body of applied knowledge had been established.

European thought on catching pike and other fish emerged, like that on fish rearing, from scattered unintentional traces of illiterate and disorganized empirical practice to coherent consideration in written, and then printed, treatises. Before the fourteenth-century no known text purports to describe or instruct in the arts and crafts of fishing; as mentioned before, our knowledge of medieval capture techniques comes from passing and often obscure references in writings done for other ends, chiefly literary or regulatory. Thereafter, however, works now extant make more visible for angling than for pisciculture the cultural process whereby a "literature" evolved from lists of prescriptions and short tracts to extended, comprehensive, and self-conscious didactic treatments.

The few brief early discussions of fish-capture techniques now known to have been written in fourteenth-century Italy, Germany, and England do not specify target species for the attractants, piscicides, baits, and gear they prescribe, but comparable or larger notes from the fifteenth century do. The pike, notably piscivorous among the easily seen European fishes of fresh waters, thus required different treatment from that for fishes susceptible to bread pastes, maggots, or live or simulated insects. A fifteenth-century Germany translator of the section on fishing from the fourteenth-century agricultural manual by the Bolognese Pietro do Crescenzi interpolated in a passage on angling the comment that a single hook baited with a small fish was good for "all predators like pike."[5] The interpolator adds that strong hooks and a line covered with wire are needed because of the pike's teeth. Several of the more numerous English manuscript tracts offer similar advice. One in a fifteenth-century paper manuscript (Harley 2389) at the British Library goes into more detail, prescribing "to catch a pyke at all tymes" a double hook mounted two fathoms below a large cork and baited with a small roach, gudgeon, or bleak that has been rubbed with camphor and oil to make it shine and with asafetida to attract by odor. Especially in May, September, and October a frog is the preferred bait, and from January through March the pike will bite at a worm, but the small fish properly anointed is otherwise the best. A monk at the Bavarian abbey of Tegernsee, who about 1500 wrote down the methods of the professional fishers employed there, described techniques like the English ones, but also mentioned the use of a hook wrapped with purple silk and a special mix of feathers.

The long Tegernsee manuscript still only listed baits, but by its time a genuine angling literature, which offered to a reading public organized treatment of the subject, was already appearing. The pamphlet printed in Heidelberg in 1493 (see above) combined advice on baits, a fisherman's calendar, and a curious satirical comparison of fish to human society ("The pike is a robber"). Its printer, Jacob Köebel, expressed surprised delight at finding a written discourse on the useful and pleasant activity of fishing. Earlier still, the anonymous English *Treatyse of Fysshynge wyth an Angle* (at times ignorantly ascribed to a mythical "Dame Juliana Berners" or "Barnes"), probably composed about 1420 and surviving in its initial form only as a fragmentary mid-century manuscript, had articulated the sporting quality of angling, described the necessary tackle, and detailed its use in general and for particular fishes. The extant portion, however, gives for pike only the recommendation to dye a chalk line brown and protect it with a wire. When the complete *Treatyse* appeared in print in the second *Boke of St. Albans* in 1496, some revision had occurred and larger coverage was given to pike fishing. This begins with moral opprobrium for the pike's predatory behavior, though these habits then explain the recommended baits and tactics: thread a roach or herring on a hook and float it in a likely pike habitat; hook a frog through the skin of the neck and cast it into those places; soak a small fish in asafetida before using it as bait; "and yf ye lyst to haue a good sporte, thenne tye the corde [with baited hook] to a gose fote [goose's foot] and ye shall se god halynge [a good tug-of-war] whether the gose or the pyke shall haue the better."[6]

With the German tract of 1493, republished dozens of times in the next century and incorporated into other continental works, and the printing of the English *Treatyse*, fishing as the practical application of observed data from nature entered the world of the public literary culture. On the European continent a tradition of angling literature subsequently faltered, but in England it grew and, with it, a cumulative angling perspective on the pike. At least some fishers read and some writers fished. In *The Arte of Angling* published anonymously in 1577 William Samuel, a Huntingdonshire clergyman, labeled the pike (here "pickerel") the "freshwater wolf" for the first time in English and noted its difference from other fishes in lacking a fear of man. Samuel advised familiar capture techniques suited to the pike's size and predatory nature: the wire-protected and heavy line; the roach, dace, frog, or large worm as bait; a drifting or still presentation. A new suggestion he offered was to hook a dead bait through the nose and move it actively in the water and then, when the pike took, to wait until it carried, released, retook, and swallowed the bait before setting the hook. The conceptions of pike and pike fishing given in both the *Treatyse* and the *Arte* became commonplaces in English angling books done about 1600 and, later, in *The Compleat Angler* of Izaak Walton. This was in part because these authors lifted whole passages from the earlier works. In angling, then, a second systematic literate tradition about pike had emerged from the changing European consciousness.

For knowledge of pike, William Samuel drew in 1577 on more than angling experience and the written precedent of the *Treatyse*. His fictive expert, Piscator, tells his neophyte companion about a reputed 267-year-old pike captured in Germany which, says he, "Gesnerus doth make report of."[7] He refers to the Swiss physician and naturalist Konrad von Gesner (1516–1565), a cofounder of modern ichthyological and modern bibliographical science. Gesner and his fellow sixteenth-century students of fishes established the third context in which European perceptions of *lucius* departed from the protohistorical and the presystematic.

This essay can provide no history of sixteenth-century ichthyology, just a sketch of how *lucius* was handled in that cultural setting. Gesner's principal work on fishes, the third volume of his *Historia animalium*, "which is on the nature of fishes and aquatic animals," was published in Zürich in 1558. Its author exploited scholarship by French, Italian, and German writers, as well as his own extensive network of correspondents. Gesner's treatment of *lucius* conformed to what had already become a standard mode of topical organization. His text begins with the nomenclature of Latin and the European vernaculars, for scientific inquiry requires consensus on the object of discussion. Thus, he cited Ausonius but rejected as synonyms for *lucius* Pliny's *esox*, Strabo's *oxrynchus*, and Aristotle's *lupus*. In his examination of recorded distribution Gesner noted the absence of pike from Spain. Physical descriptions, external and internal, follow. Gesner referred to writings of his contemporary Pierre Belon, and of his medieval predecessor Thomas of Cantimpré. After giving the latter's report on a crystal stone in the brain of pike, Gesner specified that he could not confirm this from his own observations. He then mentioned that some people saw in the head markings of the instruments of the Passion.

Further sections in Gesner's discussion treat similarly the habitat, habits, capture, and dietary value of *lucius*. This dweller in quiet fresh waters "besieges, as Ausonius says" its prey, fishes and frogs, from cover. Feeding habits are described with reference to Thomas of Cantimpré and Albertus Magnus and then amplified with contemporary reports of the pike's voracity: one from the Rhone is said to have seized the lip of a mule brought to water; a man from Kraków told of pike eating small dogs and biting the feet of servant girls who swam in a fish pond. "Ein Hecht is ein Rauber" ("A pike is a robber") is acknowledged as coming from the German "locularia piscium," the satirical comparison printed in 1493. Do pike reproduce by spontaneous generation? Gesner summarized earlier arguments and then pointed out that spawning pike and pike fry had been seen in the Elbe and in Switzerland. He listed techniques for catching pike and reported on size, season, and gear restrictions in force in various south German jurisdictions. He contrasted Ausonius's disdain for its food value with the favor of contemporary practice and writers. Gesner also offered exemplary recipes, culinary and medicinal, including some taken from his compatriot Gregor Mangolt. In this concluding section Gesner

reported both that some people eat raw pike skin as a prophylactic against fever and that pike ashes relieve pains in "shameful places," though noting that the latter claim is "uncertain."
       To develop knowledge about pike, Konrad von Gesner and his contemporaries read, observed, and catalogued.[8] They gathered data from all available sources, linked that data to the organism to which it referred, and began to sort out that data. The pike had become an object of inquiry or, if you will, of science. But sixteenth-century science was still closely connected to humanistic scholarship, for its practitioners had first to find and summarize the information in earlier writings done for whatever purpose. Hence Gesner's place as a father of bibliography (his *Biblioteca universalis* of 1545 listed some 10,000 Latin, Greek, and Hebrew works) cannot be separated from his approach to ichthyology. The flood of information released by the printing press allowed, even demanded, that knowledge become an ordered but open-ended accumulation of data for collaborative consideration and incremental change.
       Sixteenth-century shifts in the form, content, and context of scientific thinking about *E. lucius* thus replicated those then occurring in writings on the culture and capture of this fish. Information once confined to the unsystematic empiricism of illiterate practitioners or to an intellectual elite of professional scholars now became accessible to a wider array of people through publication in many identical copies. Writers of treatises and manuals sorted this data, organized it, and made it potentially subject to the tests of observation and subsequent revision. William Samuel's use of Gesner's writings and Gesner's of the 1493 tract even suggest new possibilities of cross-fertilization among hitherto separate groups interested in the pike. The "aquatic wolf" remained in the sixteenth century a creature of awe and mystery for Europeans, witness the tales of its age and ferocity Gesner thought proper to relate. Europeans now possessed about the pike, however, a corpus of shared and intentionally shaped information available to those interested in it for whatever reason—food, sport, management, or scientific curiosity.

NOTES

This article first appeared as a foreword to *An Annotated Bibliography of the Pike, Esox lucius (Osteichthyes: Salmoniformes)* ed. E.J. Crossman and J.M. Casselman (Toronto: Royal Ontario Museum, 1987). Reprinted with the permission of the Royal Ontario Museum.

Editorial policy for Life Science Publications of the Royal Ontario Museum discourages the use of footnotes. This essay provides fewer exact citations than is normal in historical scholarship. These notes therefore give detailed references only for extended direct primary quotations and for those few modern studies that have most importantly influenced the interpretations here offered. The author welcomes inquiries about the source of any evidence inadequately described here.

1. The only recorded Latin name for pike is *lucius*, which, as Ausonius says, was also a common Roman personal name. No useful explanation for the homonymy has ever been suggested. The Latin root *luc-* is subsequently attached to this fish in all Romance languages, in Gaelic, and into the seventeenth century, in English (as *luce*). French gradually abandoned the Latinate form for another of possible Gallic origin, *brochet* (literally "poker," "spear," and hence in English under a French influence, "pike"). The German *Hecht* (<*hachit*, compare Old English *haecit*) carries the same connotation. *Esox* is a Latin word derived from the Celtic term for salmon and was, until the time of Linnaeus, used not for pike but for various salmonids.

2. *The Ruodlieb, Linguistic Introduction, Latin Text, and Glossary*, ed. Gordon B. Ford, Jr. (Leiden, 1966), fragment X, lines 39–40: "Lucius et rufus, qui sunt in piscibus hirpus. Pisces namque vorant, illos ubi prendere possunt." Translation by Gordon B. Ford, Jr., *The Ruodlieb, The First Medieval Epic of Chivalry from Eleventh-Century Germany* (Leiden, 1965), 74.

3. *Le Menagier de Paris*, ed. G.E. Brereton and J.M. Ferrier (Oxford, 1981), 173, 181–183, 231–232. Late medieval French texts do not always agree on the size sequence of names given to *lucius*.

4. Christian Hünemörder, "Die Geschichte der Fischbücher von Aristoteles bis zum Ende des 17 Jahrhunderts," in *Deutsches Schiffahrts-archiv*, 1 (1975), 188–198, surveys formal scholarship in medieval and early modern times.

5. "alle rawbfisch als hechte." Kurt Lindner, ed. *Das Jagdbuch des Petrus de Crescentiis in deutschen Ubersetzungen des 14, und 15, Jahrhunderts* (Berlin, 1957), 159. This passage in Book 10, chapter 38, of the fifteenth-century translation is absent from the same section of both a

fourteenth-century German version and de Crescenzi's original (there
10:39), which make no reference to particular fish species.
    6. John McDonald, *The Origins of Angling* (New York, 1963), 220,
is a facsimile of the printed text: the manuscript passage occurs on p. 154.
    7. *The Arte of Angling 1577*, ed. Gerald E. Bentley (Princeton,
1958), facsimile fols. D.iii. verso–D.iiii recto, and modernized text pp. 46–
47. Identification of the reference to Gesner was made by D.E. Rhodes, "A
new line for the angle, 1577," in *The Library*, 5th series 10 (1955), 123–
124, who traced the passage to Gesner's *Nomenclator aquatilium
animantium* (Zürich, 1560), 316. Gesner had earlier published the tale,
however, in the dedication to his *Historia animalium, III. De piscium &
aquatilium animantium naturae* (Zürich, 1558), fols. a3 recto–a6 verso, in
which he attributed it to his own teacher, the German humanist Conrad
Celtis.
    8. These final paragraphs are influenced by Elizabeth L. Eisenstein,
The Printing Press as an Agent of Change (Cambridge, 1979), abridged as
The Printing Revolution in Early Modern Europe (Cambridge, 1983).

ANIMAL IMAGES IN GOTTFRIED VON STRASSBURG'S *TRISTAN*: STRUCTURE AND MEANING OF METAPHOR

Margaret Schleissner

In his essay "Das wunnecliche tal," Rainer Gruenter emphasizes the particular way in which Gottfried, at the climax of his poem, the description of the lovers' cave and its surrounding landscape, combines and manipulates material from two distinct and apparently mutually exclusive traditions: Christian mysticism and the antique topos of the *locus amoenus*. The effectiveness of Gottfried's nature description, according to Gruenter, lies in its ambivalence, the fact that elements that participate in seemingly contrary spheres are brought together in such a way as to effect not a sublimation of their attributes but a kind of dynamic relationship of reciprocal neutralization. Thus the sacred cave is "paganized" through the traditional rhetorical *locus amoenus* description, just as the bucolic scenery is "sacralized" through the language of Christian allegory.[1] Furthermore, Gruenter writes, the objects of the landscape are characterized more through their function than through their attributes. For example, through the device of the personification of nature, which belongs traditionally to the antique *locus amoenus* description and here informs Gottfried's metaphor of the Arthurian courtly festival (16891–16909),[2] the objects of nature participate actively as courtiers in the ideal life of the lovers. In this way, passages descriptive of condition become descriptive of action.[3]

The conscious appropriation and unique combination of elements from diverse intellectual spheres underlies Gottfried's use of animal lore and imagery as well. The same image may carry a negative valence according to one tradition and at the same time be associated with a positive or neutral valence in another. It therefore seems entirely possible that, as Gruenter suggests, the conscious play with traditional topics and the associations they evoke effect a reciprocal and therefore

77

dynamic relativization of conventional values. Such a dynamic structure underlying metaphor in turn highlights the central thematic ambiguities of the text—the tension, for example, between absolute passion and the courtly society that opposes it, or between notions of *minne* (love) and *êre* (honor).

Moreover, Gruenter's characterization of the oscillation between condition (Zustand) and action (Vorgang) in the description of the lovers' cave and its surroundings extends to Gottfried's animal images as well. Just as a kind of immediate identification between nature and human beings is effected through the device of personification in the context of the lovers' cave, so at those points in which human figures are associated with animals a similar relationship between condition and function pertains. Passages descriptive of action, in other words, in which the animal seems to have a primarily epic function, often describe condition. Conversely, where animals appear primarily as images (that is, as metaphors descriptive of condition), they often describe function or anticipate epic action.

The image of the falcon associated with Isolde, the image of the boar associated with Tristan, the two dogs Petitcreiu and Hiudan, and the action involving the two stags—the excoriation of the hart upon Tristan's arrival in Cornwall and the hunt of the marvelous stag of the Minnegrotte—are all in some measure twofold; that is, they occur in two major contexts, require signification as two opposing poles of a duality, and exhibit a dynamic structure of participation in action and condition. As will be seen, all are systematic contributors to Gottfried's interpretation of the Tristan story. The system that links the four types of animals together and advances them in pairs is a uniform concept of dynamic duality.

The Falcon

Isolde is described as bird, specifically a falcon, in two passages: the scene in which she appears with her mother before the Irish court and in the account of the effects of the love potion. The passage that contains the image of the bird to characterize Isolde's appearance at her father's court depicts her as a free, predatory bird and, simultaneously, as an artificial, feathered decoy:

suoze gebildet über al,
lanc, ûf gewollen unde smal
gestellet in der waete,
als sî diu Minne draete
ir selber zeinem vederspil ... (ll. 10897–10901)

gevedere schâchblicke
die flugen dâ snedicke
schâchende dar unde dan:
ich waene, Isôt vil manegen man
sîn selbes da beroubete ... (ll. 10961–10965)

si was an ir gelâze
ûfreht und offenbaere,
gelîch dem sperwaere,
gestreichet alse ein papegân;
si liez ir ougen umbe gân
als der valke ûf dem aste; (ll. 10996–11001)

[exquisitely formed in every part, tall, well-molded and slender,
and shaped in her attire as if Love had formed her to be her own
falcon ... Rapacious feathered glances flew thick as falling
snow, ranging from side to side in search of prey. I know that
Isolde robbed many a man of his very self! ... Her figure was
free and erect as a sparrow hawk's, well-preened as a parakeet's.
She sent her eyes roving like a falcon on its bough.]

Unbound by love, Isolde still functions here within a
conventional scheme: the standard prelude to a courtly love relationship
consists in the exchange of provocative glances. (Gottfried always
stresses either the harmony or disharmony of hearts and eyes in such
situations.) Clearly, Gottfired emphasizes the visual in these passages,
and as A.T. Hatto remarks in his article "Der minnen vederspil Isot," he
uses verbs and verbal constructions ("rapacious feathered
glances ... flew ... roving") to "activate" the image of the falcon.[4] The
image of the bird in this context refers to Isolde's simultaneous function
as bird of prey and lure: her own glances and the effect she has on those
who catch sight of her denote reciprocal action.

Hatto seems to overlook lines 10964–65, which describe the
effect of Isolde's appearance on the men at court. Thus, he discounts

Ranke's translation of "vederspil" (1091) as "Lockvogel" (artificial decoy) for poetic reasons as too static.[5] Whether or not such a translation is justified in terms of medieval hunting practice, it must be acknowledged that Isolde functions in general as a lure causing men to lose their freedom. Indeed, this recalls the fact that it was precisely the presence of hunting birds on the Norwegian merchant ship (also enumerated by name, 2201–07)[6] that lured Tristan aboard and brought him to Cornwall originally. Once in Cornwall, the homeless boy, bewailing his separation from family and friends, curses those same birds, again by name (2593–94). Then, in Tristan's second journey to Ireland, Isolde functions as a lure, drawing him toward that country— and this proves to be the source of even greater misfortune for Tristan.

Upon the return voyage from Ireland, Tristan and Isolde inadvertently drink the love potion. With this act, as Hatto notes, the image of Isolde as falcon is fundamentally changed: she is the falcon caught in the lime tree of love, the more she struggles to escape the more she must succumb. Passages describing the effects of the love potion on Isolde are embedded in images of war, ensnarement, and subsequent surrender, culminating in the epithetical phrase, "Der Minnen verderspil Isôt" (11989, "Love's falcon, Isolde"), after which the image of the falcon is dropped, its function having been fulfilled.[7]

The image of Isolde's ensnarement in the lime tree of love recalls the same image ušed in the story of Tristan's parents in connection with Tristan's father, Riwalîn (839–865). Like Riwalîn, Isolde finally capitulates by bringing heart and eyes into harmony so that they have but a single common object: "Love and the man" ("minne und man," 11844). Moreover, as in the case of Riwalîn, Isolde's surrender prepares the way for actions that fly in the face of courtly conventions.

In Hatto's analysis the parallel to the passage with Riwalîn makes one thing clear. Through the introduction of the purely literary device of the falcon, Gottfried unequivocally ascribes to the love potion the power to effect a radical emotional reversal. There can be no doubt that the potion alone has caused Tristan and Isolde to fall in love: a metaphor descriptive of condition elucidates epic action.[8]

The Boar

In four passages—Tristan's investiture as knight, the preparation for the battle with Môrolt, Marjodô's dream, and the description of Tristan and Kâedîn's method of fighting—Tristan is identified with the image of the boar. Klaus Speckenbach has described the various associations the boar might have had for Gottfried and his contemporaries.[9] Daniel's dream of the successive appearance of four beasts—lioness, bear, leopard, and boar—in the seventh book of Daniel was commonly interpreted in the Middle Ages as the doctrine of the consecution of the four world empires (*translatio imperii*). The boar signified the most powerful and hence the last of these, the Roman Empire, of which the Holy Roman Empire was but the continuation. Thus, positive value is ascribed to the boar, for instance, in the *Kaiserchronik* and the *Annolied*, as well as in numerous examples of heroic epic: the boar achieves ascendancy through its qualities as an indefatigable fighter. In contradistinction to this positive interpretation of the boar in Daniel's dream, the theological interpretation, based on Jerome's commentary, castigates the boar because it ushers in the destruction of the world. The boar is described as having eleven horns; the eleventh horn signifies the Antichrist. These divergent valuations of the boar in the book of Daniel—one secular and positive, the other theological and negative—correspond to the two major traditions regarding the boar that Speckenbach outlines: (1) the antique-Germanic tradition, based more or less on "scientific" observation, which depicts and praises the boar as an invincible warrior, and (2) the Judeo-Christian tradition, based on the only other instance of a boar in the Vulgate (Psalms 79:14) in which a boar from the woods (*aper de silva*) ravages the vineyard symbolic of the kingdom of Israel or the church of Christ. Influenced by this passage, the Christian exegetical tradition regards the boar as an exclusively negative figure, categorically as the destroyer.

As Speckenbach convincingly argues, Gottfried seems to have been fully aware of both traditions and to have played them off one against the other.[10] The changing aspect of the boar emblem, moreover, seems to correspond to the three phases of Tristan's life when the work is considered from the point of view of a Tristan biography.

In the scene of Tristan's investiture as knight at Mark's court, and again in the description of Tristan's preparation for battle with

Môrolt, we learn that Tristan's weapons carry the somewhat ridiculous combination of a shield bearing the emblem of a black boar (4940 and 6618–20) and a helmet engraved with the arrow of Venus (4943–44 and 6598). The most we can say about the emblem of the boar as it applies to Tristan in these passages is that Gottfried uses it in connection with the antique-Germanic tradition. Insofar as the story of Tristan's life in the stage before the love potion is concerned, he is still depicted as the invincible fighter who is historically and politically effective. The boar, understood as the symbol of bravery and inconquerability in battle, is relativized, however, even at this stage: the shield with the boar is mentioned only in conjunction with the helmet and its emblem of love, which clearly anticipates the next phase of Tristan's life.

In the context of a Tristan biography it is perhaps significant that the shield with the boar is destroyed (9038) in the fight with the dragon to win the hand of Isolde in Mark's name.[11] The helmet with the emblem of love, however, remains, and it is precisely by means of its reflection that Isolde discovers Tristan in the bog.

The episode with the love potion introduces the next phase of Tristan's life, in which he assumes the role of exemplary lover. This new phase begins with a short interlude in which Tristan and Isolde live their love happily and unsuspected at Mark's court. It includes the Gandîn episode and ends with Marjodô's discovery of the lovers following the dream of the boar, after which the so-called Tristan-Isolde-Minne is realized under its most characteristic feature, that of deception followed by counterdeception.

Marjodô's dream (13515–13540) occurs simultaneously with a rendezvous between Tristan and Isolde. The dream itself, in which the boar is unmistakably identified with Tristan, contains clear allusions to both the antique-Germanic and Judeo-Christian boar traditions. On the one hand, Gottfried enumerates the naturalistic attributes of the boar that contribute to the notion of his fearlessness, specifically the foaming at the mouth (13521 and 13536), the sharpening of the teeth (31521), and the boar's turning to engage the hunters face-to-face (13522).[12] On the other hand, the description of the boar from the woods (13518, literally the *aper de silva!*) that breaks into the palace of the king is an obvious allusion to the psalm passage, calculated to align Tristan with the image of the destroyer. Here it is important to note, however, that Gottfried deviates from his source in two major ways. First of all, in Gottfried's version, as opposed to that of Friar Róbert's, *Saga of*

Tristram and Isönd, the steward Marjodô appears as the frustrated admirer of the queen (13600–05). Second, in the *Saga* Mark is wounded by the tusks of the boar. In Gottfried, the dream describes not a mortal attack on Mark but merely a defilement of his bed and is therefore a projection of the steward's jealousy.[13]

Certainly, the dream is meant to reassert the question of the ethical nature of *Tristanminne* in the mind of the audience: Tristan is the defiler of the marriage bed, the sacrament of marriage and the queen. Yet he appears unequivocally as the destroyer only in the mind of the steward, not in the opinion of the narrator. Thus Gottfried's clever manipulation of both boar traditions yields the conclusion that Tristan's guilt is relativized by the subjectivity of the dreamer, who is motivated by personal revenge and condemned by Gottfried's narrator.

The fourth and final reference to Tristan as boar describes Tristan and Kâedîn's method of fighting (18894ff.) and belongs to the third and final phase of Tristan's biography.[14] In this phase of his final separation from Mark's court, Tristan appears in Arundêl and elsewhere in the role of knight, a political-historical figure, but with this condition: he now seeks *âventiure* not for its own sake, but for the sake of distraction (18723f.), and because he cannot refuse to undertake anything he is asked to do in Isolde's name. *Mutatis mutandis,* then, Tristan's boar emblem, which signifies the invincible warrior, again gains ascendancy in the third and final phase of his life.

Petitcreiu and Hiudan

In certain older versions of the Tristan legend, that of Béroul and those associated with this branch, Tristan's hunting dog Hiudan appears as an integral part of the episode in the wilderness. With the Tristan story of Thomas, however, a new dog, Petitcreiu, is introduced to the tradition.

According to the *Saga,* during his sojourn at the court of a duke of Poland, Tristan encounters a many-colored dog, whose coat changes hue when regarded from different perspectives and whose bell has the magical power to eliminate all distress. Kept and shown in lavish circumstances, the dog is a valuable present from an elf-woman. At great peril, Tristan procures the dog for his mistress, and although the gift is most precious to Isönd, it is not long before this courtly lapdog accompanies the lovers to the woods, where he proves his mettle as an extraordinary hunting hound (95–100). The two dogs are thus conflated: the "wonder dog" Petitcreiu, who functions initially as a love token in Thomas's version, nonetheless remains associated with Tristan and the hunt. Moreover, there is no indication that Isönd, after receiving the dog, tears off the bell as she does in Gottfried's version. On the contrary, beside the replica of the queen in the hall of statues is the representation of her dog, "which shook its head and rang its bell and was very cleverly made" (121). The transformation of Petitcreiu from an instrument of one-sided joy into a symbol of mutual sorrow is, therefore, Gottfried's innovation.[15]

Gottfried devotes 100 lines (15795–15894) to the presentation of Petitcreiu. Tristan's melancholy provides the immediate occasion for the dog's introduction to the story, inasmuch as Duke Gilân wishes to distract his guest with his pet (15795–804). As a present from a goddess, Petitcreiu is ascribed supernatural origin, created by and for love (15810–14). From the beginning, then, Petitcreiu is connected with *minne* as a category of existence.

There follows a description of the twofold effect generated by Petitcreiu's colors and his bell. (The description of the lovers' cave refers to the fact that both visual and acoustic pleasures could be had there.) The description of Petitcreiu's colors (15821–15848) proceeds from an unidentifiable mixture, through all phases of the color spectrum expressed as hyperboles, and toward a new and noble synthesis, a perfect unity in multiplicity, and returns to the colorlessness of the beginning.

Moreover, the fact that the dog's mechanical properties are stressed and that his colors change with shifts in perspective suggests that Petitcreiu represents a metaphor of metaphor. Petitcreiu as an image, in other words, refers to its own artificiality. In any case, the hyperbolic phrases of this passage also inform the allegory of the lovers' cave, so that in retrospect Petitcreiu emerges as an emblem of a new kind of *minne*.

In fact all of Petitcreiu's qualities—the magical charm of the bell (15849–63) and the fact that he neither whines nor barks, is obliging when it comes to play, and doesn't eat or drink (15890–93)—anticipate the lovers' cave to such an extent that he figures, essentially, as its miniature embodiment.[16]

Tristan's sense of ecstasy at the acquisition of Petitcreiu approaches his feeling of delight with Isolde, so that Petitcreiu represents for Tristan a substitute for Isolde in terms of pleasure. In this spirit, he decides to forgo the pleasure that Petitcreiu provides and to have the dog delivered to his mistress so that she too may be relieved of her sorrow. But Isolde, with the gesture of tearing away the bell, which she does in the name of loyalty (16404) to "renew her suffering" (16358, "ze niuwenne ir senede leit"), inverts Tristan's intention by denying herself the acoustic pleasure that the dog provides and creating a substitute for Tristan in sorrow. Isolde's action reestablishes an equilibrium between the lovers and, in that sense, represents the counterpart of Tristan's initial act of self-denial. Taken together, these acts form a first symbolic avowal of a selfless, spiritual love: Isolde affirms the mutuality of their suffering as an integral part of their love.

In the scene of the lovers' departure from Mark's court a second dog, Hiudan, is introduced (16650–54). Gottfried stresses that it is Hiudan, not Petitcreiu, that accompanies the lovers to the woods (16663). Like Petitcreiu, Hiudan appears initially in his natural colors, so to speak—that is, in his primarily external role as one of the pack of courtly hunting dogs probably used by Mark as well.[17] To begin with, Tristan selects Hiudan from the pack and leads him on the line himself. (Hiudan, in contrast to Petitcreiu, will remain for the most part associated with Tristan.) Tristan has been the master huntsman from the beginning, and so his departure into exile is a rather sophisticated image of his expertise in this regard: he leads his favorite hound on the line himself. As we shall see, Hiudan's external appearance allows him to function in a context symbolic of *minne*, which is separate from, yet parallel to, that involving Petitcreiu.

In our next encounter with him, in other words, Hiudan becomes thematic: Tristan teaches him to hunt noiselessly. Hiudan becomes transfigured as an integral part of a newer, more comfortable, if technically less ceremonial style of "hunting with the crossbow" ("birsen mit dem armbruste," 17250–51), which is devoid of any practical purpose and is conducted for the sake of pure pleasure. Seen through conservative courtly eyes, Tristan's new method of hunting represents an aesthetically less exacting, if not frivolous, form of hunting, radically different from Mark's more formal form of hunting (ironically, introduced as a foreign custom to the Cornish court by Tristan himself, 2933ff.).[18]

Mark's hunt occurs at the same time and in the same place
(17287–88) as that of Tristan and his beloved, but for entirely different
reasons (because of his sorrow on account of Isolde, 17283) and is thus
related to Tristan's hunt thematically. The consequent thematic conca-
tenation of *minne* and the hunt in Gottfried's text becomes explicit in
Gottfried's so-called *minne*-monologue (17104–142), in which the
quarry comes to signify a certain kind of erotic *aventiure*: the object of
the chase is the perfect union of Tristan-Isolde-Minne. Thus Tristan's
leisurely hunting is contrasted with Mark's sluggish and troubled
hunting for the sake of distraction.

Hiudan, incorporated fully into the love-hunt scheme, undergoes
a similar stylization when Tristan teaches him to track game silently,
probably the first example of de-barking in literature! As a kind of
newfangled contrivance Hiudan, like Petitcreiu without his bell
(16394–401), is deprived of his proper function. In fact, insofar as a
contradiction arises between proper role and actual role, the fates of
both dogs resemble those of their masters. Tristan and Isolde have
indeed lost their respective functions at court: Tristan as nephew and
loyal liege of Mark, Isolde as Mark's wife and queen of the realm. This
in turn supports the idea that animals in some sense figure as signs for
Tristan and Isolde, appear in pairs, and stand in a dialectical
relationship to one another, in which action and condition are mutually
reflective.

The Stag

The episode with the "strange stag" (17297), like Marjodô's
dream, represents a flight entailing discovery of the lovers. Moreover,
this second supernatural animal—like Hiudan, the falcon, and the
boar—belongs implicitly to the allegory of the hunt. Gottfried's
representation of this incident differs from that of his source in several
ways. First of all, he inserts the depiction of Mark's hunt between the
third (17143–17178) and the fourth (17351–17420) *locus amoenus*
descriptions to create a unity of time and place as well as a thematic
identification: the contrast between the pleasurable hunt of Tristan and
Mark's compulsiveness. Moreover, the *powerful* stag of the *Saga* (p.
102) becomes the *marvelous* stag in Gottfried's text, described as
having a horse's mane (17298) and as being powerful, big, and white

(17299) with short antlers (17300).[19] Gottfried reduces the epic suspense that accompanies an exact account of the chase in the *Saga* and expands the description of the animal itself in order to provide an additional reason for Mark's vexation: Mark's hunt, once the stag has escaped, is motivated less by the pride of the sportsman than by the deceptive attraction of the extraordinary (17313–17317).[20] Finally, the "strange hart" in Gottfried's text participates explicitly in the allegorical sphere of the lovers' cave, originating and ending there:

> und sîne fluht hin wider genam,
> von dannen er ouch dar kam,
> hin dâ diu fossiure was
> alder geflôch er under genas. (ll. 17309–17312)

> [and fled to where he had come from, over towards the Cave. He fled there and saved his hide.]

The appearance of the extraordinary stag, preceded by Gottfried's *minne*-monologue, in which equivalents for allegorical terms are given and embedded in descriptions of the ideal life in the wilderness, draws the allegory of the hunt to its fullest possible conclusion. Mark, the incompetent lover and cuckold, enlists the assistance of a professional huntsman in tracking the stag. In other words, he hunts by proxy. This recalls his indecision and dependence on Tristan's mediation in the past, especially in the quest for Isolde. Tristan, of course, had discovered the Cave of Lovers effortlessly and by chance when he was out hunting (16690–91), whereas Mark requires the intercession of a skilled huntsman with his hound, not to mention the stag as lure or emissary.

As in the case of Petitcreiu, the epithet "extraordinary" links the stag to the figures of Tristan and Isolde. Its whiteness applies to the lovers' cave, signifying perfection (16968), and to the lovers themselves, especially to their hands as they practice their various musical skills (3337, 3550, 8070). Moreover, Mark's huntsman mistakes the lovers' tracks in the morning dew for those of the stag (17423–27).[21] It is clear that Mark, on the other hand, despite his most anxious efforts, will remain unsuccessful. Just as he cannot manipulate the bolt at the entrance to the lovers' cave, so he will never attain the quarry which is the ideal of Tristan-Isolde-Minne.[22]

No wonder that Gottfried devotes 750 lines toward the beginning of his *Tristan* to the excoriation of the hart. Not only does this scene reveal Tristan's nature as artist, but when considered in conjunction with the second episode of the marvelous stag of the Minnegrotte, it anticipates his fate as lover as well. It is by means of this first stag and his extraordinary hunting skills that the "expert huntsman Tristan" (3322, "der jegermeister Tristan") insinuates himself into Mark's court in the first place. The stag of the Minnegrotte, then, can be seen as the counterpart of the first stag: one serves the epic function of leading Tristan to Mark, and the other leads Mark to Tristan.

Thus the marvelous stag of the Minnegrotte closes the circle of the allegory of the hunt. In a certain sense, it closes the circle of animal images in Gottfried's *Tristan* as well, since it incorporates some of the most outstanding features of each. Like Petitcreiu, this second supernatural creature is emblematic of Tristan-Isolde-Minne; like Hiudan, it functions as part of the love-hunt scheme. As a double-edged image of attraction and deception, it exhibits all the plasticity of the image of the falcon associated with Isolde, and as a primarily epic mechanism of discovery, it carries the subjective reality, the psychological consequence of the boar in Marjodô's dream.

Appearing as signs in two major contexts (Isolde as falcon at the Irish court and following the love potion, Tristan's boar emblem and the boar of Marjodô's dream, the dogs Petitcreiu and Hiudan, the stag that is broken up at the outset and the fantastic stag of the Minnegrotte), the animals in Gottfried's *Tristan* are all in some way identified with the figures of the lovers and serve to characterize the concept of *minne* in a new set of terms. They call for a twofold interpretation (Isolde as bird of prey and helpless lure; Tristan as invincible knight and destroyer; Petitcreiu as *minne* associated with Isolde in the context of the court, Hiudan as *minne* associated with Tristan in the wilderness; the two stags associated with distinct modes of hunting, courtly and uncourtly). The process by which each image attains its fullest meaning is through consideration of two poles of a duality that reciprocally illumine one another.

NOTES

1. Rainer Gruenter, "Das wunnecliche tal," *Euphorion*, 55 (1961): 396–97. For a discussion of Christian allegorical elements in the Minnegrotte episode, see Freidrich Wilhelm Wodtke, "Die Allegorie des 'Inner Paradieses' bei Bernhard von Clairvaux, Honorius Augustodunensis, Gottfried von Strassburg und in der deutschen Mystik," in *Festschrift für Josef Quint*, ed. Hugo Moser et al. (Bonn: Emil Semmel Verlag, 1964), 277–290, and Friedrich Ranke, "Die Allegorie der Minnegrotte in Gottfried's *Tristan*" (1925), in *Gottfried von Strassburg*, ed. Alois Wolf (Darmstadt: Wissenschaftliche Buchgesellschaft, 1973), 1–24. The elements of the traditional *locus amoenus* description in Gottfried's work are also discussed in Ingrid Hahn, *Raum und Landschaft in Gottfried's Tristan*, Medium Aevum 3 (Munich: Eidos Verlag, 1963), 25–34.

2. All line references are to the edition by Karl Marold (Berlin: Walter de Gruyter, 1969). Translations are from Gottfried von Strassburg, *Tristan*,. trans. A.T. Hatto (Harmondsworth: Penguin, 1960).

3. Gruenter, 397: "Der Aspekt des Zustandes wird hier überall durch den Aspekt des Vorganges ersetzt."

4. A.T. Hatto, "Der minnen vederspil Isot," *Euphorion*, 51 (1957), 303, n. 2.

5. Hatto, 305–06.

6. Hahn, 90.

7. Hatto, 303, 307.

8. Hatto, 302, 307.

9. Klaus Speckenbach, "Der Eber in der deutschen Literatur des Mittelalters," in *Verbum et Signum I*, ed. Hans Fromm et al. (Munich: Wilhelm Fink Verlag, 1975), 425–476. See also Manfred Zips, "Tristan and die Ebersymbolik," *Beiträge zur Geschichte der deutschen Sprache und Literatur*, 94 (1972): 132–152.

10. Speckenbach, 476.

11. Speckenbach (473–76) refutes the view of some critics—notably Heinrich Beck, *Das Ebersignum im Germanischen* (Berlin: Walter de Gruyter, 1965), 131–35; Petrus Tax, *Wort, Sinnbild und Zahl im Tristanroman* (Berlin: Erich Schmidt Verlag, 1961), 193 and n. 39; and Johannes Rathofer, "Der 'wunderbare Hirsch' der Minnegrotte," *Zeitschrift für deutsches Altertum*, 95 (1966): 38–40—who have claimed that the black color of Tristan's shield in the investiture passage denotes a diabolical quality and yields the equation:

Tristan = boar = devil.

12. Speckenbach, 455–56, 459, 472–73.

13. Speckenbach, 471; Zips, 147, 151. *The Saga of Tristram and Isönd*, trans. Paul Schach (Lincoln and London: University of Nebraska Press, 1973). All page references are to this translation of the *Saga*. This saga, written in

1226, is a prose translation into Norwegian of Thomas of Britain Gottfried's source.

14. 18894:

> si riten houwende under in
> als eber under schâfen.

[They rode slashing among them like wild boars among sheep.]

15. Werner Schröder, "Das Hündchen Petitcreiu im *Tristan* Gotfrids von Strassburg," in *Dialog, Festgabe für Josef Kunz*, ed. Rainer Schönhaar (Berlin: Erich Schmidt Verlag, 1973), 39; Louise Gnädinger, *Hiudan und Petitcreiu, Gestalt und Figur des Hundes in der mittelalterlichen Tristandichtung* (Zurich: Atlantis Verlag, 1971), 39; Hahn, 90–93.

16. Gnädinger, 39; and Hahn, 90–3.

17. Gnädinger, 19, 22, 46.

18. Gnädinger, 22–23 and notes 35, 36, and 37.

19. These physical attributes lead Rathofer (41–42) to interpret the extraordinary stag as a unicorn.

20. Rainer Gruenter, "Der vremede hirz," *Zeitschrift für deutsches Altertum*, 86 (1955/56), 235.

21. Rathofer, 30. Marcelle Thiébaux, *The Stag of Love: The Chase in Medieval Literature* (Ithaca and London: Cornell University Press, 1974), 130–143, sees the stag as being identified with the lovers as the victim, or the quarry.

22. Rathofer, 39.

Animals and People

MARTYRS, MONKS, INSECTS, AND ANIMALS

Maureen A. Tilley

Even people who agree that we should care for all of creation still argue among themselves about just how we ought to value the various components of the created world. Animals are a case in point. Some attribute intrinsic importance to animals, declaring all parts of creation to be of equal value. Others are more anthropocentric, insisting that humans, the rational animals, are of greater importance and value, precisely because of rationality. Other animals are valuable because they serve human beings. The earliest Christians had their own disagreements on this issue. They did not form environmental groups or put forth formal statements on ecology, but the stories they told about animals reveal how they might have addressed this twentieth-century problem.

My investigation of the early Christian attitude toward the natural world began when I was reading texts from fourth-century North Africa, the hagiography of the Donatist Christians.

The old bishop Marculus refused to recant his faith. He is about to be martyred by being thrown off a cliff onto the jagged rocks below. The author of the text was an expert at suspense. As the good bishop is thrown off the cliff and proceeds toward his doom, we read line after line about his descent—how his hair is caressed by the breezes, how his garments billow out, how his body cuts through the liquid air. On and on it goes as we wait for the climactic splat. We are further delayed as we read of the difficulty with which the soldiers and the friends of the bishop descend from the precipice to the place of death. When we all finally arrive at the base of the cliff, we look for the grisly evidence of a faith that is true even to death. We examine the jagged rocks and— *mirabile dictu*—there's no body there. Confused, the soldiers and supporters of the bishop look back up the side of the cliff. The bishop was not caught on any craggy outcropping. But as they gaze upward, they notice his profile in the clouds of the sky. Moments later, they do find his body, in the posture of sweet repose, laid out on the rocks of a nearby canyon. In witness and deference to the holiness of this martyr, the rocks themselves had refused to harm the body of the martyr.[1]

The next day I'm reading another story of Carthaginian martyrs. This time the Romans are frustrated by their own policy of persecution. The more people they martyr, the more relics the Christians have to venerate and the stronger their faith grows. So the Romans decide on an ingenious policy, one under which Christians will be executed and their bodies annihilated. The Romans load Christians and other convicts, the living and the dead, onto a ship and row several miles out into the Mediterranean, where they dump them all into the sea. Even if the tide eventually washes the bodies back to shore, the remains of the martyrs will be so disfigured by several days in the sea and so intermingled with the bodies of common criminals that the living Christians will be unable to tell the difference. They will refrain from venerating any of the bodies for fear of honoring murderers and robbers.

This case is no less wondrous. Immediately, dolphins came to the aid of the Christians and bring back only the bodies of their revered saints before the sea can take its toll.[2]

Reading stories from fifth-century Syria, I came across another case of animals assisting martyrs. A woman named Anahid was being tortured by the Persians for her adherence to Christianity. Her interrogators tried many ingenious forms of torture but were unable to break her resolve. At last she was condemned to death, and such a grisly death it was to be: she was chained by her wrists and ankles to a cliff, her body was smeared with honey, and she was left as prey for hungry animals and stinging insects. But the creatures never harmed her, for a swarm of wasps descended on the hillside. It formed a wall five arms thick to protect her. The wasps could not liberate her, but they did protect her from danger and ridicule. When the Christians came to take her body for burial, the swarm parted like a curtain.[3]

Good stories, but not simply tales of another time. There I was in the grocery store waiting in line, and I glanced at the tabloids. It was the usual: "Wild west town found on Venus," "Faith healer fixes cars by touch," "Elvis sighted in Mississippi drugstore." But Holy Ecology, Batman: "Drowning child snatched from death by heroic seal."[4] Not too much later it was "Pet rooster pulls drowning child from icy pond,"[5]

"Hero dog pulls crippled kid from swimming pool,"[6] and the story of ants that fed a toddler trapped in the jungle.[7] And there were more and more that paralleled stories of the early martyrs and ascetics. What can I say? I was hooked. I was not interested in the historical accuracy of the stories, either the martyr stories or the tabloids. What I did find interesting were the various similarities in content between the stories. Each of the stories involved a single victim in peril and a single animal (except in the case of the ants, in which it was a single anthill, analogous to Anahid and the wasps). Each told of a daring, unexpected rescue.

The similarities in content led me to contemplate similarities in audience and purpose. Neither these stories of martyrs nor the tabloids were written for the literati of their societies. The martyr stories were written to be recited aloud at the annual commemoration of these heroes and heroines of faith. The stories of the ascetics were written to encourage others who had chosen the path of self-denial. These are popular forms of literature that invite participation in the story, giving importance to one's own life. So, too, the tabloids. People read them for amusement, for titillation, to relieve the boredom of a humdrum life. Both are written to delight the reader and to confirm already held beliefs, whether those are beliefs about the nature of holiness and its manifestation in the martyrs or about the nature of Elvis and the afterlife. Both stress the ripe balance between the bizarre and the ordinary. Both involve their readers in scenarios that might well, under the right circumstances, happen to them.

How do the animals function here? In the tabloids they always seem to be rescuing young or crippled children, the innocents, the helpless. If the person is an adult, there is generally some prior contact with the animal. A dog rescued an adult woman, but the woman had been the veterinarian who had cared for the animal on another occasion.[8] In general, animals have positive relationships only with good or innocent people: children and beneficent adults. On the flip side, animals in the tabloids attack evil people or people who have invaded their territory.[9] The lesson seems to be that animals have some sixth sense about the identity of humans and they put it to good use.

But what of the stories of the saints of antiquity? It used to be a commonplace that the ascetics and the animals of Late Antiquity got on so well because the ascetics were trying to recreate Eden in this life and the animals were joining their effort. However, before jumping to any conclusions I want to look at a variety of animal stories. In this paper I will survey stories of animals from Greco-Roman sources, including Jewish and Christian sources. Each time, I'll look at folklore and theology. By examining how animals functioned in the earlier stories available to patristic writers, one should be able to detect what, if anything, is distinctive about the patristic attitude toward animals and what opinions about animals did they challenge or confirm *obiter dicta*? I hope these stories will surface issues that relate to our contemporary relationships with animals and the earth itself.

Greco-Roman Stories

In Greco-Roman stories animals exemplified justice, gratitude, and love.

Those stories that represented justice or fair play preserved a sense of order within a world in which good seemed in danger of losing out to evil. Animals, especially elephants, protected the innocent and avenged graft, adultery, and murder by their caretakers.[10]

A variant on the theme of justice were stories about the gratitude shown by animals for the favors done them. A stork fledgling had its broken wing mended by a kind woman. Later the bird repaid her with a gem it found.[11] A snake spared by a hunter rescued the innocent man from an ambush.[12] An eagle saved its benefactor from poisoning.[13] A dolphin played with the son of the elderly couple who had cared for it.[14] And, of course, there is always the story of Androcles and the lion that refused to eat him in the arena, since Androcles had previously removed a thorn from the animal's paw.[15]

There are also stories of love and devotion. Contrary to modern expectations, dogs do not figure prominently here.[16] Snakes were more widely known for combining prescience and fidelity in their care for children.[17] Again, one finds eagle stories, including one in which a bird was so devoted to its young master and lifelong companion that when the boy died, the bird threw itself on his funeral pyre.[18]

Sea mammals were the most highly praised of animals in this respect. They performed the accustomed task of saving their benefactors.[19] They went beyond justice to interspecies love, as several authors attested.[20] Plutarch said that they were the only creatures that love human beings for their own sake and not for any recompense for any kind human actions.[21] Aelian provided the love story of the dolphin that beached itself in grief over the death of its human lover, and of the seal that surpassed all other creatures by loving an ugly person who seems to have had no other friend.[22]

Is it mere coincidence that the animals are agents in the restoration of earthly equilibrium, that they seem to have gratitude, that they love human beings? Are the authors of these stories not simply anthropomorphizing animal behavior? Or do these creatures of the gods have the equivalent of human intelligence? While folklore is single-minded in its recognition of the wisdom of the animals, the philosopher-theologians were divided.

The Stoics considered animals to have a place in the natural world not unlike trees and rocks but definitely distinct from that of human beings.[23] Animals were there to be used by human beings, though not to be harmed. Even the bedbugs were there for human beings: the bugs kept people from sleeping too much.[24] But animals were not rational.[25] They did not know how to obey laws.[26] Morality itself was alien to them for the gods allowed them to eat one another.[27] They did not even have language, nor did they participate in politics, friendship, and philosophy, the *sine qua non* of the rational being (at least according to the philosophers).[28]

On the other side of the question were the Neoplatonists. Their emanationist view of the universe would not allow them to draw a sharp distinction between humans and animals even on the subject of reason.[29] Plato himself had considered animals to be the reincarnation of evil human beings. So there was a real continuum running both ways between animals and humans.[30] At the beginning of the first century C.E., Plutarch deflected much of the Stoic disdain for the abilities of animals by attributing their critiques to simple lack of knowledge. In his estimation, animals did not only rely on instinct as the Stoics claimed. The variety of abilities within even a single species was proof that they were rational and capable of learning.[31] Two hundred years later the debate was still going on. Porphyry looked at the acute sense perception of the animals, their prudence, and what he interpreted as their ability to learn, and concluded that the difference between the rationality of humans and animals was one not of essence but of degree, like that between the gods and humanity.[32] Where the Stoics had claimed that animals' lack of language was evidence of their irrationality, Porphyry answered that animals did indeed have languages but human beings had not yet learned them, as they had not yet learned the languages of all other humans.[33] He asserted that animals were part of the realm of morality for they practiced virtues and vices. The theriomorphic form of the gods of Egypt even provided them with congenial objects of worship.[34] The general attitude of the Neoplatonists was that humans and animals were part of a single web of creation.

Finally, there was the mediating point. Aelian, a third-century Greek philosopher, tended toward Stoicism in most matters, but in the animal stories he collected he found a divine providence regarding these creatures: "The gods have taken thought for them, neither looking down on them nor reckoning them of small account. For although destitute of reasoning power, at any rate they possess *understanding proportionate to their needs* [emphasis added]."[35]

Which of these positions would Christians take? Any answer would be premature before one took a look at the other major influence on the early Christians: Judaism.

Judaism

Stories of animals interacting with people are fairly rare in Judaism. Biblical stories and intertestamental literature view them as instruments of divine aid or justice. Ravens feed Elijah (1 Kings 17.6); the dogs lick up the blood of Ahab and Jezebel (1 Kings 21.19); bears killed the children who twitted Elisha as "Old Baldy" (2 Kings 2.23); and lions refused to eat Daniel but gobbled up his tormentors (Daniel 6). The Psalms of Solomon affirm that animals attack the wicked but not the just.[36] Rabbinic sources have one great animal story: When Moses and Aaron were in Egypt, servants of Pharaoh let loose lions to attack them, but when Moses raised his staff the ferocious lions traded their accustomed demeanor for that of playful puppies.[37] The animals reacted properly while their captors did not. In all these cases the animals acted better than many of the people. These irrational creatures were still wiser than the supposedly rational humans.

In general, Judaic writers presented a positive view of animals, a view arising no doubt from the belief in the direct creation of the animals by God.[38] The Jewish philosopher Philo even departed from his Neoplatonic tendencies to affirm the primal goodness of animals and their ensoulment by their creator.[39] But that positive view was tempered by two details. First, animals may have souls (i.e., a life-bearing element within them). They may also have sense perception and, therefore, a mind, but this mind is not a rational one, for animals do not have the higher reasoning powers like human beings.[40]

But even though they were not like humanity in this respect, the animals like humans were affected by the Fall. Tame before the Original Sin, they now reflected the sin of Adam and Eve. Other Jewish traditions held that there were no carnivores before the Fall and that as a result of the disorder brought by sin, the animals now failed to obey human beings.[41] But when the Messiah would come, they would revert to their original state.[42] However, even in their fallen state, some animals were better than others. The animals that Noah took onto the ark were less tainted than those that remained outside.[43]

Even in this state of imperfection, animals were valuable for three reasons; sometimes their value was intrinsic, and sometimes they were useful for some divine or human purpose.

First, animals recognized good in people and responded appropriately. In the *Testament of Job* they wept over Job's wife because of her piety.[44] In the *Testament of the Twelve Patriarchs* wild animals recognized good people and did them no harm.[45]

Second, the animals acted as witnesses to the good or evil that people do. In 2 Enoch, God preserves the souls of animals until the day of judgement so that the animals can give evidence regarding the ethical treatment of animals by their caretakers.[46] They are not preserved for any value of their own but solely to act as witnesses.[47]

Third, animals have an overtly symbolic function. In their conduct they exemplify the virtues and vices that human beings ought to have.[48]

It is just this sort of symbolism that one will find in earliest Christianity alongside the idea that animals recognize good and respond accordingly.

The New Testament and Apocryphal Literature

The New Testament contains little about animals. The birds of the air and the foxes with their dens all act as place markers for recommended or discommended conduct.[49] So too in the Gospel of Thomas. The significant exception to this is a passage by Paul, Rom.

8.18–23, which speaks of all creation in bondage waiting for redemption. The sentiment is not singular: first, it is perfectly congruent with the Jewish belief that animals suffer the results of the sin of Eve and Adam; and second, it presages the cooperation of inanimate nature with the saints.

Outside the New Testament, in the apocryphal material, we reenter the world of the folktale. Material from the second century shows the recognition of goodness by the world of nature. The *Acts of Peter* contains a story in which a dog obtained a human voice in order to bear witness against Simon Magus.[50] In the *Proto-Evangelium of James*, not only animals but also inanimate nature recognizes and responds to holiness. As the child John the Baptist and his mother Elizabeth fled the soldiers of King Herod, Elizabeth appealed to the mountains for help. They opened up and hid her and her son.[51] Meanwhile, the Baptist's father had been slaughtered in the temple by the soldiers, and "the panelwork of the ceiling of the temple wailed" at his death.[52]

From the third century come the *Acts of Thomas* and the *Acts of Paul*. These works contain the same sort of stories we have seen in the pagan literature. In the Thomas story dogs preserved the balance of justice in an incident similar to the biblical story of the death of Jezebel. Just as the apostle predicted, the animals attacked and killed a man who had insolently slapped him.[53]

Stories of the Martyrs

The stories of the martyrs contain many incidents of animals interacting with human beings. In two separate incidents in the *Acts of Paul* lions recognized the goodness of Paul and Thecla and refused to harm them just as the lion had refused to attack Androcles.[54] Animals were also on the side of the martyrs in the story of Perpetua and Felicitas. A bear brought in to torture the martyrs refused to come out of its cage, and a boar refused to attack the martyrs, turning against the Romans instead.[55] When animals could not prevent martyrdom, they could at least reverence the bodies of the holy ones, as they did in the case of Anahid and the wasps and that of the Carthaginian martyrs whose bodies the dolphins brought back to land for proper burial and veneration.

In these stories animals give up their bestial nature at the same time the persecutors of the saints are being described with feral epithets. This is no return to Eden for the animals but a role reversal with evil human beings.[56]

Inanimate nature, too, respected the martyrs. Many stories tell of bonfires prepared for martyrs. The rains soak the pyres and the martyrs are temporarily saved.[57] Divine justice was served here as it was in the story of the bishop Marculus whose body the rocks would not tear.

In general, the animals and the world of nature recognize the holiness of the martyrs and refuse to harm them.

Stories of the Ascetics

Not every story of saints and animals involves martyrdom. A much greater number are devoted to the relationship between animals and the saints of the desert, the ascetics. In these stories animals take on many roles in a mutually beneficial relationship.

The animals call on the monks for help. A hyena prevailed on the monk Macarius to heal one of her cubs which had been born blind. She recognized his spiritual power and realized it could benefit her brood. In return for his care she brought him a ram's skin to use as a bed covering.[58]

In their turn, the animals may come to the aid of the monks of the wilderness. The animals provide an atmosphere in which the monks can learn to repent for their sins,[59] and on a more mundane level, the animals help the monks with smaller tasks. The Abba Amoun called on snakes to guard his cell.[60] The Abba Helle was ferried across the river by a crocodile. However, once he had returned from the other side, he turned to the animal that had previously terrorized the neighborhood and said, "It is better for you to die and make restitution for all the lives you have taken." The animal immediately went belly up and died.[61]

This should be no surprise, for the animals were generally responsive to the preaching of the champions of asceticism. The Abba Bes in Egypt preached to both hippos and crocodiles. Inspired by his words, they ceased their ravaging of the countryside.[62]

Often the beasts simply respond to the presence of the goodness of the holy ones. Animals delighted in the presence of the holy monk

Antony. As the demons recognized his holiness and fled, the beasts approached.[63] The animals reacted more sanely than the demons.

But when the holiness of the monk departed, so also did the good relationship with the animals. The best example is the story of the monk Sabas. This holy man had a servant named Flavius. Flavius was a real Sancho to the monk's Don Quixote. The servant tended a lion that guarded the monk's donkey from other beasts of prey. One day the servant fell into sin. On that day the lion ate the donkey.[64]

Thus in the stories of the ascetics the animals assist the monks—but only as long as the monks remain holy. As in the stories from the Greco-Roman traditions, animals recognize innocence and act with proper awe and gratitude. In addition, the monks have found in the company of the animals peace and repentance and in their turn have been able to inspire repentance in the animals. These folktales all witness to some rationality or mind in the animals.

The Theologians' Responses

We now leave the realm of folktale to contemplate the response of Christian theologians to popular beliefs about animals. Many treated the animals as their pagan predecessors had. The behavior of the animals was anthropomorphized to provide object lessons for Christians in acquiring virtues and avoiding vice. The Christians took up the preaching of Jesus on the lilies of the field and the birds of the air which provided models of trust for the disciples.[65] In their attempt at utilizing the entire Bible without taking it literally, the Christians treated discussions of animals allegorically. In the division between clean and unclean animals they saw the categorization of people according to virtue and vice. At the beginning of the second century, the *Epistle of Barnabas* used this technique, which was adapted from Jews like Philo. By the end of the century Clement of Alexandria saw the clean ruminating animals as people with the proper attitude toward scripture, mulling it over in their minds.[66] Lactantius saw the command to abstain from pork as an order to avoid sin. Christians must avoid being enslaved to their appetites as swine were.[67] John Chrysostom saw the animals as visual aids in the pursuit of Christian virtues. Wise as serpents, harmless as doves, industrious as ants and spiders: each animal had something to offer.[68]

The allegorical interpretations of behavior ignored whether animals were rational. The question that had so strongly vexed Greco-Roman philosophers was no longer an issue. But not all Christians sidestepped the issue. Among those who did treat the question we find echoes of the old Stoic/Neoplatonic split. Christian folklore came down squarely on the Neoplatonic side, with a sense that the animals knew what they were doing and with whom they were dealing. Thus they acted appropriately around the saints, martyrs, and ascetics.

The theologians, on the other hand, had a strong commitment to a Stoic universe in which humans are qualitatively different from animals. The apologist Origen appeared to take the Stoic side in his dispute with Celsus. Reason, said Origen, was common to human and heavenly beings, perhaps even to God, but not to animals.[69] If animals appeared to have organizational, governmental, or military skills, these were appearances only. They did not act from reason. They could not have reason because their souls were shaped differently.[70] Yet this did not make them totally different from human beings. However, Origen's Neoplatonism would not allow him to divorce humanity from the animal world, for both participated in the divine. Since both emanated from the divine, all participated in some degree in God.[71] So Origen held in tension the Stoic and Neoplatonic attitudes toward animals.

A century and a half later that tension is still being maintained. We see it most acutely in John Chrysostom. He commented on the passage from the Book of Jonah in which the animals of Nineveh, like the people, put on sackcloth and fast (Jonah 3.10). The animals, like the people, needed to know the message of the prophet. But while the humans were rational and could perceive the message in a rational manner, the animals, being irrational, could not. So the animals in their fasting *felt* the message of God. Thus all could understand.[72]

The patristic tradition is heir to three traditions. There was the Stoic, which saw all of nature—both sensate and nonsensate—as part of the landscape, for the use of human beings. On the other hand, there was the Neoplatonic, which saw all creation—nonsensate, sensate, and rational—as emanating from the same divine principle. Christianity held these two in tension but was constantly drawn by its Jewish heritage to a consideration of animals as fellow creatures.

The results of this tension are most succinctly put by one of the desert fathers. The abbot Alonius was once asked, "What is contempt?"

He replied "To be below the creatures that have no reason and to know they are not condemned."[73] The human sinner is higher than the animal in rationality. However, when that person sins, he or she must look up to the creature with no mind, no ability to think, no ability to observe the law or to participate in politics—all those things that are human. Perhaps what makes the Christian attitude toward animals unique is the knowledge that rationality, that which separates humanity from animality, is not the grand mark of *haute culture* before God. Virtue counts much more than mental abilities.

So we return to the tabloids: "Scientific experiments reveal your pet can read your mind . . . and even detect [your] serious illnesses."[74] They can predict an owner's epileptic seizures, helping to guarantee safety for the owner and her pet. The animals, living in a web of relationships with the human animal, have understanding proportionate to their needs. Can the rational human say the same? The early Christians offer a variety of attitudes from which to choose.

NOTES

This article first appeared in the College Theology Society Annual Volume No. 36 (1990). Reprinted with the permission of the College Theology Society.

1. *Passio benedicti martyris Marculi* (Migne PL 8.766).
2. *Passio Maximiani et Isaac Donatistarum auctore Macrobio*, Migne PL 8.772–73.
3. *Holy Women of the Syrian Orient*, introduced and translated by Sebastian P. Brock and Susan Ashbrook Harvey (Berkeley: University of California, 1987), 98.
4. *Weekly World News*, 11 Oct. 1988, 1, 5.
5. *Weekly World News*, 11 April 1989, 1, 11.
6. *Weekly World News*, 18 July 1989, 1, 3; cf. "Heroic dog saves toddler wfrom drowning," *Sun*, 18 Oct. 1988, 5.
7. "Lost tot found alive inside giant anthill, *Sun*, 18 Oct. 1988, 1, 35.
8. "Hero hound rescues nurse who saved HIM 2 months earlier," *Weekly World News*, 25 April 1989, 46.
9. E.g., "Incredible photo of a killer crock attack," *Weekly World News*, 22 May 1990, 4–5.
10. Protection of the innocent: Aelian 3.46, 12.21, in Claudius Aelianus, *Aelian. On the Characteristics of Animals*, with an English translation by A.F.

Schoelfield, 3 vols., Loeb Classical Library (Cambridge, Mass.: Harvard University Press; London: William Heinemann, 1958), 1.206–209, 3.38–41. Graft: Plutarch, *De sollertia animalium (Whether land or sea animals are better)* 12, 968D–E, in *Plutarch's Moralia*, with an English translation by Harold Cherniss and William C. Helmbold, 12 vols., Loeb Classical Library (Cambridge, Mass.: Harvard; London: William Heinemann, 1957), 12.374/75. Adultery: Aelian 8.20 (Loeb 2.206–207). Murder: Aelian 8.17 (Loeb 2.202/203).

11. Aelian 8.22 (Loeb 2.208–11).
12. Aelian 10.48 (Loeb 2.344–49).
13. Aelian 17.37 (Loeb 3.368–71).
14. Aelian 2.6 (Loeb 1.192–95).
15. Aelian 7.48 (Loeb 2.166–71).
16. An exception is the story from Gelon of Syracuse of a dog that wakes its owner from his nightmares in Aelian 6.62 (Loeb 2.84–87).
17. Aelian 4.54, 6.17, 6.63 (Loeb 1.276–79, 2.30–33, 2.86–89).
18. Aelian 6.29 (Loeb 2.46–49).
19. Aelian 8.3 (Loeb 2.180/81).
20. Cf. "Don Juan dolphin tries to mate with lady trainer," *Weekly World News*, 22 May 1990, 37.
21. Plutarch, *De soll.* 3.6, 984C (Loeb 470/71).
22. Aelian 61.5, 4.56 (Loeb 2.26–29, 1.278/79).
23. Porphyry, *On Abstinence* 3.1, in *Select Works of Porphyry containing his four books on abstinence from animal food . . .* , translated by Thomas Taylor (London: Thomas Rood, 1823), 94–95.
24. Chrysippus in *Stoicorum Viterum Fragmenta* 2.1152.
25. See Howard Cherniss and William C. Helmbold in *Plutarch's Moralia*, 313.
26. Cicero, *De finibus*, in *SVF* 3.371.
27. Hesiod, *Works and Days*, 11.277–79, cited in Plutarch, *De soll.* 964B (Loeb 348/49).
28. See Philo, *De animalibus adv. Alexandrum* 45, 84, in *Philonis Alexandrini de Animalibus*, Armenian text with an introduction, translation, and commentary by Abraham Terian (Chico: Scholars Press, 1981), 87, 103.
29. Porphyry 3.6 (Taylor, 100–101).
30. Plato, *Timaeus* 42C, 91D-92C, translated by H.D.P. Lee (Baltimore: Penguin, 1965), 58, 121.
31. Plutarch 14, 970E (Loeb 12.386/87).
32. Porphyry 3.7 (Taylor, 101).
33. Porphyry 3.3 (Taylor, 95).
34. Porphyry 3.8–10, 3.16 (Taylor, 102–106, 110).
35. Aelian, 11.31 (Loeb 2.396/397).

36. *Ps. Sol.* 13.1–4, in *The Old Testament Pseudepigrapha*, edited by James H. Charlesworth, 2 vols., (Garden City, N.Y.: Doubleday, 1983 and 1985), 2.662.

37. Louis Ginzberg, *The Legends of the Jews*, 7 vols., (Philadelphia: Jewish Publication Society of America, 1937, 1966, 1982, 1983), 2.332; cf. 5.425 and 5.435.

38. Gen. 1.20–25.

39. Philo, *On the Creation* (*De mundi opificio*) 20.62–21.64, in *Philo*, with an English translation by F.H. Colson and G.H. Whittaker, 10 vols. and 2 suppl. vols., Loeb Classical Library (Cambridge, Mass.: Harvard; London: William Heinemann, 1956), 1.46–49.

40. Philo, *On the Creation* 24.73 (Loeb 1.56–59). For the distinction between mind and reasoning as they exist in human beings and in animals, see *De animalibus adv. Alex.* 12–16 and comments in Terian, 71–73.

41. Theophilus, *Theophilus to Autolycus* 2.18, in *The Ante-Nicene Fathers*, edited by Alexander Roberts and James Donaldson, 10 vols. (repr. Grand Rapids, Mich.: Eerdmans, 1983) 2.101; Novatian, *On the Jewish Meats* 2 (*ANF* 5.646); *Life of Adam and Eve* 24.4 (Charlesworth 2.283).

42. Is. 11.6–9. See the list of rabbinic references in Ginzberg, 5.102.

43. Sanh. 108a, 108b, cited in Ginzberg 1.160.

44. *Testament of Job* 40.13 (Charlesworth 1.860).

45. *Testament of Napthali* 8.4 and *Testament of Benjamin* 3.4–5 (Charlesworth 1.813–14 and 824–25).

46. *2 Enoch* 58.4–6 (Charlesworth 1.184–85).

47. *Questions of Ezra* 5 (Charlesworth 1.596, 1.599).

48. *Letter of Aristeas* 153–54 (Charlesworth 2.23); Ginzberg 1.43–46.

49. See, e.g., Mt. 8.20.

50. *Acts of Peter* 4.9–5.12, in Edgar Hennecke, *New Testament Apocrypha*, edited by Wilhelm Schneemelcher, English translation by R. McL. Wilson, 2 vols. (Philadelphia: Westminster, 1962) 2.291–92.

51. *Protoevangelium of James* 22.3 (Hennecke 2.387).

52. *Protoevangelium of James* 24.3 (Hennecke 2.388).

53. *Acts of Thomas* 5, 8 (Hennecke 2.445, 2.447).

54. *Acts of Paul* 7, 26 (Hennecke 2.372, 2.360).

55. *Passio Perpetuae* 19.5, in *The Acts of the Christian Martyrs*, introduction, texts, and translations by Herbert Musurillo (Oxford: Clarendon, 1972), 126–27.

56. For a catalogue of such stories and a structuralist analysis, see Alison Goddard Eliot, *Roads to Paradise: Reading the Lives of the Early Saints* (Hanover, N.H., and London: University Press of New England for Brown University, 1987), 149–50.

57. E.g., *Passio Sanctorum Montani et Lucii* 3.3, in Musurillo, 216–17.

58. *The Lives of the Desert Fathers: The Historia Monachorum in Aegypto*, section 21.15–16, translated by Norman Russell, introduction by Benedicta Ward (London and Oxford: Mowbray; Kalamazoo, Mich.: Cistercian, 1981), 110.

59. *Ephraemi Syri, Rabulae, Balaei aliorum opera selecta*, edited by J.J. Overbeck (Oxford, 1895), 117, cited in Arthur Vööbus, *History of Asceticism in the Syrian Orient: A Contribution to the History of Culture in the Near East.* Vol. 2: *Early Monasticism in Mesopotamia and Syria* (Louvain: Secretariat du Corpus SCO, 1960), 2.27.

60. *The Lives of the Desert Fathers* 9.7 (Russell, 81).

61. *The Lives of the Desert Fathers* 12.7–9 (Russell, 91). A similar story is found in Palladius, *Historia Lausiaca* 59 (Migne PL 73.1167).

62. *Lives of the Desert Fathers* 10 (Russell, 66).

63. Athanasius, *The Life of Antony* 53, in *Athanasius, The Life of Antony and the Letter to Marcellinus*, translation and introduction by Robert C. Gregg, Classics of Western Spirituality (New York: Paulist, 1980), 70.

64. Eliot, 156, citing Cyril of Sytholopolis, *Life of Saint Sabas* 3.2, from A.J. Festugière, *Les Moines d'orient: Introduction au monachisme oriental* (Paris: Cerf, 1961), 65.

65. Mt. 6.28–33, Lk. 12.24–31.

66. Clement of Alexandria, *Stromata* 7.18 (*ANF* 2.555–56)

67. Lactantius, *The Divine Institutes* 4.1 (*ANF* 7.119).

68. *Homilies on the Statues* 12.5–6, in *A Select Library of the Nicene and Post-Nicene Fathers of the Christian Church*. Vol. 9: *Saint Chrysostom: The Priesthood; Ascetic Treatises; Select Homilies and Letters; Homilies on the Statues* (New York: The Christian Literature Co., 1894), 419–20.

69. Origen, *Contra Celsum* 4.85, in *Origen: Contra Celsum*, translated and edited by Henry Chadwick (Cambridge: Cambridge University, 1980), 251; cf. *De principiis* 3.1.3 in *ANF* 4.303.

70. Origen, *Contra Celsum* 4.81–83 (Chadwick, 249–50).

71. Origen, *De principiis* 1.3.6 (*ANF* 4.253).

72. John Chrysostom, *Homilies on the Statues* 9, 358.

73. *The Desert Fathers*, edited by Helen Waddell (Ann Arbor: University of Michigan, 1957), xxxvi.

74. *National Examiner*, 20 March 1990, 29.

THE SHADOW OF REASON: EXPLANATIONS OF INTELLIGENT ANIMAL BEHAVIOR IN THE THIRTEENTH CENTURY

Peter G. Sobol

Human understanding of animal behavior has from the beginning followed a double path. On the one hand, the webs of spiders, the nests of birds, and the industry of ants made animals into models of prudence and wisdom. Proverbs 6:6 advises, "Go to the ant, O sluggard. Consider her ways and be wise." On the other hand, neither the Greeks nor the heirs of their intellectual traditions allowed that animals came by their wisdom in the same way that we humans come by ours. The scholars of late medieval Europe, who saw the incarnate soul in Aristotelian terms and the soul after death in Christian terms, believed that humans alone possessed the mental and spiritual power to act wisely and well. They expressed little interest in discovering how animals, endowed only with sensory powers, can lead such admirably temperate and prudent lives. Yet the question was not entirely overlooked. Throughout the thirteenth century, scholars discussed animal behavior either in passing or, as in the case of Albert the Great, in a dedicated treatise. The more closely animals were studied, the more difficult it became to uphold the rigid distinction between the mental powers of animals and humans.

Aristotle remarked on the mental life of animals in several works. In *De anima* and the *Parva Naturalia* he examined the abilities that distinguish living things from the rest of terrestrial nature. He separated these abilities into three groups, based on the apparent differences between plants, animals, and humans. The vegetative powers of nutrition, growth, and reproduction, he concluded, belong to all living things.[1] The sensitive powers belong in varying degrees to animals and humans,[2] although all animals require the sense of touch.[3]

Humans alone possess mind. Unlike the vegetative and the sensitive powers, mind requires no organ to function. Mind is potentially everything that can be thought, and hence when not thinking mind exists only potentially. Any actuality in the resting mind would limit its ability to become something thinkable.[4] In a brief and difficult passage, Aristotle implied that part of the thinking mind is unchangeable and immortal.[5]

In Aristotle's natural philosophy, each physical object consists of substance, which makes it what it is, and accidents or qualities that can change without changing the object's identity. A human may get a dark suntan, a flower may lose its odor, a sharp knife may become dull, all without ceasing to be what they were. Animals' sensitive powers provide access only to qualities, not to substances. As Aristotle wrote, "the percipient is not acted upon by the perceived as such."[6] Each of the five external senses has for its proper object a quality that it alone can detect. Only vision senses colors, only hearing senses sounds, only smell senses odors, only taste senses flavors, and only touch senses such qualities as hot and cold, wet and dry, and hard and soft.[7] The common sensibles—such as size, shape, multiplicity and unity, and motion and rest—can be detected by more than one sense.[8] Aristotle relegated objects themselves to a third category called indirect or incidental sensibles. Because we have no direct perception of substance, our willingness to extrapolate from our proper sensation of, for example, redness to our indirect sensation of a rose always entails the possibility of error. We have no direct or error-free awareness of the substance of things.[9]

Aristotle recognized that the external senses alone could not explain every experience of sensation. If vision reacts only to color, how are we aware of darkness? How are we aware of an act of vision? How are we able to recognize that the whiteness we see and the sweetness we taste are different? There must be a faculty that receives from the five external senses in the same way as they in turn receive from the outside world, a faculty that can detect the absence of a sensible, that can be aware of acts of sensation,[10] and that can recognize that two qualities such as whiteness and sweetness, though often associated, are different.[11] In *De juventute et senectute*, Aristotle called this power the common sense.[12] Some animals also share with humans an ability to be guided by, and to manipulate, images of sensed objects, an ability Aristotle named *phantasia*, or imagination. The power of memory, although associated with imagination and common sense, warranted its own treatise in the *Parva naturalia*.[13] In the closing chapters of *De anima*, Aristotle pondered the origin of animal motion and concluded that imagination, combined with appetite—the drive to pursue what is pleasing to the senses and avoid what is unpleasant—guides the behavior of animals. Humans too are moved by imagination and appetite. They are also moved by their practical mind and thus can experience conflicting desires between the urges of the sensitive appetite and the will.[14]

Common sense, imagination, memory, and appetite could easily form the basis for an explanation of how ants, bees, dogs, and elephants do what they do. Yet Aristotle attempted no such explanation in *De anima* or the *Parva naturalia*, and understandably so. The more appropriate place to apply these powers would be the books explicitly devoted to animals. The *Historia animalium*, however, which contains many reports of animal behavior especially in its eighth and ninth books, does not explain these reports with reference to the internal powers of sense. Instead, Aristotle pointed out that animals seem to emulate humans in the qualities of their mental life.[15] Passages in *Historia animalium* include "intelligent" (*phronema*) among the many dispositions evident in the animal kingdom.[16] Near the beginning of Book VIII, Aristotle wrote, "Just as in man we find knowledge, wisdom, and sagacity [*techne, sophia,* and *synesis*] so in certain animals there exists some other natural potentiality akin to these."[17] Yet Aristotle did not trace this emulation to the shared powers of common sense, imagination, memory, and appetite. In *De partibus animalium*, he again referred to intelligence in animals and again made no use of internal sense powers to explain it. Instead, he correlated intelligence to the properties of the blood or blood-analogue. "If it [i.e., blood] tends to be thin and cold, it is conducive to sensation and intelligence [*noeroteron*]. The same difference holds good with the counterpart of blood in other creatures."[18] Hence the intelligence of bees.[19]

Had the *Historia animalium* inspired as many medieval commentaries as did *De anima*, the early history of comparative psychology might have been much different, as scholars struggled to reconcile the two works. As it was, *De anima* attracted many more commentators, and no wonder. A commentary on the nine-book *Historia animalium* would be a massive undertaking, and less pertinent to human life than the three-book *De anima*, especially in a Christian context. Commentators on *De anima* who chose to pursue the question of animal behavior could focus on the internal powers of sense and ignore the *phronesis* of the zoological books.

By the thirteenth century, students of *De anima* had more to draw upon than Aristotle alone. The intense activity of twelfth-century translators that had brought Aristotle to the Latin west had also made available a host of other works by Greek, Jewish, and Arabic philosophers and commentators. Preeminent among these newly acquired authors was the Persian philosopher and physician known to the west as Avicenna. European medical schools used Avicenna's *Canon* as a text until the seventeenth century. Parts of his encyclopedic *Kitab al-Shifa* were translated separately and were also closely studied in the universities. Book VI of the *Shifa*, on the soul, was translated into Latin as *De anima* or *Sextus de naturalibus*.[20] In that work, Avicenna discovered no less than five internal senses.[21] He used his knowledge of cerebral anatomy and his experience with diseases and wounds of the head to locate each internal sense in one of the cerebral ventricles. In the process, he articulated the problem of animal behavior in a way that guided academic discussion for the next 700 years.

Like Aristotle, Avicenna had compiled a large text on animals. He too recognized that much animal behavior involved reactions that cannot be based on sensory qualities. To use the familiar example, why does a sheep run away from a wolf even when it has never seen one before? Not because the color of the wolf harms the sheep's eyes or because the odor of the wolf harms the sheep's nose. Rather than attribute such behavior to prudence or intelligence, Avicenna proposed that among the internal senses was a power that allowed animals to assess objects based on something other than the qualities detectable by the external senses. Avicenna's word for that "something" became in Latin *intentio*, or intention. The power that perceived intentions became in Latin *estimativa*.[22] Avicenna divided the function of the *estimativa* into three groups of phenomena. In instinctive animal behavior, intentions arrived at the perceiving animal in much the same way as sensible qualities arrived. An intention, however, passed undetected through the sensory apparatus until it arrived at the *estimativa* in the middle cerebral ventricle, where a judgment about the value of the perceived body to the perceiving animal occurred. A sheep seeing its first wolf discerns harm in the intention arriving from the wolf, and the sheep runs away.[23] The second group of phenomena consisted of learned behaviors, in which intentions are created in the animal brain by the linking of two sensory images. For example, a dog that has been beaten with a stick learns to recognize that sticks are dangerous, because the image of a stick and the image of pain are linked in the dog's memory, creating an intention, a judgment that sticks are bad. The next time the dog sees a stick, the dog's *estimativa* recognizes the link between that form and pain, and the dog runs away.[24]

The third group of phenomena consisted of judgments that an object with one sensible quality will have other sensible qualities. Suppose that an animal has experienced an object that is yellow and sweet, such as honey. When the animal perceives a new yellow object, its *estimativa* recalls the link between yellow and sweet and judges that the new yellow object is also sweet.[25]

Many Latin scholars adopted Avicenna's concept of an internal sensitive power possessed by humans and animals that informed them of the value of sensed objects by means of intentions, not by means of sense images. Dominicus Gundissalinus, the twelfth-century translator of Avicenna's *De anima*, also wrote a *De anima* of his own, which borrows not only ideas from Avicenna but large chunks of text as well. Frequent borrowing occurs in the section on the internal senses, and it is tempting to conclude that, faced with this difficult text, Gundissalinus here threw up his hands and bequeathed the task of explicating Avicenna to posterity.[26] Few scholars would have done differently, for Avicenna's theory grants to animals one of the powers of mind: to know that individual objects belong to universal classes. The intention that allows a sheep to recognize danger in one particular wolf also allows it to recognize danger in another. How is this possible unless a sheep can recognize danger as a quality divorced from any particular? Learned behavior in Avicenna's theory also requires an animal to recognize an object as a member of a class. A dog that has been beaten with a stick develops an aversion to all sticks, not just to the one with which it was beaten. Hence that dog in some way possesses the universal of "stick."[27] Even the ability to judge that what is yellow is also sweet requires that the percipient recognize that what it sees belongs to the class of yellow things.

John Blund addressed this question in a treatise, *De anima*, written around the year 1210, when he left off teaching arts at Oxford to study theology at Paris. Blund drew his understanding of the *estimativa* and his definition of "intention" from Avicenna.[28] Using the scholastic method to make precise his concept of the *estimativa*, he posited that the *estimativa* does allow animals to recognize (*apprehendere*) universals and also to recognize the truth or falsity of propositions.[29] A sheep that flees from a wolf seems able to recognize the individual wolf as a member of a class of objects that should be avoided. Because the sheep actually flees from the wolf, the sheep also seems to *know* that wolves are harmful, as if, by its flight, it were assenting to the proposition "wolves are harmful."[30]

To debunk this conclusion and restrict to humans the recognition of universals and of the truth or falsity of propositions, Blund explained that when a sheep sees a wolf and recognizes its harmful intent, it does not reach the conclusion in a universal sense, of all wolves, but only of the present one.[31] His explanation for why the sheep is unaware of the truth of its perceptions of the wolf consists of no more than stating that perception of truth or falsity is by definition only possible by means of intellect.[32]

Granting Blund's claim that a sheep in the presence of a wolf reacts only to the present individual and not to the entire class does not restrict the sheep's ability to react to the danger posed by any single wolf. Before the sheep can flee from the present wolf, it must have some means of determining that the present thing is indeed a wolf, or at least that the present thing is an object to be avoided. In either case, however, the sheep has mimicked the human intellect: it has recognized that an individual object belongs to a universal class.

If Blund did not successfully deny animal knowledge of universals, he deserves credit for having at least raised the problem. Few medieval scholars after Blund probed the challenge to exclusive human mental powers latent in Avicenna's theory of animal behavior.

One exception was Roger Bacon. Although mystery shrouds most of Bacon's life, we know that he lectured on Aristotle's natural philosophy in the arts faculty at Paris. He may then have gone to Oxford, where he joined the Franciscan order. Soon after that, Bacon began to seek patrons, with little success, to fund a major scholarly project. He believed that the Church had failed to recognize how powerful an instrument natural philosophy could be in the service of the true faith. His fellow friars, angered by his acerbity and wary of his tolerance for the apocalyptic writings of Joachim of Fiore, gave him no encouragement. In 1267 or 1268, Bacon forwarded in secret to Pope Clement IV two books, the *Opus maius* and the *Opus minus*, in which he made his case for natural philosophy. No evidence suggests that these books had any impact on the Church or on the universities.

Historians of science continue to grapple with Bacon's legacy, having made of him at one time or another everything from a prophet of modern science to an undistinguished representative of thirteenth-century natural philosophy. His reputation as a prophet derives from part 6 of his *Opus maius* in which he describes a "science of experience" (*scientia experimentalis*), a way of learning about nature equal in veracity to divine revelation.[33] Bacon believed that God had revealed the truths of nature to ancient sages and that the record of that revelation survived in their written works.[34] Centuries of copying and translation had, however, damaged the record's integrity and introduced any number of false statements. One of the "prerogatives" of the science of experience was to purge the record of such errors as the claim that only goat's blood can break a diamond and that hot water freezes faster than cold.[35]

If experience can verify the record of revelation, then understanding the process of experience assumes a central importance. Bacon was especially interested in visual perception.[36] One of the first Latin scholars with access to Arabic optical works, he established the study of vision, or *perspectiva*, as a distinct part of natural philosophy in the West. Because Bacon sought to discover how vision leads to knowledge, his description of vision does not end with the eye but continues with the roles of the optic nerve and the internal senses, providing the occasion for a few words on animal behavior. The instinctive fear that animals evince at the sight of a wolf or at the roar of a lion cannot, Bacon felt, be a response to quality alone. What the perceiving animal fears is not a color or a sound, but the wolf or the lion itself. Consequently, the perceiving animal must receive something of the substance along with what it receives of the accidents of perceived bodies. The external senses, the common sense, and the imagination perceive accidents, hence a further internal sense, the *estimativa*, must perceive substance.[37] Bacon defended this departure from Aristotle by claiming that it was no departure at all. Poor translations of Aristotle's works had so obscured his meaning that the more reliable translations of Arabic followers such as Avicenna offered the best glimpse into the mind of the Philosopher.[38] If, as Avicenna claimed, external senses could not detect intentions, then intentions could not represent qualities. If intentions do not represent qualities, they must represent substance. Hence Aristotle must have believed that animals could directly perceive substance.

Bacon also invoked poor translation to remove from perspectivist literature an apparent admission of reasoning power in animals. The Arabic polymath known to the West as Alhazen, Bacon's chief source for perspectivist theories, had divided sensory cognition into three modes, depending on what powers were brought to bear. Bacon adopted these three modes in his own work. The perception of light and color, which required only the external sense of vision, he called "cognition by sense alone."[39] More complex perceptions required the exercise of internal senses. When I see a person, I am able to recognize both that what I see belongs to the universal category of "person" and that the person is or is not known to me.[40] Using this second mode of cognition, which Bacon called "cognition by resemblance" (*cognitio per similitudinem*), animals can distinguish universal classes from one another, and they can distinguish individuals from universals and from each other. The third mode of cognition entailed a process resembling logical discourse (*quasi quoddam genus arguendi*).[41] Animals used this process to perceive distance, motion, and magnitude.

Despite the apparent overlap of human and animal mental powers entailed in these modes of cognition, Bacon insisted that humans were the only incarnate creatures truly capable of knowledge and reason. Bacon's names for the second and third modes of cognition were purposeful departures from the Latin text of Alhazen, in which the perception of visible objects is described as taking place "by vision and prior knowledge" and "by vision and syllogism."[42] Bacon denied that knowledge and syllogism, "as commonly understood," belonged to the sensitive part of the soul.[43] The translator of Alhazen had erred when he borrowed "knowledge" and "syllogism" from the human mental vocabulary and applied them to animals. An animal's ability to recognize and distinguish universal categories and individuals derives not from the human kind of knowledge but from the activity of its internal senses. Human syllogism is also distinct from the discursive process that takes place in animals. When humans syllogize, they recognise a difference between premises and conclusion. In an animal, the discursive process is instinctive and unconscious.[44] Bacon thus admitted the ability of animals to recognize universals and to draw conclusions while, at the same time, he defended the special status of humans.

Wherever Bacon may fit in the intellectual world of the thirteenth century, his admission that animals reason and recognize universals is unique in medieval scholastic thought. And his focus on the awareness of mental acts as a means of distinguishing human thinking from animal thinking is eerily prescient of Renaissance arguments that culminate in the Cartesian animal machine.

Bacon's polemics on behalf of his own brand of natural philosophy led him to criticize several contemporary philosophers and theologians, sometimes by name and sometimes not. One recurring target of Bacon's scorn and almost certainly the brunt of many of his attacks on unnamed persons was the *doctor universalis*, Albert the Great.[45] In passages from several works, Bacon belittled Albert for his lack of formal training in the arts. Ironically, Bacon's reforming zeal led him to attack Albert, one of the few natural philosophers who shared his conviction that the study of nature demanded experience as well as book learning. Albert and Bacon both acquired posthumously the reputation for dabbling in magic that sprang up around anyone with a hands-on approach to natural philosophy.

Albert's lack of formal training did not stop him from commenting upon or paraphrasing virtually every work attributed to Aristotle. Throughout his long and prolific career, he touched upon the question of animal behavior several times. In his *De anima* Albert wrote that both humans and animals needed a power that could do what the five senses could not: recognize relationships and make value judgments not only of benevolence and danger but also of filiation and maternity.[46] Like Avicenna before him, Albert attributed recognition of relationships in animals and humans to the *estimativa*, which fulfilled its role by eliciting "intentions which are not written in sense."[47] And, like John Blund, Albert recognized that the *estimativa* seemed to confer on animals, despite their lack of intellect, the ability to know universals. Yet if they possessed such an ability, Albert argued, animals would learn as humans learn, "through discovery, doctrine, and study,"[48] which, clearly, they do not. Humans alone, by virtue of their exclusive possession of intellect, and *not* by virtue of their *estimativa*, can derive universals from their sense experience and, by contemplating those universals, construct arts and sciences.

In Book XXI of *De animalibus*, on the other hand, Albert qualified both the meaning of "universal" and the exclusive human possession of knowledge. Following Avicenna, Albert claimed that their intellect made humans the most perfect animals, not because of the intellect itself but because the presence of intellect in humans improved and ennobled their sensitive and even their vegetative powers.[49] But while Albert would not allow animals to possess intellect, he did not here maintain the clean distinction made in *De anima* between the mental powers of animals and humans. "Certain animals," he wrote, "seem to have a little of the ability to learn from experience . . . And we see that many animals besides man have some experiential cognition in singular things."[50] Some animals achieve a level of cognition that makes them appear rational.[51] But of course, Albert went on to say, animals cannot use experience to arrive at a universal, and hence they cannot have knowledge in the same sense that humans do.[52]

Among animals capable of experiential cognition, the highest place belongs to the pygmies. In many ways, pygmies resemble humans. Their upright stance confers upon them, as it does upon humans,[53] a certain amount of spiritual clarity. Pygmies have rounded heads, brains with three ventricles, and immobile ears. Their hands closely resemble human hands. They have a language in which they can discuss particular things.[54] But they lack the ability to elicit universals; their society has no laws. They are clearly higher on the scale of perfection than other animals although the power that so elevates them "is not named by philosophers." In his attempts to locate this power, Albert proposed that reason (*ratio*) consisted of two functions. The first of these two functions involved sense, memory, and *estimativa*; the second involved intellect. The latter he named the light of reason, and the former, its shadow. Pygmies, he stated, possessed the shadow of reason, not its light.[55] Albert went on to remind his reader that an experienced thing had universal content in two ways: (1) insofar as it allows the intellect to know the quiddity or truth of a thing and (2) insofar as it bears on what the percipient should pursue or avoid.[56] The pygmy mind, therefore, although incapable of abstracting intellectual universal content from the particulars of its sense data, nevertheless still compares these particulars with the contents of its memory and thus achieves experiential cognition. With this a pygmy can construct an imperfect induction and recognize, at some quasi-universal level, the value of a perceived object.[57]

Pygmies thus occupy a place on the scale of perfection between humans and the rest of the animal kingdom. Apes are incapable of bringing memory to bear on experience, yet apes have what might be called a transpecific *estimativa*.[58] Seeing one small ape show to another its mother's breasts, an ape will then, if possible, show to a boy a woman's breasts.[59] No other animal can recognize homologous values in another species. Apes are also the only animals that can be taught by vision and, in fact, will immediately imitate any human action.[60] All other trainable animals must be trained by sounds.

Albert's discussion of quadrupeds, birds, and fish focuses on their trainability. Only animals with hearing and memory can be trained, and their success depends on their estimative power. Albert suggested that sounds and spoken words contain a *forma operabilis* that listening animals can detect and use as a basis for action to the extent that they are endowed with *estimativa*. A dog pursues the sound of a deer because the dog's *estimativa* detects in the sound an "operable form" that stimulates the dog's hunting appetite. "Operable forms" detected by a sheep in the sound of a wolf stimulate flight; in the sound of the shepherd's voice, they stimulate the desire to approach. Thus trained animals need not understand their trainer's language. The need only discern the "operable form" in his voice to determine whether he is pleased or angry, and they will adjust their behavior accordingly.[61]

Albert's comparative psychology thus qualifies in several ways the standard psychological theory set forth in thirteenth-century *De anima* commentaries, including Albert's own. Faced with experiential cognition in pygmies, apes, and other animals, Albert allowed not only that animals possessed some part of *ratio*, but also that things have a universal content detectable by animals. Faced with the trainability of certain animals, he introduced the *forma operabilis*, which has a function equivalent to the function of intentions with the added ability to convey a human trainer's state of mind. Indeed, the Albert of *De animalibus*, Book 21, wrote as if virtually all animal behavior were learned behavior.[62] He did not deny that higher animals could react without experience, but he invoked unlearned behavior only when discussing the behavior of the cuttlefish and polyp. He described this behavior as so primitive, so immediate, that it did not require the participation of the *estimativa*.[63] In the single passage in which Albert mentioned *instinctus*, he referred not to a source of unlearned behavior but to a necessary condition for learning.[64]

Albert's willingness to depart from standard psychological theory in Book 21 follows from Aristotle's willingness to discuss the mental life of animals in *Historia animalium* without reference to the powers of the sensitive soul delineated in *De anima*. It may also be true that the departures in Albert's comparative psychology derive from a realization that the standard psychology, with its rigid restriction of intelligence to humans, could offer no adequate explanation of animal behavior.

If the disciple who does not surpass his master fails his master, then Thomas Aquinas certainly did not fail Albert the Great. The breadth and depth of Thomas's authority in theology and philosophy earned him the title of Doctor of the Church in 1567, and Thomism is alive and well today. Yet the success of Thomism did not mean success for Albert's particular approach to nature, as Thomas's treatment of animal behavior makes clear. Thomas attributed animal behavior to a natural tendency or instinct. Humans, too, lived under the influence of various kinds of instinct. An *instinctus diaboli* could drive humans to sin.[65] But while humans possess the free will to resist an instigation toward sin, animals are completely controlled by their instincts. Any apparent wisdom or prudence in animal behavior is simply a manifestation of God's creative genius, just as a clock reflects the creative genius of its human builder.[66] Thomas pressed the mechanical analogy by noting that "all creatures of the same kind behave in the same way,"[67] just as all clocks operate the same way. One example of a behavior common to all individuals in a species is the response to danger. Avicenna and Albert had noticed that animals respond to the utility or danger in objects that could not be conveyed by the object's sensible qualities. Thomas, too, insisted that a sheep does not flee from a wolf because of its color or shape but because of its danger,[68] and that the sheep's instinctive reaction to the wolf is as inevitable as the upward motion of fire.[69] But although Thomas believed that these were similar reactions, he did not make them equivalent. Fire has no choice but to rise and does not know what it is doing. A sheep that sees a wolf must judge that the wolf is dangerous and then must run away.[70] Unlike the fire however, the sheep knows what it is doing. Humans also make judgments about what they sense, but because of their intellect, humans have the freedom to respond any way they choose.[71]

Of learned behavior Thomas had little to say beyond naming sight and hearing as the senses by which learning occurred. Thomas's virtual omission of learned behavior and Albert's attention to the same subject illustrate their different approaches to the study of nature in general. In addition to the twenty-six books of *De animalibus*, Albert wrote the five books of *De mineralibus et lapidibus* and the seven books of *De vegetabilibus*. These are the labors of a man for whom nature was a subject worthy of study in its own right. His foray into comparative psychology was a necessary part of an Aristotelian study of animals. Thomas, however, was always a theologian; animals interested him only insofar as they furthered his understanding of the place of humans in creation. The instinctive behavior of animals filled a gap in Thomas's scale of nature between minerals and plants, which lacked awareness and free will, and humans who possessed them both. Animals were aware of their acts of judgment even though these acts were not free. Instinctive behavior thus revealed God's workmanship in the animal kingdom. Learned behavior, Thomas may have felt, could reveal no more, and hence need not detain the student of nature.

The medieval inquiry into animal behavior faced two obstacles: one slight, the other severe. The slight obstacle was the acquisition of accurate reports of animal behavior. The development of theories of animal behavior was limited by the few phenomena admitted as genuinely in need of explanation. The regularity with which scholars trotted out the sheep and the wolf to illustrate instinctive behavior suggests a dearth of trustworthy alternatives as well as a respect for tradition. Bestiaries brim with intriguing stories that rarely appear in academic discussions of instinct because scholars recognized that bestiaries were pedagogical rather than zoological. Scholars also chose not to draw upon their daily experience of familiar animals, perhaps because to do so would be to violate the essentially literary nature of the medieval scientific endeavor.

The severe obstacle was the insistence that intelligence and immortality are can only occur together. Aristotle had suggested that because the human soul can become all thinkable things, some part of the soul must be unchangeable and immortal. Christians believed that when the body died, the immortal human soul went to its reward as a consequence of choices it had made during its incarnate life. To make choices, the soul needed free will and intelligence. The mortal soul of an animal, however, faced no judgment and hence had no need of free will or intelligence. Intelligence in an animal would be superfluous, and God does nothing in vain. Thus the mortality of animals prevented medieval thinkers from admitting that intelligence could play a role in animal behavior. Yet when Blund, Bacon, Albert, and Thomas faced the problem of animal behavior, they could not maintain the denial of animal intelligence enforced upon them by both their philosophy and their theology. Roger Bacon made the largest concession. He could not limit intelligence to humans, so instead, he limited the *awareness* of discursive processes to humans. Albert the Great admitted that animals could detect a universal nature in objects. John Blund had refused to make such an explicit admission, even though the Avicennan theory requires that animals recognize classes of objects. Thomas Aquinas argued that intelligent animal behavior did not demand the presence in animals of free will. Yet even if an animal's response is automatic, an animal must still first determine if a thing is beneficial or harmful. Rather than discover how animals accomplished that determination, Thomas and many of his followers were content to give it the name "natural instinct" and to pursue it no further. Not until the Middle Ages had yielded to the Renaissance did the concept of instinct face more critical scrutiny. Descartes's mechanization of instinct, foreshadowed by Thomas, drew animal behavior to the center of a profound debate on the relationship of humans to the rest of nature that continues to this day.

To suggest that medieval scholars were encumbered by their unwillingness to grant intelligence to the mortal souls of animals is not to suggest that theology impeded the advance of comparative psychology. Well before the advent of Christianity, intelligence had become an exclusive prerogative of humans. Even in the twentieth century, with theology having long ago yielded to Darwin its influence in university science departments, we have yet to discover just how differently humans and animals think. If the medieval inquiry into animal behavior was hampered by preconceived notions, it was no more so than our own.

NOTES

1. *De anima*, II.3, 415a2; III.12, 434a22.
2. *De anima*, II.2, 414a3–4.
3. III.12, 434b14, 435b4–7, b19, 413b5–8. Humans have the best sense of touch, II.9, 421a20–27, and a poor sense of smell, II.9, 421a12.
4. III.6, 429a21–27. In II.3, 414b16–19, Aristotle restricted *nous* and *dianoetikon* to "man, and any other being similar or superior to him." (*De anima*, trans. W.S. Hett, *Loeb Classical Library*, Cambridge, MA: Harvard Univ. Press, 1975, 83.) Cf. *De memoria et reminiscentia*, 1, 450a15–17. In III.3, 428a22–23, Aristotle denied *pistis* to animals; in III.3, 428a24–25, he denied *logos* to animals; in III.10, 433a12, he denied *noesis* and *logismos* to animals.
5. *De anima*, III.5, 430a23.
6. II.6, 418a24; Loeb, 103.
7. II.6, 418a12–14; Loeb, 101, 103.
8. II.6, 418a17–20.
9. Medieval scholars such as Roger Bacon (see below) and William of Ockham would find this an intolerable limitation and propose ways in which a percipient could be affected by a thing's substance.
10. In *De anima* III.2, 425b17 (Loeb, 147), Aristotle seemed willing to allow self-aware external senses (cf. Clarence William Shute, *The Psychology of Aristotle* [New York: Columbia University Press, 1941], 95), but not in *De somno*, 2, 455a18 (Loeb, 327).
11. Aristotle allows that this power "thinks and perceives," (*noei kai aisthanetai*). III.2, 426b23; Loeb, 151, 153.
12. 3, 469a12–13, *koinon aestheterion*.
13. Memory is associated with imagination according to *De memoria et reminiscentia*, 1, 450a23.
14. 434a13–15; Loeb, 193.
15. IX.7, 612b18.
16. *Historia animalium*, I.1, 488b15 (Loeb, 19); IX.6, 612a3. Of hind, IX.5, 611a15. Of crane, IX.9, 614b10.
17. *The Works of Aristotle Translated into English* (Oxford: Clarendon, 1910), vol. 4, *Historia Animalium*, translated by D'Arcy Thompson Wentworth, VIII:1, 588a30 (no pagination).
18. *De partibus animalium*, II.2, 648a2–5; Loeb, 119, 121.
19. Despite their being unteachable due to lack of hearing. *Metaphysica*, I.1, 980b21–24. The lengthy *Historia animalium*, IX.40, is devoted to the habits of bees. IX.1, 608a20–21, suggests that even deaf animals may be taught, by sight. Aristotle denied imagination to bees in *De anima*, III.3, 428a11, Loeb, 159. Albert attributed this denial to a translator's error: "Puto autem non ex vitio esse Philosophi, sed ex vitio translationis: quia Translator non intellexit nullum animalium quae dixit Aristoteles phantasiam non habere, et loco eorum

transtulit formicas et apes, et corrumpit veritatem mala ex translatione." *De anima*, III, tract. I, ch. 7. Borgnet (ed.), *Alberti magni opera omnia*, vol. 5 (1890), 324b.
20. G.C. Anawati states that this excerpt "enjoyed an extraordinary success in the Latin Middle Ages." *Dictionary of Scientific Biography*, 15:497a.
21. Harry Wolfson traced the use of the term *sensus internus* to Augustine and Gregory the Great. Arabic philosophers also spoke of internal senses. "The Internal Senses in Latin, Arabic, and Hebrew Philosophic Texts," *Harvard Theological Review*, 1935, 28:69–133.
22. F. Rahman, *A History of Muslim Philosophy*, states, "The doctrine of *wahm [estimativa]* is the most original element in Ibn Sina's psychological teaching." Quoted in *Avicenna Latinus: Liber de anima seu Sextus de naturalibus*, ed. S. van Riet (Louvain/Leiden: E.J. Brill, 1972), 37, in the note for lines 19–57. Wolfson believes that the *estimativa* is traceable to Aristotle. "Internal Senses," 88.
23. The ability of the *estimativa* to make this judgment derives from celestial influence. "Praeter hoc etiam animalia habent cautelas naturales. Cuius rei causa sunt comparationes quae habent esse inter has animas et earum principia quae sunt duces [a note here states, "duces: confusion probable entre *qa'ida* (duces) et *da'ima* (semper).") incessantes, praeter comparationes quas contingit aliquando esse et aliquando non esse, sicut considerare cum intellectu et quod subito in mentem venit: omnia etenim illinc [a note states "illinc: *ar.* «de là-bas», du monde des *principia* ou substances célèstes."] veniunt. Et per istas cautelas apprehendit aestimatio intentiones quae sunt commixtae cum sensibilibus de eo quod obest vel prodest; unde omnis ovis pavet lupum, etsi numquam viderit illum nec aliquid mali pertulerit ab illo." *Avicenna Latinus*, 38:28–39:36. Venice 1508, f. 19 rb.
In a French translation of the Arabic text: "De même, les animaux possèdent des instincts naturels. La cause en est aux rapports existant entre ces âmes, et que les principes des rapports sont constants, non interrompus, autres que les rapports auxquels il arrive une fois d'être ou de ne pas être, exemple la perfection de l'intelligence, et exemple l'idée du juste. Car toutes les choses viennent d'ici-bas." *Psychologie d'Ibn Sina (Avicenne) d'après son oeuvre Aš-Šifā*, éditée et traduite en français par Ján Bakoš (Éditions de l'Academie Tchécoslovaque des Sciences), Prague, 1950, II:130. Cf IV:2; van Riet, 13; Bakos, II:120.
Albert stated in his *De animalibus*, libri XXVI, herausgegeben von Hermann Stadler (Beitrage zur Geschichte der Philosophie des Mittelalters, 16), 1325:15–16.
24. "Alius autem modus est sicut hoc quod fit per experientiam. Animal etenim cum habuerit dolorem aut delicias, aut pervenerit ad illud utilitas sensibilis aut nocumentum sensibile adiunctum cum forma sensibili, et descripta fuerit in formali forma huius rei et forma eius quod adiunctum est illi,

et descripta fuerit in memoria intentio comparationis quae est inter illas et iudicium de illa, scilicet quod memoria per seipsam naturaliter apprehendit hoc, et deinde apparuerit extra imaginativam forma ipsa, tunc movebitur per formam et movebitur cum illa id quod adiunctum fuerat illi de intentionibus utilibus aut nocivis, et omnino procedet memoria ad modum motus et perquisitionis quae est natura virtutis imaginativae; sed aestimatio hoc totum sentiet simul et videbit intentionem per formam illam, et hic est modus qui accidit per experientiam; unde canes terrentur lapidibus et fustibus et similia." IV:3; *Avicenna Latinus*, 39:39–52.

25. "Aliquando autem ab estimatione adveniunt alia judicia ad modum similitudinis: cum enim res habuerit aliquam formam conjunctam cum intentione estimationis in aliquo sensibilium quae <non> conjuncta est semper cum omnibus illis, cum visa fuerit forma videbitur eius intentio." IV.3; *Avicenna Latinus*, 40. Cf. IV.1; van Riet, 7:88–8:94; Venice, f. 17va-b.

26. J. T. Muckle, "The treatise *De anima* of Dominicus Gundissalinus," *Mediaeval Studies*, 1940, 2:23–103. For the borrowed sections cf. *Avicenna Latinus*, IV:3, *passim*, which refers to the pages in Muckle's text of Gundissalinus's *De anima*.

27. One solution would be to claim that learned responses to individual objects result from the third of Avicenna's three estimative functions. Albert hinted at such an explanation in his *Quaestiones de animalibus*, *Alberti Magni Opera Omnia*, edited by B. Geyer, vol. 12 (1955), 189.

28. "Intentionem appelat Commentator [sic] qualitatem singularem non cadentem in sensum, que est vel rei nocitiva vel expediens." John Blund, *Tractatus De anima*, edited by D.A. Callus and R.W. Hunt (London: Oxford University Press, 1970), 69:2–4.

29. "Item. Ut dictum est superius, per estimationem tum fit compositio tum divisio. Sed non est secundum estimationem componere aliqua nisi prius apprehendantur extremitates illius compositionis. Ergo cum ovis secundum estimationem componit in eius anima hoc, scilicet lupum esse fugiendum, prius apprehendit hoc ipsum 'fugere' et rem designatam per hunc terminum 'lupum'. Sed hoc ipsum 'fugere' est universale, et ille terminus 'lupum' significat universale. Sic ergo per estimationem apprehenduntur universalia. Possunt ergo bruta animalia apprehendere universalia." Blund, 70:9–17.

30. Cf. *De anima*, III.7, 431a8 ff.; Loeb, 175.

31. "Unde secundum vim estimativam non apprehenditur quod a lupo sit fugiendum, sed apprehenditur quod ab hoc lupo sit fugiendum, qui est in sensu, vel prius fuit in sensu; et cum per hunc terminum, 'hoc lupo,' significetur singulare, illud quod significatur ulterius per hunc terminum 'fugiendum' trahitur ad singulare per hanc determinationem 'ab hoc lupo.'" Blund, 70:27–32.

32. "Non enim apprehendunt veritatem vel falsitatem, cum intellectu careant et ratione." Blund, 71:6–7.

33. I follow Stewart C. Easton in translating *scientia experimentalis* as "'science of experience' rather than experimental science, which suggests some kind of experiments in our modern sense." *Roger Bacon and His Search for a Universal Science* (New York: Columbia University Press, 1952), 175.

34. "Ergo oportet quod intellectus hominis aliter juvetur, et ideo sancti patriarchae et prophetae, qui primo dederunt scientias mundo, receperunt illuminationes interiores et non solum stabant in sensu. Et similiter multi post Christum fideles. Nam gratia fidei illuminat multum, et divinae inspirationes, non solum in spiritualibus, sed corporalibus et scientiis philosophiae." *Opus Maius*, VI.1; Bridges, II.169. These sages included Pythagoras, Socrates, Plato, and Aristotle. *Opus tertium*, ed. J.S. Brewer, Rerum Britannicarum Medii Aevi Scriptores, vol. 15, p. 81. In Easton's words, Bacon "wanted to separate folklore and magic from the genuine data of revelation." *Roger Bacon*, 175.

35. "Nam multa scribunt auctores, et vulgus tenet per argumenta quae fingit sine experientia, quae sunt omnino falsa. Vulgatum enim est apud omnes quod adamas non potest frangi nisi sanguine hircino, et philosophi et theologi hac sententia abutuntur. Sed nondum certificatum est de fractione per huiusmodi sanguinem, quanquam elaboratum est ad hoc; et sine illo sanguine potest frangi de facili. Hoc enim vidi oculis meis; et necesse est hoc, quia gemmae non possunt sculpti nisi per fragmenta huius lapidis." *Opus maius*, VI.1; Bridges, II.168. Bridges refers to Pliny 37.7 on goat's blood. On hot water freezing faster than cold, in which many people today believe, see Aristotle, *Meteorologica*, I.12, 348b32–349a4.

36. *Opus maius*, V.1.1; Bridges, II.3.

37. *Opus maius*, V.1.4, Bridges, II.8, refers to *qualitates complexionales*. Bridges revealed in a note that only one ms. had this reading; others had *qualitates substantiales*. At V.1.5, Bridges II.11, Bacon referred to "qualitas complexionalis nocivae vel utilis, seu magis ipsa natura substantialis utilis vel nociva." The *estimativa* is harmed by what it receives from a dangerous object in the same way that the external senses are harmed by what is noxious to them. *De multiplicatione specierum*, I.2; Lindberg, 24:73–79.

38. *Opus maius*, V.1.5; Bridges, II:10.

39. "cognitio solo sensu." *Opus maius*, V.10.3; Bridges, II:79.

40. *Opus maius*, V.10.3; Bridges, II:80. V.3.2; Bridges, II:104.

41. *Opus maius*, V.10.3; Bridges, II:81.

42. "Visibile percipitur aut solo visu, aut visu et syllogismo, aut visu et anticipata notione." Federico Risner, *Opticae thesaurus*, Alhazeni arabis libri septem (Basileae, 1572), 30.

43. "Sed haec nomina non sunt propria, quia virtutes animae sensitivae habent has cognitiones, quibus non debetur scientia nec syllogismus ut communiter accipiuntur." *Opus maius*, V.10.3; Bridges, II:82.

44. *Opus maius*, V.3.8; Bridges, II.129.

45. Jeremiah M.G. Hackett, "The Attitude of Roger Bacon to the *Scientia* of Albertus Magnus," in James J. Weisheipl (ed.), *Albertus Magnus and the Sciences* (Toronto: PIMS, 1980), 53–72.

46. *De anima* III:1.2; Borgnet V:317a. Also mentioned in the dubious *De apprehensione*, Borgnet, V:581.

47. "intentiones quae in sensu non sunt scriptae." *De anima*, III:1.2; Borgnet, V:317a. George Peter Klubertanz, *The Discursive Power: Sources and Doctrine of the* vis cogitativa *according to St. Thomas Aquinas* (St Louis: Modern Schoolman, 1952), 270, attributes innate intentions to Albert, but the majority of passages suggests they were adventitious.

48. "Si ergo bruta animalia perceptiva essent universalium, perceptiva etiam essent scientiarum per inventionem et doctrinam et studium, quod falsum est." I.39.2; De Homine, Borgnet, XXXV:338a.

49. *De animalibus*, XXI.1.1. Stadler, 1322:9–11. "virtutibus hominis propter consortium rationis accidat aliquid propter quod virtutes eius interiores differunt a virtutibus animalium." Avicenna, *De anima*, IV:3; *Avicenna Latinus*, 36:4–8.

50. "Quaedam autem animalia videntur aliquid licet parum experimenti participare. Experimentum namque ex multis nascitur memoriis quia eiusdem rei multae memoriae faciunt potentiam et facultatem aliquid experimenti: et nos videmus quod multa animalia praeter hominem aliquid experimentalis habent cognitionis in singularibus." *De animalibus*, XXI.1.2; Stadler, 1327:28–32.

51. Ibid.; Stadler, 1326:13. Ch. 3, Stadler 1332:15–16.

52. Ibid., ch. 2; Stadler, 1327:35–38.

53. Ibid., ch. 1; Stadler, 1324:29–32.

54. Ibid., ch. 2; Stadler 1328:15–17.

55. Ibid; Stadler, 1328:23–24.

56. Ibid; Stadler, 1329:12–20.

57. "Inductionis autem aliquid videtur participare pigmeus in hoc quod experimenti parum participat secundum sillogismum operativum quem practicum Graeci vocant, sed perfecte non inducit quando non progreditur usque ad universalis acceptionem." Ibid., ch. 3; Stadler, 1332:3–6. Thomas used *syllogismum practicum sive operativum* to mean any syllogism with a singular conclusion that suggested action. See esp. *Sententia libri Ethicorum*, 6.9.

58. According to H.W. Janson, *Apes and Ape Lore in the Middle Ages and Renaissance* (London: Warburg Institute, 1952), 85, Albert grouped pygmies with apes on a level beneath humans and placed all remaining animals on a third lower level. Yet Albert stated, "Pycmeus igitur secundum praeinducta quasi medium est inter hominem divinum intellectum habentem, et alia muta animalia in quibus nichil divinae lucis esse deprehenditur." Ibid., ch. 2; Stadler, 1329:25–27. Albert continued, however, by saying, "Reliquarum autem symiarum genera," suggesting that pygmies were a genus of apes. Ibid., ch. 3; Stadler, 1329:36.

59. Ibid; Stadler, 1331:26–28.

60. Thus can they be trapped. XXII.2.1; Stadler 1422:14–16.

61. XXI.1.2; Stadler, 1327:14–20. On quadrupeds, pp. 1334–35; on birds, pp. 1336–37.

62. Including self-medication: "sicut quod mustela pugnans cum serpente vulnerata contra venenum accipit folium endiviae quae a quibusdam rostrum porcinum vocatur." Ibid., ch. 2; Stadler, 1327:32–34.

63. "Istae tamen providentiae sunt omnium animalium et causantur a sensu conferentis aut nocivi potius quam a praecognitione aestimationis." Ibid., ch. 6; Stadler, 1340:22–24.

64. "Est autem praeter omnia quae inducta sunt observandum quod nullum omnino animal disciplinabile est nisi cum instinctu naturae." Ibid., ch. 3; Stadler, 1330:25–26.

65. See, e.g., *Summa Theologica*, I.114.3.

66. "Sicut autem comparantur artificialia ad artem humanam, ita comparantur omnia naturalia ad artem divinam ... Et propter hoc etiam quaedam animalia dicuntur prudentia val sagacia, non quod in eis sit aliqua ratio vel electio; quod ex hoc apparet quod omnia quae sunt unius naturae similiter operantur." *Summa theologica*, I–II.13.2. *ad* 3.

67. "quod ex hoc apparet quod omnia quae sunt unius naturae similiter operantur." Ibid. Thomas also mentioned the similarity of behaviors among individuals within a species in his commentary on *Physics* II:8 and VIII:4. Cf. Albert's commentary on *Physics* II.1.2.

68. "Sed necessarium est animali ut quaerat aliqua vel fugiat non solum quia sunt convenientia vel non convenientia ad sentiendum sed etiam propter aliquas alias commoditates et utilitates, sive nocumentum ... Necessarium est ergo animali quod percipiat huiusmodi intentiones quas non percipit sensus exterior." *Summa Theologica*, I.78.4.

69. "Ad secundum dicendum quod brutum animal accipit unum prae alio, quia appetitus eius est naturaliter determinatus ad ipsum; unde statim quando per sensum, vel per imaginationem repraesentatur ei aliquid ad quod naturaliter inclinatur eius appetitus, absque electione movetur ad ipsum; sicut etiam absque electione ignis movetur sursum et non deorsum." *Summa theologica*, I–II.13.2 *ad* 2.

70. "Judicat enim ovis videns lupum eum esse fugiendum naturali judicio, et non libero, quia non ex collatione sed ex naturali instinctu hoc judicat." *Summa Theologica*, I.83.1.

71. Animals have "cognitio finis"; humans have "cognitio rationis finis." *Summa Theologica*, I–II.6.2.

THE GODDESS NATURA IN THE OCCITAN LYRIC

Veronica Fraser

The troubadour lyric, which flourished in the twelfth and thirteenth century in southern France, celebrated in song and in verse the beauty and perfections of the lady, and the primacy of love. The nature topos is widely used in the love song, in particular in the opening stanza, in which it forms a suitable framework for the invitation to love. The celebration of nature is closely tied up with the celebration of love, but the imagery contained in the spring opening is not merely a commonplace, an ornament of style; it is frequently further developed by the poet to form an allegorical framework for the whole song, which thus presents the lady in terms of the goddess Natura, a powerful divinity of fertility and renewal, strongly rooted in popular and classical mythology. The lady possesses many qualities of the goddess, in particular her ability to heal and restore, to bring joy and renewal of life. She is furthermore the source of the poet's creative ability and encourages and promotes moral and spiritual improvement. Nature imagery is incorporated into the love request addressed to the lady as part of the rhetoric of persuasion by means of which the lover invites the beloved to enjoy physical union and the fullness of love.

Medieval views on the creation of the universe and the role of the goddess Natura are contained in treatises on natural science and philosophy, many of which were commentaries or adaptations of the *Timaeus* of Plato. Plato's myth of creation had been transmitted to the medieval west by Chalcidius, who translated the first fifty-three chapters of the *Timaeus* and added an extensive commentary.[1] In the twelfth century there was a renewed interest in the *Timaeus*, and many commentaries were written on it, such as the *Glosae super Platonem* of Bernard of Chartres.[2] Other works on the creation that were influential at the time of the troubadours were the *Cosmographia* of Bernard

129

Sylvester and the *De planctu Naturae* of Alan of Lille. These two works describe in detail the goddess Natura and her role in the process of creation.

Bernard Silvester's *Cosmographia*, an adaptation in poetic form of Plato's dialogue, was composed between 1145 and 1156.[3] It is divided into two sections, the *Megacosmos* and the *Microcosmos*; the first describes the creation of the world (including the planets, stars, and other celestial bodies), and the second deals specifically with the creation of man, the supreme work of the creator. Although the eternal Godhead is the prime mover and overseer of creation, he is assisted by a number of goddesses, each with her own duties to perform. Of these female deities, Natura, Noys, Endelechia, and Physis are the most important figures. Each represents a different aspect of the female ideal—physical, intellectual, and spiritual: nurturing and propagation, in the case of Natura herself; ordering in the case of Noys, who is the female intellect; and spiritual in the case of Endelechia, who represents the world soul. The fourth goddess, Physis, has practical qualities; she is the craftswoman, responsible for the final shaping of man. It is Natura who sets everything in motion, as we see at the beginning of the poem in her initial complaint to her mother Noys. She requests that Sylva, who represents formless matter or chaos, be ordered and made more beautiful. Sylva, or Hyle, is the womb of the world, from which all else proceeds. Noys agrees to bring about harmony and cultivation in the universe, and she does this with the help of the other female deities. Endelechia, for example, provides the light that will later form the substance of human souls to be infused into the bodies formed by Physis. Noys creates the stars and heavenly bodies and then fashions the earth using the matter found in Sylva. The animals and plants are made, as well as everything necessary for healing and propagating. Nature herself creates the grove, a different one in every land, a type of ideal landscape where all is luxuriant and abundant. All has been provided to ensure the constant renewal of creation through the union of the male and female elements of propagation.

In the second book of the *Cosmographia*, the *Microcosmos*, in which man is carefully fashioned, the goddess Physis has the most important role. Bernard describes the work of Physis in Granusion, or paradise, where she is helped by her two daughters, Theory and Practice. Physis has knowledge of herbs and minerals that may heal man. Natura arrives in Paradise and informs Physis of her task, to complete creation with the human species who will rule over all other creatures. At the arrival of Nature in her chariot, the whole earth teems with life and acknowledges her as the mother of generation. She aids in the creation of man by joining the body, formed by Physis, to the soul, provided by her sister Urania.

Bernard ends his treatise with a celebration of propagation, in which he describes the male genitalia and praises their use, which is both necessary and enjoyable. Through them man may fight against death and thus ensure the continued existence of the universe. The powerful phallus and the shining sperm are Nature's weapons against man's frailty, since he is subject to decay.[4]

In Bernard's treatise Natura has the task of overseeing the creation of the universe and of man; she undertakes a journey through the spheres to do this, and with the help of her companions she is able to ensure the creation of man and the continuation of his species.

One of the sources for Bernard's poem on the universe was the Hermetic text the *Asclepius*, as has been shown by Brian Stock and Peter Dronke.[5] The *Asclepius*, which is part of the *Corpus Hermeticum*, was translated into Latin from the Greek between 100 and 300 A.D.[6] This anonymous work is in the form of a dialogue between Hermes Trismegistus and his pupil Asclepius and contains information on the occult sciences, revelation, and the physical and spiritual nature of man and the universe. As well as Egyptian, Greek, and Judaic elements, there are Gnostic Christian influences in the text, such as are found in the Cathar religion, which flourished in the Occitan region at the time of the troubadours.[7] In the *Asclepius* man is presented as an integral part of the universe, possessing both divine and material properties, with the particular duty of overseeing the cultivation of the earth and the ordering of the world. In this task he is assisted by demons, who are halfway between God and man. The divinity is bisexual; God possesses the two sexes, as do all created things.[8] Fertility and reproduction are venerated; the union of the two sexes ensures eternal reproduction and the continuation of the species. Sexual union is therefore sacred, a divine mystery, by means of which nature is filled with the creative activity of God. Human sensuality and sexuality are celebrated as part of the divine plan in this essentially non-Christian work.

In the twelfth century, as A.D. Nock has shown, many authors were familiar with the *Asclepius*. As well as Bernard, Alan of Lille quotes from the *Asclepius* in his *Contra haereticos*. The views on nature expressed in the Hermetic work, and in particular the veneration of human sexuality and reproduction, are also found in Alan's poem *De planctu Naturae*, which was written about the year 1165. Alan spent some time in Languedoc and was a teacher at Montpellier, and it is possible that his work was known to the troubadours.[9] In *De planctu* the goddess Natura has a prominent role in encouraging human regeneration and the physical union of man and woman. Both Alan and Bernard exalt procreation, though whereas Bernard has ended on an optimistic note in praise of man's reproductive capacities, Alan begins with a lament that man has strayed from his proper path and is neglecting the duties assigned to him. Natura appears to the poet in a dream, weeping and disheveled because man is not respecting her laws. For this she blames Venus Monstruosa, unnatural love, which does not lead to procreation and which cannot ensure the continuation of Nature's plan. All other vices on earth result from this prime sin of excessive and fruitless lust. Alan's poem is didactic; Natura is angry with those who have transgressed. She explains that the hammers must not get detached from the anvils. For this reason she comes back to earth to put things to rights. She summons the help of her Priest Genius, who is also her son, and her husband Hymen, the god of marriage. At her arrival on earth all creatures rejoice and greet her with hope and renewed vitality. The male virtues are also presented in the form of her charioteer, who is a model of male perfection, both moral and physical. Genius, her priest, does his mother's bidding and proceeds to excommunicate all those who have transgressed. The male and female principles must be honored for the earth to flourish and renew itself.

In both of these treatises the healing power of nature is stressed. In the *De planctu* Nature arrives and embraces the poet, who is suffering and afraid, and restores him with her kiss. In the *Cosmographia* Natura brings about harmony and unity to the megacosmos as well as the microcosmos. These same qualities of healing, abundance, fertility and renewal, and harmony and unity are to be found in the representations of the goddess in the vernacular literatures of the Middle Ages, for example, in Chaucer and in the *Roman de la Rose*, as previous studies have shown.[10] In these works Natura is personified and has a role in the narrative, as in those of Alan and Bernard. In the Occitan lyric Natura is also present, but not as a personification. Images relating to nature and to themes of fertility and healing form part of the traditional love request addressed to the lady.

In some instances the lady has the same qualities as the goddess; she is a source of healing and abundance, of youth, and of joy. The metaphors and allegories relating to Natura add further erotic connotations to the love request, the desired union of the two lovers. The poet-lover has his part to play to complete the equation, as the complimentary element of the life force, normally represented as the seed or the spark of life. He invites the lady to participate in the renewal of the cycle of creation and to follow Nature's lore.

It is in this framework that we should see the traditional spring opening of many of the *cansos*, or love songs, both in the courtly tradition of the *chanson courtoise* and in the popular genres, such as the *alba* and the *pastorela*, which also use a great deal of nature imagery. Most of the poets restrict the nature topos to the opening stanza of the song, where it constitutes an appropriate motif for what is to follow: a celebration of the lady's beauty and a request for love's reward. However, in some cases the nature topos is developed throughout the whole canso, in the form of the trope *allegoria*, an extended and obscure metaphor, which provides a unifying structure to the whole canso. This may be seen most strikingly in the songs of Arnaut Daniel, Peire Vidal, Jaufre Rudel, and Bernart de Ventadorn, though many other poets make extensive use of the theme of nature. These poets have considerably developed the use of nature imagery to the extent that it forms part of a latent message of erotic persuasion. The following examples will serve to show how the attributes of the goddess Natura are applied to the lady and are incorporated into the celebration of physical union.

In one of Peire's cansos, in which he celebrates his "Car'amiga dols et franca," the lady is described as a tree producing fruits of joy that ripen on the branch:

Quar vos etz arbres e branca
On fruitz de gaug s'asazona. (XV:9–10)

[For you are the tree and the branch / where the fruit of joy ripens.][11]

She is the source of abundance and also of healing. Through her the poet may be healed and restored, if she will grant him her love:

Quar vostr'amors segurana
Gueris e.m reven e.m sana. (13–14)

[For your sincere love / heals me and restores me to health.]

In another canso Peire uses nature imagery throughout again in the form of an allegory or extended metaphor forming a unifying structure to the whole composition. He presents the lady as the source of joy, healing, and abundance, and also suggests that the two lovers renew their past love. A celebration of nature and fertility provides a suitable context for the traditional love request.

In the opening stanza the nature theme is introduced with the evocation of springtime as a suitable setting for love. The trees, the flowering branches, and the bird-song all rejoice with the lover at the arrival and renewal of nature. In the following stanza the lover compares himself to the fruit on the branch, invigorated and expectant:

Qu'ab joi longamen
Viu e renovell
Co.l fruch el ramell. (XXVIII:17–19)

[Like the fruit on the branch / I am renewed through joy and live long.]

A reference to the love he has already enjoyed is expressed by means of a metaphor in the same register of flowering and renewal:

Qu'en mon cor ai fuelh'e flor
Que.m te tot l'an en verdor. (21–22)

[In my heart I have leaf and flower / which keep me all year round in verdure.]

In the central stanza of the poem the metaphor is extended to include the whole tree, branches, leaves, fruit, and flowers, to express the full flowering of love in accordance with Nature's decrees:

Ben aurai d'amor
Fuelh'e frug e flor
E ram e verdor. (37–39)

[From love I shall receive / leaf, fruit, and flower / branch and greenery.]

The sexual connotations become more frequent and more evident as the lady is identified more closely with the images of nature. If she grants him a kiss, she will bring joy and the hope of some further flowering of love:

> Plus gais que l'auzell
> Serai, si l'es bell
> Qu'un dous bais novell
> Me don per amor,
> Qu'anc d'altre ramell
> No vuelc culhir flor,
> Ni fruit ni verdor. (49–55)

[I shall be happier than a bird / if she deigns to give me for love / a sweet new kiss / because from that branch alone / I desire to pluck the flower / the fruit and the leaves.]

The precise nature of the flower he desires and the renewal that will follow becomes more evident as the canso progresses. He once possessed the flower but no longer is able to enjoy it; his constant desire is to regain it and thus to be renewed in vigor and health.

> Tener me pot longamen
> En valor et en bon sen
> Gai e cortes e novell,
> Cum bella flor en ramell. (93–96)

[She can keep me for a long time / in good health and vigour / gay and courtly, constantly renewed / like the sweet flower on the branch.]

The lady is here clearly presented in terms of the goddess Natura, the powerful earth goddess, source of renewal and vigor, of growth and abundance.

In Arnaut Daniel the sexual connotations relating to Natura are even stronger. One could cite numerous examples, but it will suffice to present here instances of erotic nature imagery, which Arnaut, like Peire, incorporates into the love request. Both male and female elements of procreation are celebrated, and Arnaut begins his song of springtime and renewal by a reference to the zodiac signs that encompass this season, from April to June.

Entre.l Taur e.l doble signe
Don doutz tems nais e.l freitz secha,
Per que.l clars critz d'auzels d'arma
Justa.lz prims cims e.lz vertz brancs,
Ai el cor un joi don fermi
Jausenz motz clars, cars e certz. (19:1–6)

[Between the bull and the double sign / when the sweet season is born
and the cold dries / so that the birds' clear song may ring forth / as far as
the high treetops and the green branches / this brings such joy to my
heart that I must / compose songs that are clear, rich, and precise.][12]

The sexual imagery is apparent from the opening stanza with the
reference to the bull and the twins, Taurus and Gemini, suggesting male
sexuality. We are reminded of Bernard Sylvester's praise of virility in
the *Microcosmos*, in which the twins have the task of ensuring eternal
reproduction.[13] Arnaut continues his song in praise of springtime and
the joy that urges the lover to sing in imitation of the birds in the
treetops. The sweet season brings forth his song and also his desire,
which grows firmer and more certain. The male imagery of fire that
ignites and begins the process of nature and renewal follows the
description of the lady's perfections. The lover presents himself as
being worthy of them, since he is valiant and firm and does not waver
or lose his strength.

E pel doutz tems baut, benigne,
Brandis si mos chans sa flecha
C'a pauc focs no.n sall, can s'arma,
Per issir d'entre.lz dos flancs;
. . . E.m sent ferms d'un tal fozil
Don totz jorns mon sen afil. (19–22; 26–27)

[And in this sweet, benevolent season / my song shoots forth its arrow /
as fire flares up when ignited / to surge forth between two thighs;
/. . . and I feel myself hardened by this flint / which daily sharpens my
senses.]

Phallic symbolism may be seen in the arrow (*flecha*) and the stone
(*fozil*), recalling the hammer and anvil imagery in Alan of Lille's *De
planctu*.[14] Arnaut is more openly erotic than Peire, who uses subtle
persuasion rather than explicit description. Laura Kendrick has studied

the possible gestural accompaniment to these types of erotic invitations, which would considerably enhance the sexual context.[15] The lover does not hold back in addressing his request to the lady; he is quite graphic about the desired result of his song of nature and renewal; fearlessly he stands upright and firm and makes no mystery of his desired aim:

Per que.m do, jauszens, estancs
Lai on dreitz tenc e confermi;
Mos desirs fatz francs e certz. (31–33)

[Joyfully I stand firm, upright, and solid / and in so doing I make my desire known / openly, and without hesitation.]

Arnaut has opened his song with reference to the renewal of nature, the celebration of the female principle of fertility and generation traditionally found in the flowering and renewal of foliage and blossom, but he quickly changes the focus of his song to include the male elements of propagation and thus to invite the lady to union and fulfillment, in the context of Nature's lore.

There are many other instances of the nature topos in Arnaut's songs, in particular in the opening stanza; in the following example, the sights and sounds of nature encourage the poet to compose a song of joy and love and to color it in imitation of nature:

Er vei vermeills, vertz, blaus, blancs, gruocs
vergiers, plans, plais, tertres, e vaus,
e.il votz dels auzels sona e tint
ab doutz acort maitin e tart.
So.m met en cor q'ieu colore mon chan
d'un aital flor don lo fruitz sia amors,
e jois lo grans, e l'olors d'enuoc gaindres. (13:1–7)

[Now I see scarlet, green, blue, white , yellow / orchards, meadows, hedges, hills and vales / and the trill of the bird-song rings out / with sweet harmony morning and evening. / For this I desire to color my song / with such a flower of which the fruit will be love / and joy the seed, and the scent a shield from harm.]

Here we see Ceres covering the earth with her colors, the visible and audible signs of nature, which are then metaphorically transferred to the song, using the same imagery of flower and fruit, seed and scent, all the elements of propagation from the beginnings in the seed to the final product, the fruit. All the senses are invoked to ensure joy and to ward off ill, and thus to help the poet in his creative endeavors. Nature and creative activity are linked, man's creative capacities reflecting those of Nature. The theme of love follows this introduction, by means of the male image of fire, the spark that ignites the world, described by Bernard in the *Megacosmos* as the ethereal fire, a lover or a husband, drawn to the lap of Earth, his bride.[16] In this stanza, as in the previous one, Amors is equated with Natura:

> D'amor mi pren penssan lo fuocs,
> e.l desiriers doutz e coraus,
> e.l mals es saboros q'ieu sint,
> e.il flama soaus on plus m'art, (8–11)

> [With these thoughts the fire of love takes me / with a sweet and heartfelt desire / and the pain that I feel is a pleasure / and the flame is gentle the more it burns me.]

The fire of love scorches and enflames him with desire for his lady, who is then celebrated in the remaining stanzas of the song. She is the inspiration and purpose of his art, as Nature has been the initial instigator of it. Arnaut has not developed an allegorical framework for the lady, as Peire has done, but for him nature is seen as the prime mover, the source of creation and also of creativity.

Bernart de Ventadorn uses the spring opening more than any other troubadour, though he does not develop the nature topos in the same way as Peire or Arnaut. Bernart's evocations of springtime and the rebirth of nature are limited to the opening stanza, in which they have the traditional function of providing a framework for celebrating the beauty of the lady and the upsurge of joy and desire in the lover. The following example recalls that of Peire Vidal, in which the lover himself is presented in terms of the flowers and fruits of love; he blossoms and renews himself, following the example of Natura:

> Lancan folhon bosc e jarric
> e.lh flors pareis e.lh verdura
> pels vergers e pels pratz,
> e.lh auzel, c'an estat enic,
> son gai desotz los folhatz,

autresi.m chant e m'esbaudei
e reflorisc e reverdei
e folh segon ma natura. (24:1–8)

[When the woods and the copses are in leaf / and the flowers and greenery appear in meadows and orchards / and the birds, who have been sad, / are happy amongst the foliage / I also sing and rejoice / I bloom again and renew myself / and I produce leaves according to my nature.][17]

Man is part of nature and follows the lore of the goddess as poet and as lover; in his own way he flowers and rejoices by composing a new song and by celebrating his lady in the service of love. Nature encourages love and procreation, the physical union of the lovers that ensures man against death and extinction; she also encourages the lover's art by inspiring his creative powers.

Such spring openings abound in the works of the troubadours, where they are used to introduce the theme of love and the beauty and perfection of the lady as reflections of Nature's perfections. Nature also has the function of a teacher, instructing the lover and encouraging him to imitate her, both in his art and in his actions. In a song of Jaufre Rudel, Nature provides both male and female teachers, which may be found in the fields, the blossoms, and the bird-songs. All the elements of propagation are there to help the poet compose his song and also to attain his lady's love.

Pro ai del chan essenhadors
En torn mi et ensenhairitz:
Pratz e vergiers, albres e flors,
Voutas d'auzels e lays e critz,
Per lo dous termini suau; (III:1–5)

[I have both male and female teachers of song / meadows and orchards, trees and flowers / bird-song and lays and cries / throughout the sweet, soft season.][18]

Nature encourages him to sing in praise of love, and shows him how to do it by following the indicators she provides in the spring, the sweet season of renewal. At the end of the song another traditional role of nature is introduced, that of healer. The lady, like Natura, has the power

to heal and to restore; a kiss may renew health better than any
physician:

> Que tan no fauc sospirs e plors
> Que sol baizar per escarit,
> Que.l cor mi tengues san e sau.
> Bona es l'amors e molt per vau
> E d'aquest mal mi pot guerir
> Ses gart de metge sapien. (51–56)

> [I do not have need of sighs and tears so much / as a single kiss / which
> would keep my heart safe and sound. / Love is good and precious / and
> it can heal me from this sickness / without the art of a learned doctor.]

Nature as healer and as teacher is found in the Greek concept of
Physis, in the Aristotelian view of nature as provident, beneficent, and
always informing, ordering, and teaching.[19] This same concept is
incorporated into the later traditions of Bernard and Alan. The
troubadours present the lady in terms of Natura, in particular her power
to heal and restore, to bring joy, and ultimately to triumph over death
through renewal. The optimism of Bernard's portrayal of Natura in the
Cosmographia is echoed here in the song of the troubadours.

Although nature imagery is widely used in the songs of the male
troubadours, there are virtually no instances of it in the works of the
female poets, or trobairitz. They do not present the beloved in terms of
nature imagery, nor do they use the sights and sounds of nature as an
invitation to love. The "amic" is not seen as a source of abundance,
healing, and renewal. However, there is one example in the song of a
female poet in which nature, or rather the absence of it, is invoked in
the cold, dead season of winter. Azalais de Porcairagues uses the
reversal of the spring opening to introduce a lament for the loss of love.
Here the register is not one of optimism and renewal, but rather of loss
and deprivation, the absence of joy and of hope, which is reflected in
the the images of winter:

> Ar em al freg temps vengut
> quel gels el neus e la faingna
> e.l aucellet estan mut,
> c'us de chantar non s'afraingna;
> e son sec li ram pels plais
> que flors ni foilla noi nais,

Ni rossignols noi crida,
Que l'am e mai me reissida. (1–8)

[Now that the cold weather has come / with ice and snow and mud / the
birds are silent / and one no longer is inclined to sing; / the branches in
the meadows are bare / neither flower nor leaf grows; / I no longer hear
the song of the nightingale / which so sweetly revives me in May.][20]

In this lament nature is dead and love is therefore absent, reflecting the
cruelty of the beloved in the harshness of nature. The birds are silent,
nothing grows, and the poet, too, is unable to celebrate love in her song.

All the examples of the nature topos mentioned so far are to be
found in the *canso*, the courtly love song, but there are also many
examples of similar evocations of nature in the popular genres, such as
the *alba* and the *pastorela*, many of which are anonymous and could
have been composed by either a male or a female poet. In these poems
the spring awakening is frequently coupled to the invitation to love. In
many cases it is the female voice that is heard, inviting her "amic" to
join her in celebrating the spring. In this *alba* the young girl invites her
beloved to embrace her one last time before the dawn breaks:

Bels dous amics, baisem nos eu e vos
Aval els pratz on chanto.ls auzelos;
Tot o fassam en despeit del gilos;
Oi deus, oi deus, de l'alba! tan tost ve.
Bels dous amics, fassam un joc novel,
Ins el jardi on chanton li auzel,
Tro la gaita toque son caramel.
Oi deus, oi deus, de l'alba! tan tost ve.

Per la douss'aura qu'es venguda de lai
Del meu amic bel e cortes e gai,
Del seu alen ai begut un dous rai;
Oi deus, oi deus, de l'alba! tan tost ve. (8:9–20)

[Dear sweet friend, let us embrace / there in the fields, where the birds
sing / let us do everything to spite the jealous ones / Oh God! how the
dawn comes too soon. / II. Dear sweet friend, let us enjoy a new game /
there in the garden where the birds sing / until the watchman plays his
pipe / Oh God! how the dawn comes too soon. / III. The soft breeze

comes to me / from my handsome young lover / I have drunk from his
sweet breath / Oh God! how the dawn comes too soon.][21]

In this portrayal of nature and love we have a picture of the
young lovers embracing in the fields, following the plan laid out for
mankind by the goddess Natura, whose lore they have accepted
joyfully. In this song the two elements of procreation unite, as is shown
in the third stanza in the metaphorical allusion to physical union "un
dous rai" that the girl has received from her young lover. There is a
narrative progression from the kiss of the first stanza, "baisem nos," to
the new game of love in the second stanza, "un joc novel," which
culminates in the sweet draught that she has drunk in the last stanza,
representing the full enjoyment of love.

The nature topos, which is normally considered to be merely a
commonplace of the love lyric, with little more than an ornamental
function, is considerably extended and amplified by some poets to
provide a complex context for the love request, and to serve as a means
of erotic persuasion. In the courtly love song the poet praises the lady in
terms of the goddess Natura; he celebrates her powers of regeneration
and renewal, the essential female component of the life cycle. In the
examples of Arnaut Daniel, the poet also presents himself in terms of
male nature imagery relating to male forces of reproduction that
complete the cycle of renewal. The song may be seen as an expression
of the cult of Natura, which had both learned and folkloric sources, and
which was strongly entrenched in the medieval consciousness. As we
have seen in the *De planctu Naturae* of Alan of Lille, the role of the
goddess Natura is to ensure mankind's victory over death and decay by
bringing about the union of the male and female elements of creation.
This expression of physical harmony and celebration of the life force is
incorporated into the Occitan love lyric in the popular as well as the
courtly traditions, where it is presented in the guise of the powerful
figure of the goddess Natura.

NOTES

1. Calcidius, *Plato Latinus*, Translation and Commentary on the
Timaeus, ed. P.J. Jensen and J.H. Waszink (London: Warburg Institute, 1962),
vol. 4.

2. Bernard of Chartres, *The Glosae super Platonem of Bernard of Chartres*, ed. Paul E. Dutton (Toronto: PIMS, 1991). For the importance of Calcidius in the transmission of the *Timaeus*, see also Paul E. Dutton, "Illustre civitatis et populi exemplum: Plato's *Timaeus* and the Transmission from Calcidius to the end of the twelfth Century of a Tripartite Scheme of Society," *Medieval Studies* 45 (1983): 79–119.

3. Bernardus Silvestris, *Cosmographia*, ed. Peter Dronke (Leiden: E.J. Brill, 1978). An English translation is to be found in Winthrop Wetherbee, *The Cosmographia of Bernardus Sivestris* (New York: Columbia University Press: 1973).

4. *Microcosmos* XIV:161–162. "Cum morte invicti pugnant, genialibus armis / Naturam reparant, perpetuantque genus."

5. Brian Stock, *Myth and Science in the Twelfth Century* (Princeton: Princeton University Press, 1972). Stock deals at length with the various sources of the *Cosmographia*. For a discussion of the Hermetic elements see pages 102–105. Also Dronke, *Cosmographia* 16–28.

6. [Hermes] Trismegistus, *Corpus Hermeticum: [Asclepius]*, ed. A.D. Nock and A.-J. Festugière (Paris: Les Belles Lettres, 1960), tome II, v.

7. On the sources and influence of the *Corpus Hermeticum* see W.C. Grese, *Corpus Hermeticum XIII and Early Christian Literature* (Leiden: Brill, 1979).

8. *Asclepius* 20, 321: God is "solus ut omnia, utraque sexus fecunditate plenissimus."

9. Alan of Lille, *The Plaint of Nature*, trans. James J. Sheridan (Toronto: PIMS, 1980), 7.

10. See George Economou, *The Goddess Natura in Medieval Literature* (Cambridge, Mass.: Harvard University Press, 1972).

11. Peire Vidal, *Poesie*, ed. D'Arco Silvio Avalle, 2 vols. (Milano: Riccardo Ricciardi, 1960).

12. Arnaut Daniel, *The Poetry of Arnaut Daniel*, ed. James J. Wilhelm (New York: Garland, 1981).

13. *Microcosmos* XIV:159–160. "Ad Genios Fetura duos concessit—et olim / Commissum geminis fratribus—illud opus."

14. *Plaint*, Prose 5, 155–156. Venus is charged with the task of ensuring heterosexual union. Natura instructs her that she must "not allow the hammers to stray away from their anvils in any form of deviation."

15. Laura Kendrick, *The Game of Love* (Berkeley: University of California Press, 1988), 165.

16. *Megacosmos* IV:11–14. "Ignis namque ethereus, socialibus et maritus, gremio Telluris coniugis affusus, generationem rerum publicam, quam de calore suo producit ad vitam, eam inferioribus elementis comodat nutriendam."

17. Bernart de Ventadour, *The Songs of Bernart de Ventadorn*, ed. Stephen G. Nichols (Chapel Hill: University of North Carolina Press, 1972). This example of Bernart may be compared with that of Peire Vidal above, 8–9, XXVIII:17–19, and 95–96.

18. Jaufre Rudel, *The Songs of Jaufre Rudel*, ed. Rupert T. Pickens (Toronto: PIMS, 1978).

19. See Wolfgang Schadewaldt, "The Concepts of Nature and Technique according to the Greeks," in *Research in Philosophy and Technology*, vol. 2 (1979): 159–171.

20. Meg Bogin, *The Women Troubadours* (New York: Paddington Press, 1976).

21. Pierre Bec (ed.), *Anthologie des Troubadours* (Paris: Union Générale d'Editions, 1979), 57–59.

WILD FOLK AND LUNATICS IN MEDIEVAL ROMANCE

David A. Sprunger

On the imagined borders between the animal and the human, one finds the medieval wild folk, who populate many medieval romances. Often the heroes of these works undergo and overcome bouts of madness, during which they suffer a visual and behavioral transformation, described with characteristics common to the race of wild folk. Neither clearly human nor clearly animal, these wild people, mythic inhabitants of unexplored woods and distant worlds, combine distinctive qualities of the animal and the human at one time. To understand better the perplexing madness sequence common in romances, we may examine the iconographic tradition of wild folk and realize the multiple implications suggested by this single symbol.

As a group, the wild folk represent at one time both the animal and the human. They can suggest the low, animal side of human potential with its violence, its lust, and its raw struggle for survival. They can also suggest the heights of human potential: through a solitary, Edenic life away from the distractions and corruptions of the city, the wild men attain a kind of holy grace and redemption.[1] Thus, the romance episodes in which the mad hero takes on the qualities of a wild man gain a special significance, for they encapsulate in a single image this complex set of potentials. The madman's inner turmoil becomes externalized through his wild appearance and through his wild life away from civilization, yet at the same time, the wild folk image suggests penance and eventual restoration.

An iconographic tradition for the hairy wild folk existed independently of the romances. Figure 1 introduces us to the tradition, an entire wild family seen here in a tableau of about 1500 attributed to Jean Bourdichon. The tableau's context as one of a series of scenes depicting the four conditions of human life (the wild, the poor, the

145

Figure 1. Jean Bourdichon, L'état Sauvage, ca. 1500. Paris, École Nationale
Supérieure des Beaux-Arts, Bibliothèque, Miniature 90.

working, and the noble) makes an explicit human link, as do specific details within it. Overall, this picture illustrates the most positive aspect of the wild folk. The very grouping of the three figures suggests the holy family, and it is a pose repeated in other depictions of wild families. The male stands erect like a human, grasping with an opposable thumb a massive staff or cudgel. In medieval Islamic thought, it was such hands—in particular, fingers with broad nails rather than claws—that helped define the wild folk as more human than animal.[2] His mate sits upright on the ground, suckling their child in an equally human manner. And most human of all are the family's faces: the male's long but generally tidy hair, his trimmed beard, the female's rosy cheeks, and her bound hair all suggest definitely human models.

At the same time, though, these beings are not fully human: they are clearly separated from the city, which stands far distant from their wilderness retreat. Nor do they share in the technological advances of the city and civilization. Instead, the wild folk survive with natural tools, indicated here by the giant club. They seek shelters in forests or natural caves (although this particular cave has a suspiciously square, tomblike door). Nature supplies them with pure drinking water from an inviting and convenient spring. The family demonstrates also the most distinctive visual characteristic of wild folk: shaggy body hair, although in this picture that hair resembles a tattered, removable union suit with frayed collar and cuffs and holes in the chest, knees, and elbows.

This basic combination of animal and human traits is repeated in other visual depictions of the wild folk: hairy covering, solitary existence, natural tools or weapons. Although the Dutch gablestone in Figure 2 dates from the sixteenth century, it illustrates a late form of this medieval notion of the wild man.[3] The text clearly labels a wild man, but he displays a very human bearing, from the way he carries the club on his shoulder like a soldier with a weapon at rest to the way his shaggy covering appears to be a removable tunic belted with a vine. The wild man's adaptation of vegetation for clothing suggests a link with the related genre of the green man, a personification of man's link with the plant world.[4]

In any case, while the Dutch wild man shows more human than animal countenance and bearing, in an enamelled wild man perched like King Kong atop a silver ewer from the late fifteenth century animal features predominate, though with positive implications (Figure 3).[5] Notice again the distinctive bare patches on the large flexible joints: the

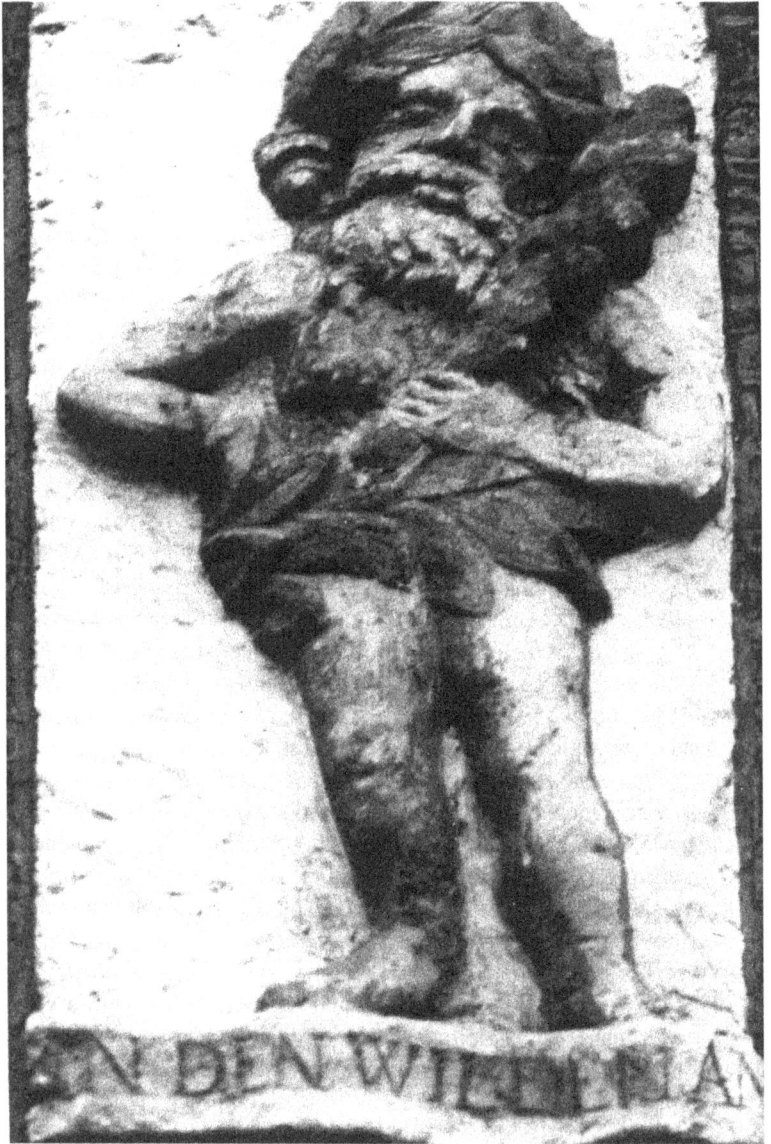

Figure 2. Gablestone located at 45 N.Z. Voorburgwal, Amsterdam. Late 16th century.

Figure 3. Filial on a ewer from the Treasury of the Teutonic Knights, Vienna, late 15th century. Cloisters Collection of the Metropolitan Museum of Art, New York (accession nos. 53.20.1 & 2).

elbows and knees. These bald areas suggest the dual potentials, the simultaneous animal and human qualities, that one finds conjoined in the wild folk. His hair is worn away on the knees and elbows as if he has been crawling on all fours like a beast, a posture in which one often finds some wild folk. Yet, despite this evidence of a former animal stance, the wild man now stands erect with a human bearing. The vertical emphasis establishes the wild man as a potential *homo erectus*, with a posture allowing him to contemplate the heavens and look up to God while the beasts, in contrast, go about studying the ground and their bellies.[6]

In medieval thought, posture provided an important distinction between beast and human. St. Basil had noted, "Man the heavenly plant, excels as much in the shape of his body as he does in the worthiness of his soul. Of what sort is the shape of the quadruped? Their heads droop to the earth, look to the belly, and belly's pleasure is in every way pursued. Your head is raised to heaven, your eyes look to those things above."[7]

While wild folk may look like animals, many illustrations show them engaged in activity normally associated with humans, although possibly for satiric purposes. For example, a Book of Hours in the Beinecke Library depicts on almost every page marginalia of wild folk engaging in human activity: hunting, jousting, dancing. Figure 4 illustrates this capacity for organized human behavior. An elderly wild man directs the roasting of some animal while the younger ones watch. The harnessing of fire for cooking food stands in sharp contrast with the wild folk's typical vegetarian or raw-meat diet, and as such these scenes stress the positive human side of the wild folk, although in such illustrations their existence is again clearly removed from the town and castle standing off on the horizon.[8]

More typical than these carnivorous wild folk is their portrayal in peaceful coexistence with the animals that normally avoid humans. In Figure 5, a marginal illustration from an Alexander romance, a wild man brandishing a club makes his getaway on a stag while a crowned king gives hot pursuit. The fact that the wild man seems to be kidnapping a completely human woman suggests another animal characteristic sometimes associated with wild folk: unbridled animal sexuality.[9] Freed from human society's restrictions of sexual discipline, the wild folk give free reign to their libidos, indulging their whims.

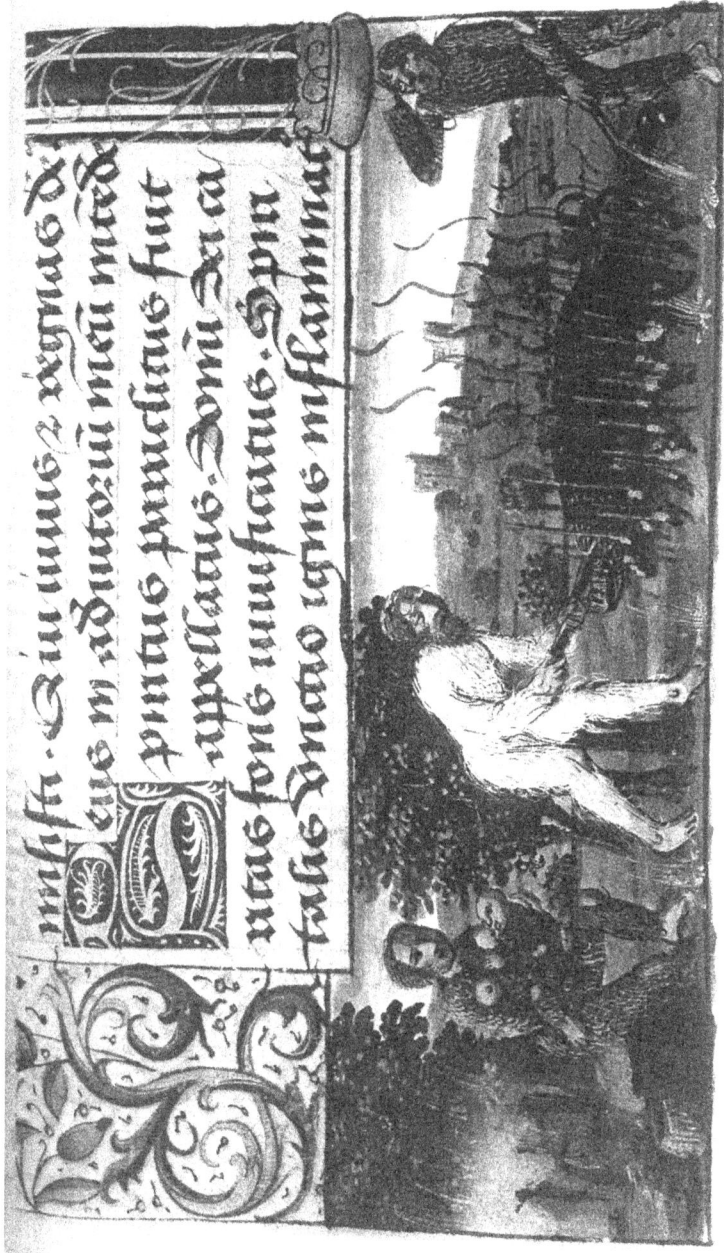

Figure 4. Marginal illustration from a Book of Hours, use of Rome, by the shop of Jean de Montluçon. France, Bourges, ca. 1500. Yale University, Beinecke Rare Book and Manuscript Library Ms. 436, fol. 72v.

Figure 5. Wild man pursued by a king. Marginal illustration in a Romance of Alexander, illuminated by Jehan de Grise, Bruges, ca. 1338–44. Bodleian Library, University of Oxford, Ms. Bodley 264, fol. 69v.

Of great popularity during the Middle Ages were romances of King Alexander and his conquest of the known world. During his campaign to India, Alexander meets some wild folk, and these encounters again underscore an ambiguous response to their animal and human identity, especially in the wild people's interaction with animals and beings set in instinctive opposition to humans. In one encounter, the wild men are allied with animals and other monstrous races, and they attack Alexander and his troops, wielding human weapons and fighting from behind the protection of shields. At the same time, however, the wild folk remain linked to uncivilized nature by their lack of speech and by their military alliance with the wild boars, an animal held to be particularly wary of human encounter and deadly when approached too closely.

Figure 6 shows a scene in which Alexander captures a wild man. Although details of the episode vary from version to version, Alexander first tests the wild man by presenting it with a nude woman, the scene shown in the left of the frame. The wild man either rips her apart and eats her or merely shows great excitement and attempts to seize her, both responses again underscoring the wild folk's bestiality and sexuality. When Alexander determines it to be mute and without reason and thus like a beast, he has it incinerated, a punishment typically reserved for human heretics.[10]

Thus far my discussion has stressed the animalistic and more negative side of the wild folk, especially as it occurs in discussions of the wild folk as types. When we turn to the folklore of popular religion, however, we find cases of individuals who became wild folk and are portrayed very positively. For example, a narrative tradition endows certain ascetic hermits whose clothes have rotted away with a compensatory layer of hair for protection and modesty. The transformed saint is clearly linked to the wild folk visually although not in behavior. In this tradition we find, among others, St. John Chrysostom, St. Christopher, St. Mary Magdalene, and St. Mary the Egyptian.[11]

A significant difference between the romance hero–wild folk and the saint–wild folk is that the saint enters the wilderness and the ascetic life voluntarily and rationally while the romance hero flees there in madness. The medieval legend of St. John Chrysostom, for instance, tells of a man who as conscious penance for raping and supposedly

Figure 6. *Le livre et la vraye histoire du bon roy Alixandre*, France, early 15th century. London, The British Library, Ms. Royal 20.B.XX, fol. 64r.

murdering a young princess chooses to crawl on all fours and observes a vow of silence; after some fifteen years of this behavior, he sprouts a protective coat of hair. After he fully atones for his sins, this hair falls away during the happy ending.[12]

The longest of the legends dealing with the "hairy anchorite" is that of St. Mary the Egyptian. Mary was a prostitute from Alexandria who traveled to the Holy Land, plying her trade to sailors for the price of her passage. When converted by the Holy Spirit in Jerusalem, she fled to the barren desert where she lived in solitude for many years (forty to fifty in most versions). As her clothes decay, they are replaced by a natural covering of wool-like hair. Her sole companion is a lion, who guards her herb garden against animal predators and who uses his powerful claws to dig her grave in the hard desert after her death.[13]

In all these cases, a person who has sinned but repented takes on the visual appearance of the wild folk, always as a precedent to moral restoration. A gift from God, the wild exterior prefigures penance and eventual restoration.

The medieval romances that describe their mad heroes as wild men clearly draw on these dual traditions of the wild folk. Rather than draw on the iconography of insanity with its emblematic baldness, chains, and demons, however, the romance authors instead describe the hero in terms suggestive of the wild folk.[14] Two possibilities might explain this shift in focus. First is the connection often posited between madness and wildness. In English, folk etymology contributed to this perception because the Middle English term for madness was "wode," and thus a "wode man" could be either one who was mad or one associated with the woods. A further connection emerges from descriptions of madness as a chaotic disruption of a once ordered mind, an opposition similar to that between random wilderness and the ordered town.[15] The connection between mental, internal wildness and geographic, external wildness alone cannot adequately explain why the romance authors chose to describe their mad heroes as wild men. It is to the dual potentials of the wild folk that we must turn to complete the puzzle.

As the hero's mental faculties are impaired—usually in response to intense grief or to mutually exclusive chivalric obligations—his external appearance undergoes an accompanying symbolic transformation away from the human and toward the bestial. In some cases, the linking to wild folk is quite explicit: when he goes mad, Suibhne from the Old Irish *Suibhne Geilt*, for example, sprouts feathers—as stylized hair—over his body, which recede when he recovers his wits. In the Mabinogion's "Lady of the Fountain," Owein's madness, paralleling Yvain's, also involves rapid, universal hair growth:

> And he was wandering thus till his clothes perished, and till his body was nigh perished, and till long hair grew all over his body; and he would keep company with wild beasts and feed them till they were used to him. (174)

Hartmann von Aue's Iwein apparently becomes black, although details of his transformation aren't clear: "wart gelîch einem Môre / an allem sînem lîbe" [became like a Moor on all his body] (3348–49). In the Middle English *Ywain and Gawain*, Ywain whelks about "in þhe forest, / Als it wore a wild beste" (ll. 1653–54). Sir Orfeo becomes "lene, rowe, and blak" (l. 459), and Malory's Lancelot and Tristram similarly grow hairy in their exile, although not in such specific, tip-to-toe ways.

While the hairiness indicative of wild folk could be an exaggeration of the grooming experienced on a prolonged wilderness stay, the romance hero's wild external appearance as indicative of an internal mental state has ample precedent in medieval religious literature. The Book of Daniel recounts the fall of the Babylonian King Nebuchadnezzar, who declines to remember the Lord and suffers a humiliating seven years as a beast of the field, crawling on all fours, lowing, and foraging like an ox. For protection from the elements, he sprouts a shaggy coat of "dewy eagle feathers," although the artist of Figure 7 has chosen to illustrate these feathers with the more traditional thick hair instead, a practice common in Nebuchadnezzar iconography.[16]

Notice in the illustration of Nebuchadnezzar the underlying notion of the *homo erectus* again. After Nebuchadnezzar repents of his pride, he is cured of his madness, and in this illustration that cure is represented by God's angel helping him to his feet, returning him to an upright position and thus to full humanity. Again, this transformation was both a punishment and part of the vehicle by which the sinner is purified, restored, and brought back to God.

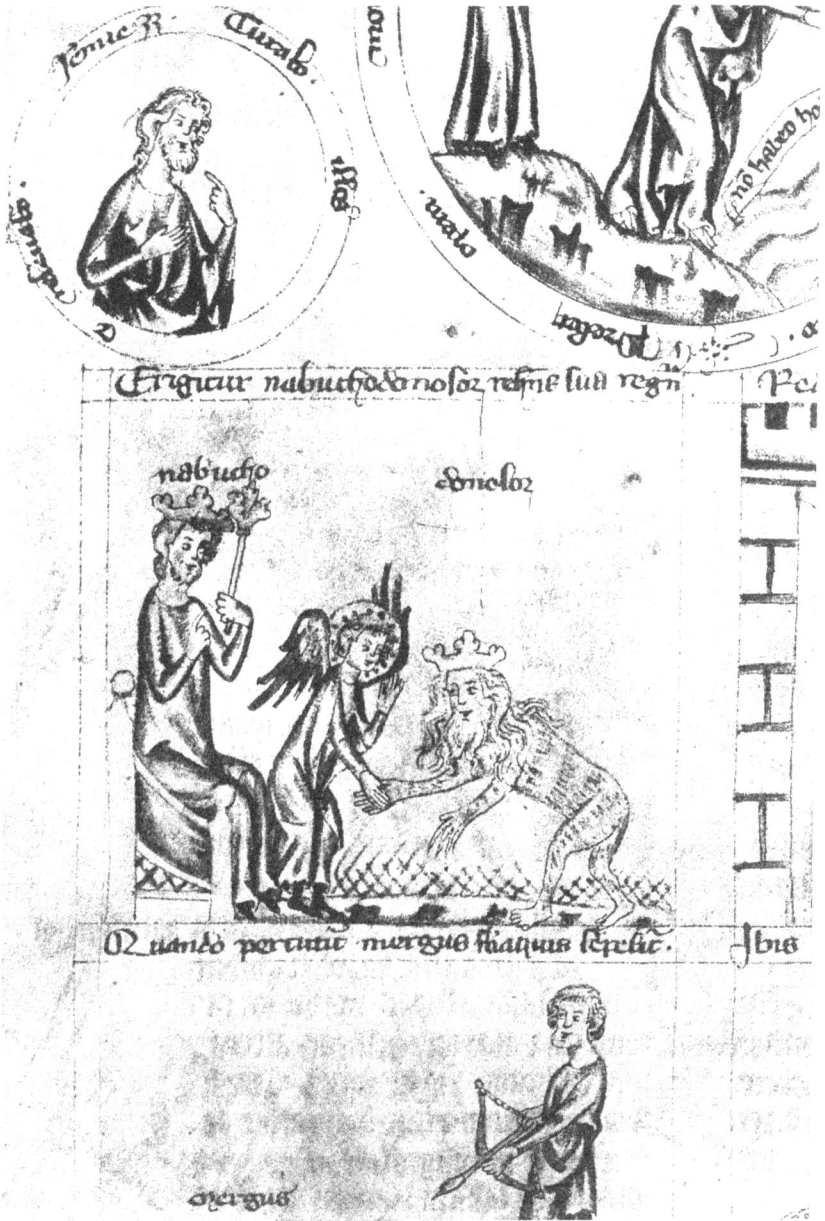

Figure 7. The cure of Nebuchadnezzar. Ulrich von Lilienfeld, *Concordantia cartatis* (after 1351). Stiftsbibliothek Lilienfeld (Austria) Ms. 151, fol. 40r. (Reprinted with permission of Akademische Druck- u.

A similar cure occurs in a German romance, *Der Busant*, in which a benevolent duke undertakes to restore a captured wild man, a onetime prince who turned into a wild man following accidental separation from his beloved. When the prince becomes a wild man, he begins to crawl through the forest on all fours; his cure involves, among other therapies, learning to walk again on two feet.[17]

The mad hero also takes on many of the wild folk's animal living conditions: he flees from society into the forests and takes up instead a life of aimless wandering, Michel Foucault's distinctive marker of madness in the Middle Ages before the confinement the Renaissance imposed on its insane.[18] He becomes mute or incomprehensible, unable to communicate with other humans. Finally, he forages for food, eating uncooked whatever he does find.

Each of these elements is of literary significance. The existence in the woods provides a symbolic link to the hero's psychological state. In a tradition stretching back to classical poetry, a character's physical location can suggest his emotional state, and movement from the ordered social world into the wilderness reflects emotional dislocation.[19] In sharp contrast to our modern notion of forests as idyllic retreats to which one escapes the conflicts of city life, medieval thought considered forests to be harsh, unpleasant locales fraught with dangers innumerable. Protagonists who move from the organized civilization of the city into the chaotic woods enter a dangerous liminal state over which they must triumph or from which perish. Thus, Dante the Pilgrim, for example, begins his journeying in a "selva oscura" (dark woods), a place of despair from which he seeks escape.[20] The madman's horizontal dislocation from the ordered world to the chaotic parallels his mental disruption.

The mad hero's involuntary muteness also separates him from the human world. St. Augustine notes in *The City of God* that common language is the bond that joins humans into useful fellowship; without it, two humans have nothing in common:

> If neither knows the other's language, it is easier for dumb animals, even of different kinds, to associate together than these men, although both are human beings. For when men cannot communicate their thoughts to each other, simply because of differences of language, all the similarity of their common human nature is of no avail to unite them in fellowship.[21]

England's Wild Man of Orford was marked by a similar muteness. This hairy man was supposedly captured by fisherman in 1161 and kept in captivity, being fed a diet of raw fish and meat. Although his captors tortured him in attempts to make him speak, he could not or would not, and eventually he escaped.[22]

Unable to communicate verbally with the humans he meets, the madman cannot signal his identity or his intentions, which thus prevents him from reclaiming his former station in society. When the hero does have contact with humans, he must take a role at the bottom of the social chain. Thus, we find Yvain gathering food for the benevolent hermit he finds in the wood, Tristan playing the fool for shepherds, and Lancelot acting as a jester at a remote castle. In each of such roles, the hairy hero is never a social equal to the humans around him.

The lunatic's life in the forest also incorporates a more bestial diet of roots and nuts, following perhaps the pattern of the transformed King Nebuchadnezzar, who foraged for grass like a cow. Although it does not involve a madman, one finds in *El Cid* (ca. 1140) a conscious use of such vegetarianism to represent social humbling. As part of his reconciliation with the king, the Cid approaches him, "knelt down on his hands and knees on the ground and with his teeth pulled up a mouthful of grass."[23] Returning to the mad heroes, we find bestial dining reaching its zenith in the Yvain cycles, in which the hero regresses so far as to eat raw flesh. Such detail is consistent with Levi-Strauss's distinctions between the raw and the cooked as markers of civilized life. Isolation from fire thus provides an obvious symbol for separation from full human existence.

In the Middle English version, "Ywain and Gawain," this diet is not bestial but therapeutic: Ywain "drank of þe warm blode, / and þat did him mekil gode " (1669–70). In her study of medieval madmen, Penelope Doob suggests another possibility, that Yvain is following the example of some animals in attempting self-medication through drinking blood.[24] A medical tradition did suggest that the ingestion of blood, one of the body's four humors, would restore an individual's equilibrium and prevent any health problems. Thus, France's Louis XI (1461–83) reportedly drank the blood of several infants in a vain attempt to prolong his life, and Pope Innocent VIII allegedly drank the blood of three young boys, who all died from complications during donation.[25]

Just as the hero loses his reasoning ability—the distinguishing "sapiens" of human identity—he comes in danger of losing his humanity entirely and becoming a mere beast. His mind whirling, he journeys away into the woods from his former existence, shedding everything that once made him unique: his name, his reputation, his network of relatives and friends, his weapons, his clothing, and his visual identity. And as in many folktales—and indeed, in much of literature from any age—by losing himself, he paradoxically comes to find himself.

Though the mad hero's journey is a horizontal one, out and back, it provides a metaphoric journey of descent and ascent, a pattern that Northrup Frye identifies in *The Secular Scripture* as one of the essential radicals of romance structure.[26] This up and down movement is achieved through what Frye calls the "motif of amnesia," a significant "break in consciousness" that "may either be normally internalized as a break in memory, or externalized as a change in fortunes or social context" (102). The mad hero does both. His identity is unrecognizable, even to those who knew him, and he enjoys at best a hazy knowledge of his former self and, more often, exhibits a total amnesia. Even the recovery from madness takes on the short, sharp shock that the folk tradition associates with the recovery from amnesia: Yvain's brisk massage, Tristram's baths and hot suppings, Lancelot's exposure to the Holy Grail, Orfeo's glimpse of Heurodis.

The transformation of the hero to his ambivalent condition of partially human, partially bestial being helps calibrate him at his lowest possible position in the scale of human perfection. The wild folk's life in the state of nature—with its simultaneous implications of low bestiality, sexuality, and savagery and of high holiness and upward potential—makes a perfect symbol for the confused hero. From such depths, his gradual but inevitable—if not surpassing—recovery of his former mental, social, and economic condition makes his inevitable triumph all the more victorious. By reviewing the wildness without—as captured in the visual depictions of the wild folk—we can better understand the complex nature of the wildness within.

NOTES

1. Two books that examine the multiple implications of the wild folk are Richard Bernheimer, *Wild Men in the Middle Ages: A Study in Art, Sentiment, and Demonology* (Cambridge, Mass.: Harvard University Press, 1952), and Timothy Husband, *The Wild Man: Medieval Myth and Symbolism* (New York: The Metropolitan Museum of Art, 1980).

2. Nizami al-Arudi, *Chahar maqala*, Gibb Memorial Series 11 (1921): 9. Quoted by Bernheimer 190, n. 10. The other characteristics that defined the human status were the upright posture and the hairy head.

3. This wild man is located at 45 N.Z. Voorburgwal, Amsterdam. Additional examples of the wild man motif in the Amsterdam appear in J.H. Kruizinga, *Zag U Dit in Amsterdam*, n.d., 50–53. For discussion of the wild man's heraldic role at the end of the Middle Ages, see Bernheimer 176–88.

4. See William Anderson, *Green Man: The Archetype of Our Oneness with the Earth* (London: Harper Collins, 1990).

5. The ewer on which this wild man stands is one of a matched pair from the Treasury of the Teutonic Knights, Vienna. Each ewer stands 25 inches tall and is 8 ¼ inches at the widest point. The set was purchased in 1953 by the Cloisters Collection of the Metropolitan Museum of Art, New York (accession nos. 53.20.1 & 2.).

6. See C.A. Patrides, "Renaissance Ideas of Man's Upright Form," *Journal of the History of Ideas* 19 (1958): 256–58.

7. Basil, Homilia IX in *Hexaemeron* II, *Patrologica Graecae* 29.192.

8. More illustrations from this fascinating manuscript can be found in Husband, 32, and in Barbara Shailor, *The Medieval Book: Illustrated from the Beinecke Rare Book and Manuscript Library*, Medieval Academy Reprints for Teaching 28 (Toronto: University of Toronto Press, 1991), 45.

9. Bernheimer devotes an entire chapter of his work to this quality: "The Erotic Connotations," 121–75.

10. For some accessible versions of Alexander's capture of the wild man, see "Historia de Preliis," Recension J1, in *The Romances of Alexander*, trans. Dennis Kratz, Garland Library of Medieval Literature 64 (New York: Garland Publishing, Inc., 1991), 65–66, and *The Greek Alexander Romance*, trans. Richard Stoneman (Harmondsworth, U.K.: Penguin Books, 1991), 116. For general information on Alexander legends of the Middle Ages, see David J. Ross, *Alexander Historiatus: A Guide to Medieval Alexander Literature* (1963; Frankfurt am Main: Atheanum, 1988), and George Cary, *The Medieval Alexander* (Cambridge: Cambridge University Press, 1956).

11. For a thorough discussion of saints as wild folk, see the Charles Allyn Williams' three-part series on the Hairy Anchorite: "Oriental Affinities of the Legend of the Hairy Anchorite, Part I: Pre-Christian," *University of Illinois Studies in Language and Literature* 10 (1925): 187–242, "Oriental Affinities of

the Legend of the Hairy Anchorite, Part II: Christian," *University of Illinois Studies in Language and Literature* 11 (1926): 429–510, and "The German Legends of the Hairy Anchorite," *University of Illinois Studies in Language and Literature* 18 (1935): 1–140.

12. Williams summarizes this legend (and many others) in "Oriental Affinities . . . Part I: Pre-Christian," 10–11.

13. Williams gives a generic version of this legend in "Oriental Affinities . . . Part II: Christian," 477–79.

14. Instances of such mad heroes can be found in the following texts: *Buile Suibhne (The Frenzy of Suibhne) being The Adventure of Suibhne Geilt, A Middle-Irish Romance*, ed. and trans. J.G. O'Keeffe, Irish Texts Society 12 (1910) (London: David Nutt, 1913); "The Vita Merlini," ed. and trans. John Jay Parry, *University of Illinois Studies in Language and Literature* 10 (1925): 250–380; "Lancelot" and "Tristan" in *The Works of Sir Thomas Malory*, ed. Eugène Vinaver, 3d ed., 3 vols. (Oxford: Clarendon Press, 1990); Chrétien de Troyes, *The Knight with the Lion, or Yvain (Le Chevalier au Lion)*, ed. and trans. William W. Kibler, Garland Library of Medieval Literature 48 (New York: Garland Publishing, Inc., 1985); "The Lady of the Fountain," in *The Mabinogion*, trans. Jeffrey Gantz (New York: Dorset Press, 1976), 192–216. Hartmann von Aue, *Iwein*, ed. and trans. Patrick McConeghy, Garland Library of Medieval Literature 19 (New York: Garland Publishing Company, 1984); *Ywain and Gawain*, ed. Albert Friedman and Norman Harrington, EETS O.S. 254 (London: Oxford University Press, 1964); *Sir Orfeo*, ed. A.J. Bliss (Oxford, 1954). Citations of page and line numbers from these works will appear parenthetically in the text.

15. Further ideas on wildness, madness, and the interiorization of wilderness appear in Hayden White, "The Forms of Wilderness: Archaeology of an Idea," in *The Wild Man Within: An Image in Western Thought from The Renaissance to Romanticism* (Pittsburgh: University of Pittsburgh Press, 1972), 3–38.

16. See, for example, the illustrations in Penelope Doob, *Nebuchadnezzar's Children: Conventions of Madness in Middle English Literature* (New Haven: Yale University Press, 1974).

17. "Der Busant," in *Gesammtabenteur. Hundert altdeutsche Erzählungen: Ritter-und Pfaffen-Mären, Stadt-und Dorfgeschicten Schwänke, Wundersagen und Legenden, meist zum erstenmal gedruckt*, ed. Friedrich Heinrich von der Hagen, 3 vols. (Stuttgart: J.G. Cotta'scher Verlag, 1850) I, 333–66. The story follows the French tale "Peter of Provence."

18. Michel Foucault, *Madness and Civilization*, trans. Richard Howard (New York: Random House, 1965), especially 7–13.

19. See, for example, K.W. Grandsen, *Virgil: The Aeneid* (Cambridge: Cambridge University Press, 1990), 12–13. Grandsen sees Virgil's Eclogue 2 as the genesis of this tradition.

20. Dante, *The Divine Comedy*: Inferno, canto 1, line 2. For discussion of the literary uses of forests, see Marianne Stauffer, *Der Wald: Zur Darstellung und Deutung der Natur im Mittelalter*, Studiorum Romanicorum Collectio Turicenisis 10 (Bern: Francke Verlag, 1959). For symbolism of landscape in general, see Marjorie Hope Nicholson, *Mountain Gloom and Mountain Glory: The Development of the Aesthetics of the Infinite* (Ithaca: Cornell University Press, 1959).

21. St. Augustine, *Concerning the City of God against the Pagans*, ed. David Knowles, trans. Henry Bettenson (Harmondsworth: Penguin Books, 1972), 861.

22. The anecdote is reported in Christina Hole, *English Folklore* (London: B.T. Batsford, Ltd., 1940), 103–04. She credits as her source Ralph of Coggeshall.

23. *The Poem of the Cid: A Bilingual Edition with Parallel Text*, ed. Ian Michael, trans. Rita Hamilton and Janet Perry (Harmondsworth: Penguin Books, 1975), second cantar, ll. 2021–22, pp. 128–29.

24. See Doob 38, n. 58.

25. David Riesman, *The Story of Medicine in the Middle Ages* (New York: Paul B. Hoeber, Inc., 1935), 327.

26. Northrup Frye, *The Secular Scripture: A Study of Structure of Romance* (Cambridge, Mass.: Harvard University Press, 1976), 97.

People and the Land

THE LAND, WHO OWNS IT?

John Hilary Martin, O.P.

When our modern legal establishment speaks of ownership of land nowadays, it refers to owning a bundle of rights. If you own land in the full sense, you can control who comes onto your property and who is kept off, who can dig for minerals and drill for oil. When the Bay Area Rapid Transit (BART) system was under construction, the City of Berkeley found that it could acquire the right to rent out, of all things, the air space above the subway corridor that ran underground through the City Center. One particularly enterprising property owner in the Monterey area has claimed to own the rights over any photographs made of a particularly beautiful cypress tree found on his property (but that is in the courts). I won't even bother to go into the bundle of property rights that you might think you hold over your property but no longer do because of decisions made by various planning and zoning commissions at the state and local level. Ownership of property is in bits and pieces. Hearing this, medievalists might first reply, Aha, feudalism still lives. Feudal property rights also took the form of contractual arrangements between master and tenant, which enmeshed property in a series of duties and obligations, rights and privileges, and liens and freedoms of one sort or another. Modern arrangements might almost look feudal, but a second glance reveals that the present-day arrangements about property are really not the same. Modern ownership, in theory at any rate, does not assume that rights and obligations are between particular individuals (a local contract, so to speak), but rather assumes that the parcelling out of specific rights over property applies universally. Within the legal pigeonholes that you (and your property) happen to find yourselves, all owners are bound equally. If we set aside the contractual aspect of medieval land tenure, we find that the medieval mind held a much more unitary view about the ultimate right of possession than we do nowadays.

Three general attitudes can be listed about the origin of ownership over land (although you would not find them set out as such in medieval texts). I can say that the land is mine because (a) I saw it first before anyone else did; (b) I was the first to occupy it, or rather I inherited or acquired it from people who said they were the first to occupy it; and (c) it's mine because I conquered it by the sword.

The most celebrated example of the last type of claim was made for William the Conqueror, who seized England in 1066 from the Saxon line of kings. After the Conquest he claimed to possess England both as the successor of the previous kings and as the victor in conquest.[1] In consequence, he had the right to confirm (or deny) old customs and, more significantly, to distribute land to his own followers. Under his dispensation the new owners became his tenants-in-chief, with the result that land was possessed not absolutely, but in service to the Crown. William's claim in England was not unique, and was imitated elsewhere as the Middle Ages advanced.

Right of conquest, of course, is simply replacing one person's rights with another's. What about claims that were based not on conquest but on original possession? What about claims to ownership based on being the first person to lay eyes on the place? Under this rubric, I suppose, the best claimants for possessing land would be Adam and Eve, since they saw all of it first. But they have left no records about their claims, and no one has appealed to them. In crowded medieval Europe the common claim for possessing parcels of land was either by gift of a recent conqueror or by acquiring it from someone who could legitimately claim that they or their predecessors had always possessed it time out of mind.[2] Toward the close of the Middle Ages new opportunity presented itself for a rash of claims to ownership of land based on the principle of the "first to lay sight of," or the "first to set foot on" principle as it is alternatively called. The grand explorers working in the service of rulers of Portugal, Spain, France, and England, to name the main ones, claimed the lands of the newly found worlds of America and Asia for their sovereigns on the grounds that they had discovered them. Discoverers sometimes claimed that what they had found was *terra nullius* (i.e., empty lands without inhabitants), and so the land could truly be called "the land [belonging to] no one."[3] In a few cases this was perhaps true (isolated islands, for example), but more often than not people were living there. When it was pointed out that there were in fact some people already living in those places, further arguments were required. Although the Church and the royal governments were cautious in phrasing their claims, a frequent answer to the objection that the newly discovered lands could hardly be called the lands of no one (there were inhabitants living there) was that, despite appearances, the inhabitants were not really human, or if they were human, they were at a lower rung of the ladder of civilization and so their presence did not really count. In any event they were non-Christians with wicked and unnatural customs, so they had forfeited whatever natural rights they might have once possessed. The new lands, therefore, were open to those Europeans who first discovered and laid claim to them.

Alert readers of the article may have already noticed that while all three of the foregoing positions might serve as a useful rule of thumb to determine ownership for pragmatic purposes, none of them establishes a very solid basis for erecting a general theory of land possession. As so much in the Middle Ages, this problem will have two aspects: religious grounds for possessing land and a basis in the law of nature. A general theory of possession at the time of the explorers would take us too far afield, and frankly would go beyond the research that I have been able to do.[4] For the natural law basis I shall restrict myself to authors of the mid-thirteenth century who wrote after Aristotle became available and before the influence of William of Ockham began to be felt. I will concentrate on the attitudes of Thomas Aquinas because he was familiar with pre-Aristotelian traditions (he had been trained in them as an undergraduate) and he knew the writings of Aristotle as thoroughly as any of his contemporaries.[5] For the religious grounds I shall search a bit farther afield and look into late patristic and early medieval commentaries on the occupation of the Holy Land. Let us turn first to Thomas Aquinas for the natural law arguments.

Thomas deals with the natural law aspects of ownership in the second part of his *Summa*. This lengthy section of the *Summa* deals with human nature as created in the image of God and so is dedicated to presenting a careful balance between humanistic and religious values. Like God, the origin of all human creativity will involve free will and the choices it makes. The goal of human creativity is eudaemonistic, a search for personal happiness, for the fulfillment of legitimate human desires. Thomas's arguments to show that no created good or any combination of them could ever fulfill human desire are too well known to be canvassed here. The fact that created goods are not ultimate goals does not make them illegitimate as temporary goals, however. Land and chattels are such. Although they rank among the more ephemeral things of this earth, they are, nevertheless, means by which we can move toward happiness. If used wisely, they can draw us closer to our goal of happiness, which consists in friendship with God, who alone is the fulfillment of all desire. But lands and chattels are not easy to use wisely. When Thomas gets around to dealing with the ownership of property, he puts possession, along with theft and rapine, among the vices that can militate against our practice of the virtue of justice. The case for ownership of property does not start on a very positive note. Having private property is something on the order of having a just war. It can be justified, but the case for having it must be proven and must be nuanced carefully. Thomas asks two questions: "Is the possession of the goods of nature (exteriorum rerum) natural to a human being? Secondly, if so, is it permitted for an individual to possess something as their very own (propriam possidere)?"[6]

Thomas finds that it is not unnatural to possess things. The human community can have dominion over nature (*res exteriores*), provided we understand what is meant by "dominion." It goes without saying that the physical world of nature is not at the beck and call of individuals or even of the whole human community, but rather of God, who is the creator. But in a certain sense it is natural for human beings to be put in charge of things and given dominion over them by the Creator. Why is this so? Because human beings, by intelligent choices, can organize everything for their advantage just as if they were made for them. But why does mere human utility give human beings the right to have dominance over everything? It does so, Thomas argues, because what is lower is always ordered to the advantage of what is higher, as philosophy teaches us.[7] The same idea is expressed in Genesis where we read, "Let us make man in our image, after our own likeness, and let them have dominion over the fish of the sea . . ." (Gen. 1:26). While God always has primary dominion over everything, God has subordinated some things to sustaining human life according to providence. The principle of human predominance over creation is no passing idea in Thomas's writings. It is repeated frequently in various contexts so that it seems fair to say that for him the whole physical world came into being for the use of the human community.[8] The idea is repeated by other schoolmen, such as Bonaventure, who teaches that all sentient beings have been made for humanity.[9] Scotus would modify this only to the extent that the world was made to provide a suitable environment for the Incarnate Christ. The notion was not seriously disputed at the time.

Even if we agree that it is quite natural, and so not morally wrong, for the human community to dominate the earth, this obviously is no brief to justify one person's, or one group's, claim to possess some portion of the earth more than the next person's. Genesis seems to suggest that all human beings were to share the earth communally. To prove the legitimacy of personal possessions, Thomas employs a different line of argument. He makes the distinction between dominion and use. It is one thing to have the power to acquire and dole out things to others, and quite another to make use of them for oneself. It is perfectly all right to possess things as your very own, storing them and handing them out to others. In fact, it is absolutely necessary that someone be in charge of material possessions if human affairs are going to run smoothly. Everyone, after all, is more solicitous about acquiring something for themselves than working for something that will be held in common. Things run better when each takes care of his or her own possessions. If things are held indiscriminately (*indistincte*), there will inevitably be confusion over who should do what. Finally, experience shows that fights arise more frequently among people who hold things in common. Life is more peaceful, Thomas believed, and Aristotle before him, when each one rests content with his or her own possessions.[10] However, while private possession of property may be appropriate for a variety of practical reasons, the use of things is another matter. Here the communal aspect of the goods of the earth should be preserved. From the point of view of their use individuals shouldn't consider things as exclusively their own, as if they held some kind of absolute dominion over them, but should quickly put their possessions at the disposal of those who need them.

Is Thomas's presentation anything more than a pious hope? A form of wishful thinking? It is certainly in the genre of advice to the good citizen, but his argument goes beyond that to suggest a structure. Since the land and all goods of the earth were given to the human community by the Creator, they must be available for the common benefit of all humanity, but this by no means implies that they should be left untended and open to all. Some distinction of property should be made, but it should be made according to the way in which humans relate to each other (*secundum humanum condictum*) in the real world. There is nothing in nature that says that this field belongs to this person and that field to another. This is achieved through public law (*ius positivum*).[11] For Thomas, this involves not so much a government decree as a carrying out of the political process.[12] This process, if properly carried out, will produce laws that are rational formulations designed to promote the common good and not the expressions of an arbitrary will.[13]

Human beings are social animals, but this means much more than that we happen to enjoy each other's society. Human beings are social in the fundamental sense that they require mutual assistance in order to survive. Some in a community must till the fields, some must bake the bread, some must weave, some must build, some must manufacture, some must trade, some must teach school, some must be administrators, some must mind the church, some must be politicians, and so on. The land is the basis for any human organization and in a very important sense is always held in common. Whoever is in charge of the community (and for the medieval this can be emperor, prince, elected magistrate, or communal assembly) must determine the positive laws that arrange for distribution of its wealth and services. Now particular arrangements can be forced according to the principle that the "firstest with the mostest" wins the day, but things cannot be legitimately apportioned out in that way. Land, and everything else, is divided justly in a community insofar as it contributes to the common good. The bottom line of this approach is that legal title, the just title to land or the goods of the earth, does not belong to first possessor, or to the discoverer, or to victors in conquest, but to a community working for the common good—which includes the common good of all who come into working contact with that community.

Armed with this theory all would have been, if not well, at least neat and tidy, if it were not for the fact that lands and chattels had been given to a particular community by the command of God. A reader of Scripture in the medieval period, as in any other, could hardly avoid noticing that gift of land was an important theme. The land given Israel (*ha 'aretz*) was essentially a promised land.[14] It could be given by God to this particular people because it was owned by God in the first place, and so it became theirs. The land of promise and the terms of that promise is perhaps one of the most important theological themes pursued through the whole of the Pentateuch and Josue. Whether the overriding importance of living in the promised land is a product of the last stages of the formation of the Pentateuch (late Exilic) or a more primitive idea need not concern us.[15] The Book of Josue states the case, and it was not the only locus. The book begins with the blunt statement that gives a modern reader cause to pause and, apparently, gave medieval authors cause to pause as well. "Moses my servant is dead. Now therefore arise, go over this Jordan, you and all this people, into the land which I am giving to them, to the people of Israel. Every place that the sole of your foot will tread upon I have given to you, as I promised Moses."[16] The book goes on to order Josue by divine mandate to attack without mercy, kill all the inhabitants of the land, and take no spoil, but divide and occupy the land forever. The land of Canaan is given and delivered to the Israelites (Jos. 1:6) so that it can be possessed by them (Jos. 1:11) as a permanent inheritance (Jos. 11:23). Possession of the land, moreover, means dispossession of the local inhabitants. They are, in effect, denied entitlement, reduced to the status of slaves, threatened with genocide, and placed under a perpetual ban.[17] To argue that Josue was written long after the event and that things did not really happen like that may be historically quite correct, but it is beside the point. What is being presented here is divine authorization for land occupation without any reference to understandings of justice, medieval or contemporary. Taken in isolation the book of Josue, with its stark orders to seize lands, is a difficult book. To soften its statement, it is customary to point out that the occupation of Canaan is intelligible only if it is taken in the context of Yahweh's redeeming his promises. To understand it we need to refer back to Exodus, in which the Lord God promised Moses that he would lead the people out of Egypt into a good and spacious land, a land flowing with milk and honey, the land of the Canaanites, etc.[18] These promises were built on still older promises made to Abraham and his descendants. In Genesis, "The Lord said to Abram, . . . 'Lift up your eyes, and look from the place where you are northward and southward and eastward and westward; for all the land that you see I will give to you and your descendants forever. I will made your descendants as the dust of the earth; so that if one can count the dust of the earth, your descendants also can be counted.'"[19] The land that is promised to Abraham, the land he is gazing at and encouraged to walk about in, is presented as a specific place, a well populated region, the historic land of Canaan with its cities and villages. In Genesis the reason why this land is assigned by God to

Abraham is simply because of his trusting faith. Abraham's faithfulness to God is demonstrated at various times, and on these occasions the promises are repeated and reinforced. We could say that figures like Moses and Josue could refer back to these promises to justify their later occupation of Canaan if *justify* were not such a strong word to modern ears. Better to say the promises provided the reasons why they kept going back to that place that had become, a holy place, a holy land for them.

In these passages exegetes are presented with a golden opportunity for enlarging on their discussion of the religious ownership of specific lands. Medieval exegetes never seem to have taken up the challenge. Instead of coming to grips with reasons why Abraham, Moses, and Josue could justly taking the land of Canaan from the local inhabitants, they doggedly followed the trail of authors writing in the patristic period, who simply spiritualized the entire issue. We have only to think of the figurative and otherworldly interpretation of the third-century exegete Origen. As we might expect, Origen had precedents for his treatment of land from other Christian writers, but he also looked to Jewish authors, like Philo and rabbinic commentators.[20] He opens his commentary on Josue by reminding us that Josue is a name with the same meaning as Jesus. It is significant, therefore, that after Moses' death it was a Josue who succeeded him. Just as Moses is the figure of the Old Testament, so Jesus is the figure of the New. This parallelism sets the tone of his whole further commentary, and for medieval commentary as well. At first reading the events that are described in the book of Josue appear to tell us what happened to Israel "after Moses, the servant of the Lord, was dead" (ch. 1, v. 2). If we wish to grasp the higher meaning, however, the book must be read as figurative statements of the work of Jesus, the new Moses. What shall we say, then, about the land being given to Josue? What shall we make of the promise that the people will acquire "every place where the sole of your foot will tread?" When we speak in figure, we are, of course, no longer particularly concerned with the land of Canaan as geographical spot on the shores of the Mediterranean. We are no longer talking of the land that Moses saw, but that which God now gives the people through Jesus.[21] What is that land, then, and where are all those places on which the people's feet will tread? The land is "the land [*terra*] which the meek will inherit," as stated in the beatitudes.[22] The places are the footsteps of the new Josue which his followers will tread. To properly understand this, Origen argues (as will many others after him), you have to leave aside the letter of the Law and ascend to its spirit, you must proceed from history to a higher insight. Earlier in his commentary on Genesis Origen had argued that if Abraham had lived only carnally, he would have fathered only one nation and one promise would have sufficed: the promised land of Canaan. But because Abraham believed in God, he was destined to be the father of all those who are of faith. The original promise was renewed and broadened at the time of the passion of Isaac (another figure of Jesus) to apply to those people who would be saved by the passion and resurrection of Christ. The first promise is of the land, but the second is of heaven.[23] Seen in this light the occupation of historic Canaan becomes of little religious interest. Conversely, we might add, under the influence of this mentality arguments from the religious viewpoint tend to have little to contribute to any discussion of the concrete ownership of land.

Early medieval authors such as Isidore of Spain (d. 636), the Northumbrian Bede (673–735), Rabanus Maurus (d. 856) of Germany, the *Glossa Ordinaria* (at one time attributed to Walafrid Strabo, d. 849, but in fact constructed much later, in the twelfth century), and the Low Lander, Rupert of Deutz (d. 1130), to take a representative sampling,[24] all speak of the handing over of Canaanite land to the Chosen People in the highly allegorized and mystical terms employed by Origin. Isidore, as we remember, was the author of the highly regarded *Etymologies* and a major source for the transmission canon law collections to the medieval church, as well as a notable commentator on Scripture. In his writings the echoes of Origen's method, and even its content, can clearly be heard. The burden of Isidore's argument is that with the death of Moses the Law is now dead as well, its legal precepts cease, and it is Jesus who holds the authority. He leads the people into the land spoken of in the beatitudes (i.e., "the land the meek will inherit").[25] We read that Josue sent two spies to look over Jericho prior to attacking it, razing it to the ground, and destroying all its inhabitants. The destruction was to be total, even to keep anything from the town would call down the Lord's wrath. Only Rahab, the harlot, and her family were to be saved from the general destruction because she had hid the two spies in her household. Following the lead of Origen, this horrendous picture was quietly transformed. To begin with, we should understand that Jericho is a type of the world. The spies are the Two Testaments, which scrutinize the life and morals of the world's inhabitants, finding good and evil. Rahab, the harlot, is a type of the Church, and members of her household will be saved by escaping the doomed city through the window of confession (i.e., confession of the faith). To take booty from Jericho, as some disobedient soldiers did, justly earns God's punishment because it symbolizes the introduction of worldly customs back into the camp, that is, back into the church. The commentary on Josue found among the writings of Bede (although not in fact from his pen) includes large sections taken from Isidore verbatim, which, if nothing else, are a witness of the widespread diffusion of these ideas.[26] The *Glossa Ordinaria*, the standard gloss that all serious students throughout the medieval period would have been familiar with as a beginner's guide to the Scriptures, simply paraphrases Origen. Rabanus Maur, who was given the rather grand title of preceptor of Germany, only adds a few original comments to long implicit citations taken from Origen.[27] Rupert of Deutz is more original in his presentation of Josue, but again does not enter into the question of justifying the physical possession of the land. The important point for him is that with the death of Moses, the significance of "Sion" has ceased.[28] To cross the Jordan is to leave the Old Law and its ceremonies behind. While he admits that the literal sense of the text defines a particular stretch of land (i.e., "from the wilderness and this Lebanon as far as the great river, Euphrates, all the land of the Hittites to the great sea") (Jos. 1:4), the spiritual sense defines a territory of quite another sort. In his commentary Rupert proceeds to use the geographic limits as a literary device for classifying the various sorts of people who either receive or reject the Savior.[29] Rupert's work is interesting because it underscores the notion that land in a geographic sense need be of no concern for readers of the Book of Josue, since the promise of physical land has been superseded. The widely read *Historia Scholastica* of Peter Comestor (d. 1179), a kind of set text in the early thirteenth-century university curriculum, which purported to give an outline of the history of the whole world paralleling sacred with secular events, has nothing to say about the land of Canaan beyond the bare statement of the original gift.[30] As we read these medieval exegetes we draw a blank just where we might expect them to discuss divine mandate as justification for ownership of territory. As far as they are concerned the promises of specific grant of land made by God to an individual or a specific group, something done for Abraham and Israel, had lapsed. They know of no others.

If medieval exegetes effectively bypassed the large issue of whether specific lands could be owned by divine fiat, the smaller issue of whether God permitted, or even ordered, the expropriation of chattel property belonging to another was regularly discussed. The favorite passage came from Exodus. They read there that during the flight from Egypt the Israelites took gold and silver vessels and items of clothing from the Egyptians (Ex. 12:35–6; also Ex. 3:22, 11:2). Despite the somewhat euphemistic phrasing of the event in the text of Exodus itself,[31] the incident was commonly referred to by the Church Fathers simply as "the despoiling of the Egyptians." Was this seizure of valuables a case of simple theft (something prohibited by the seventh commandment) or was it an instance that could be used to show that ownership sometimes arose from divine mandate? Occasionally our authors state briefly that it was not an unjust action because God commanded it and whatever God never orders is never unjust, but their main interest lay in drawing up allegorical explanations.[32] For Isidore (whose text again reappears almost verbatim in Bede) the gold and silver vessels and the vestments that the Israelites took from the Egyptians must be seen in a figurative sense. What the vessels signify are the academic disciplines that the gentiles were accustomed to study and, Isidore notes, "not without profit." When figurative meanings are given for a text, we are not limited to offering one. The vessels and clothes can also signify the precious souls liberated from the thrall of Egypt (a symbol of worldly evil) and added to the people of God. The articles of clothing become the bodies attached to these souls. By seizing the vessels the Israelites appropriate the learned disciplines and liberated them from the use made by the Egyptians.[33] This symbolic interpretation reported by Isidore and the pseudo-Bede Rabanus Maurus speaks of God's commandment while the *Glossa Ordinaria*, looking to the authority of Augustine, says that God can never be an unjust judge and so his commands are not to be examined but simply complied with.[34] It is only Rupert of Deutz who justifies the seizure, giving some concrete reasons. The taking of valuables by the Israelites as they left Egypt on their exodus was not unjust because the Egyptians had violently oppressed them. They were, therefore, quite justified in despoiling their oppressors, "not as brigands plundering their overlords" (an idea that few in feudal Europe would want to see justified) but as victors over a true enemy.[35] While the seizure of land can be purely spiritualized, justification of title to personal property (chattels) attracts a mixture of arguments, some allegorical but some applying to justice in a concrete, physical world.

By the middle of the thirteenth century a new defence of the, by now, classic case of the "spoliation of the Egyptians" seems to have been required. It was no longer in the form of high allegory or of simple divine fiat, but was now in terms of an uneasy combination of divine and natural law. Interest in applying natural law was most probably the result of renewed reading of the *Ethics* and *Politics* of Aristotle, an author who was not much interested in religious, still less in allegorical, answers to practical problems. While Thomas was not the only medieval author to make use of natural law arguments, his discussion set the pace. In his exposition of the Exodus story about the "spoliation of the Egyptians" Thomas argues that the Israelites cannot be accused here of stealing (i.e., taking the property of others) even if we admit that what they were taking from Egypt were real and tangible gold and silver objects.[36] Relying on the general principle that God has dominion (i.e., ownership over all things), the Israelites cannot be called thieves, since they were not taking something owned by another. Theft, Thomas reminds us, consists of taking the property that is owned by another. But whoever takes anything under orders from God is not taking anything against the will of the owner because the Lord is, after all, the primary owner of everything. Besides, God, who is the judge of all things, saw how the Israelites were oppressed in Egypt without cause and judged in their favor. By the decision of a judge the items of gold and silver that they took were now rightly assigned to them. In such cases no actual theft is being committed.[37] This leaves the door open to admitting that in a some cases, at least, positive law (*ius positivum*), which assigns property to one person rather than to another, law normally made in a community for the common good, may in some cases be a positive law of divine origin. But how are we to know of the existence of laws like this? For believers, it is an easy matter. For them, a clear statement in a scripture or by a religious authority would be enough to decide the issue—if there be such. But to decide ownership (to establish title) for a particular thing or for a piece of land is by no means an easy matter purely from the standpoint of natural law. All that can really be done is to appeal to the general principle that lands are the possession of the entire human community and distribution is to be left to the political process.[38] The issue of how religious claims to specific parcels of land were to be decided was not resolved by medieval authors.

The theory outlined above, or perhaps it might be better to say the theories offered, do not lead to a neat result in the practical realm. From a purely natural law point of view, a given acre of ground, one valley, one specific region is not absolutely related to any particular person or group. If positive laws or communal decisions are to determine questions of title, then, a theory of community and who can speak for a community is desperately needed. Sadly, this means that possession of the land, even national possession of territory, is bound to be unstable inasmuch as human communities from village to nation are always in the process of change. In addition to the ambiguities of the political process there remained the nagging possibility that one acre, one valley, one region might have been assigned to one community by divine dispensation after all. The Old Covenant, with its promise of land, had been ended, but a New Covenant had been begun. Its promise was primarily spiritual, but couldn't some residual promise of land be included still? Medieval theologians liked to speculate about the character of the world before the Fall of Adam and Eve, when all was innocence and reasonability. In this idealized world of reasonable men and women the distribution of work and duties and the division of lands to facilitate all these good efforts would have come about easily and naturally. History has taught, both before and after the Middle Ages, that ease is the last word to use when deciding such thorny issues. During the period of the Great Explorations of the sixteenth century, when the Europeans took a collective decision to occupy and settle the new lands previously unknown to them, the issue of who owns a land had to be faced with urgency. The principles of natural law and the tradition of a divine covenant, coupled with generations of European experience, had to be rethought and refashioned to give some justification for a colonialization process.[39] The notion that the earth is radically the common property of all (from natural law) and that specific parcels are given out by the victorious prince (the experience of the European community) and the sleeping tradition of a divine covenant, was, needless to say, a dangerous formula in the hands of the ambitious. The postcolonial experience of the West amply attests that that necessary reshaping and rethinking was not complete.

In pondering the question of who owns the land, we might do worse than combine simultaneously an expression from the wisdom of the Talmud with another adage repeated by Christian leaders. From the Talmud we read that "where there is perfect justice, there is no peace; and where there is perfect peace, there is no justice." The statement of Christian leaders complements this: if you want peace, then you must work for justice. At their best, medieval thinkers argue that you can obtain and hold land and chattels in peaceful possession, even hold them as your very own, but only as long as they are held with the common good of the community in mind.

NOTES

1. William's government justified the invasion of England by appealing to the grant made by Edward the Confessor, the previous king but one, and to the support of the Pope, but it was his military victory over Harold that attracted the imagination of his contemporaries, for it appeared to come as a gift of God. The victory gained for him the land of England and allowed him to hold it in the manner that he did. While he at first permitted the old customs to continue, they acquired legal standing in the kingdom because he confirmed them. In most cases the old customs did not last long. In the Domesday Book (i.e., by 1086) only 8 percent of the great landowners were still of the old Saxon class. The truly novel feature of William's rule was that it introduced a tight landed and military aristocracy into England, which assured Norman control. We are not interested so much in that as in the fact that land tenure now depended on service to the Crown, which remained the real owner. See, David Douglas, *William the Conqueror* (London: Eyre & Spottiswoode, 1964), 279–81. Warfare was endemic in early medieval society and, according to Marc Bloch, was for many centuries to be regarded as the normal tread of every leader's career, *Feudal Society* (Chicago: University of Chicago Press, 1964), I:151.
2. Many, indeed most, individuals in medieval Europe never actually possessed land at all, but lived on the land, bound to it or to their lords by various obligations.
3. This was a favorite argument of those who claimed Australia for the British Crown in 1788, and of those who subsequently claimed bits and pieces of it from the Crown. Aboriginal people abounded throughout the Continent, but the argument was made that they did not really live there, since they never tilled the soil nor built any lodgings but simply passed through from time to time on the way to other places. It was further alleged that aboriginals did not have any concept of private property, so none of the land could belong to them—views that can no longer be sustained.

4. I refer those interested in pursuing this further to the work of Professor James Gordley, who is preparing a text on comparative legal history, which will be published by the University of California Press this year.

5. Thomas began a commentary on the *Politics* of Aristotle, but it apparently bored him because he broke it off after the third book. The part completed is somewhat disappointing because it is little more than a summary of the statements made in Aristotle's text. For the dates of, purposes of, and occasions for Thomas's writings, cf. J.A. Weisheipl, *Friar Thomas d'Aquinas* (Garden City, N.Y.: Doubleday & Co., 1974), 380–1.

6. *Summa*, 2–2, q. 66, aa. 1 and 2. For a collection of Thomas's texts in English translation, see *The Political Ideas of St. Thomas Aquinas*, ed. Dino Bigongiari (New York: Hafner Publishing Co., 1953).

7. I *Politics*, ch. 3, 1256. n. 6. The principle could be assigned Neoplatonic roots as well.

8. He sees three good reasons for subordination. There is a kind of natural progression in the world of nature from the imperfect to the perfect so that the superior thing is made for the lower, viz., plants use the earth for their nutrition, animals use plants, and human beings use them both. This pattern is also reflected in the way in which God governs the world: although God directs all things, he shares his power so that angels communicate with men and women and they, in turn, govern animals. Finally, this ordering is also reflected in our difference from animals. Brute animals act from blind instinct, although at times their instincts may give the impression of wise choice. Human beings, on the other hand, truly make wise choices, since they can foresee in universal fashion what will happen in any given case, and so make an appropriate decisions. Whatever participates in a quality (for example, instinct, which shares in the quality of wise choices) is subordinate to that which possesses that quality universally and absolutely. *Summa*, 1, q. 96, a. 1.

9. Bonaventure, Sent. Bk., d. 15, a. 2, q. 1, *Opera Omnia*, II:250a; see also 382a.

10. *Summa*, 2–2, q. 66, a. 2 c. Earlier, Thomas gave a more elaborate explanation of this example (cf. *Summa*, q. 57, a. 3). If we look at a field absolutely (i.e., just as a bit of ground), there is nothing that tells us it belongs to one person more than to another. If we look at a field as an opportunity for cultivation, it bears a relation to one person more than to another (cf. II Pol. ch 2, lesson 4 & 5). In this context Thomas divides natural law as an absolute (with its reference to the inner nature of things) from natural law as the custom of peoples (the *jus gentium*). The latter makes reference to a reasoned consideration of the interrelation of humanity and nature as observed and analyzed over a long period of time in the light of common human experience. In both these ways natural law will clearly differ from statutory law (*ius positivum*), which is the result of local decisions made from time to time by particular communities in the light of their own special needs. We can expect

that statutory law will differ from place to place. Natural law considered absolutely can pertain, and often does pertain, to animals and to human beings. (Both men and animals must eat to live, procreate in order to survive as a species, etc.) It is only when we consider the interrelation of human beings (individuals and communities) with all that is found in the human environment, when we examine all the possibilities and test all the consequences of human activity in a reasoned way that we uncover the law that is proper to humanity. Its common values will be discovered through experience. That there will be common values rests on two assumptions: we are always dealing with human beings, and we are dealing with the physical cosmos. It is only in this sense that Thomas will say that natural law is what is according to nature.

     11. *Summa,* 2–2, q. 66, a. 2 ad 1m.

     12. There are two ways in which something can be said to be justly divided: (1) from the nature of the thing itself (when equal values are exchanged) or (2) by arrangements agreed on by mutual consent. Again this can occur in one of two ways. The mutual consent can be purely private as between two private persons, or it can be by a public agreement, either by agreement of the whole population or as ordained by the prince who has charge of the whole community. For Thomas, these arrangements are called positive law (*ius positivum*), *Summa,* 2–2, q. 57, a. 2.

     13. Thomas's general notion of land as a formulation of reason can be found in his *Summa,* 1–2, q. 91, a. 1–2.

     14. W.D. Davies, *The Land and the Gospel, Early Christianity and Jewish Territorial Doctrine,* (Los Angeles: University of California Press, 1974), is a masterful account of the different attitude toward the promised land in Judaism and the New Testament. In his conclusion he draws attention to the Epistle to Diognetus (c. 150), which essentially describes Christians as people at home anywhere, aliens everywhere. While Jews sought a homeland, Christians became aliens by choice in this world. Davies concludes, "The history of Judaism has generally ... witnessed a continued, and for many an increasing, attachment to the land, that of Christianity, despite the Crusades, has largely been that of detachment from it." 374–5.

     15. Gerhard von Rad, *The Problem of the Hexateuch and other Essays,* trans., E.W.T. Dicken, (New York: McGraw-Hill, 1966), land is central 79 *seq.* See also A. Graeme Auld, *Joshua, Moses and the Land: Tetrateuch-Pentateuch-Hexateuch in a Generation Since 1938* (Edinburgh: T. & T. Clark, 1980). David Clines, *The Theme of the Pentateuch,* (Sheffield: JSOT Press, 1982), argues somewhat differently, wondering if the Book of Joshua should be regarded as one in theme with the Pentateuch. Clines believes that the theme of land is far less central, since the Penteteuch should be read as a unit without seeing Joshua as its completion.

     In *The Territorial Dimension of Judaism* (Los Angeles: University of California Press, 1982), W.D. Davies has shown the undeniable historical diversity of Jewish attitudes toward the meaning of promised land as a concrete place or as a Messianic hope., esp. 54 *seq.*

16. Josue 1:2. The book of Joshua presents itself, *prima facie*, as an historical narrative, but that does not mean that we must read it that way, or that medieval commentators read it that way either. In any event, medievals regarded the literal (i.e., the historical) meaning as the mere husk of Scripture. They were preoccupied with its kernel, which held the moral and spiritual meanings of the text. Considerable work has been done on interpreting the meaning of Joshua recently. See A. Graeme Auld, *Joshua, Moses and the Land. Tetrateuch-Pentateuch-Hexateuch in a Generation Since 1938*, already cited; N.K. Gottwald, *The Tribes of Yahweh* (Maryknoll, Orbis, 1979), with its liberation theology method; or even the popularized, E. John Hamlin, *Joshua, Inheriting the Land* (Grand Rapids, Mich.: Wm. B. Eerdmans Publ. Co., 1983). These authors need to be read with the usual cautions. See the review of Auld in *The Expository Times* 93 (Oct. 1981): 24, and of Hamlin in *Vetus Testamentum*, 34, (April 1984): 254–5.

17. See Habel, Norman, "Conquest and Disposition: Justice, Joshua and Land Rights," *Pacifica*, 4.1 (Feb. 1991): 76–92. Habel presents his case in the most stark way. For Habel, Josue simply cannot be read in the light of modern principles of justice and fair play. He brushes aside the traditional justifications for Josue's actions, for example, that Canaan was an oppressive society and that its people were abnormally evil and corrupt and so justly visited with divine retribution. These excuses do not appear in the biblical text, he argues, and it never tries to justify the command to go to war on any grounds of that kind. It is a genocidal war that is justified only because God ordered it and in which failure to be thoroughgoing in conducting it was regarded as a sin of disobedience, either to God or His servant Josue. Habel concludes, "The kind of process and principles associated with contemporary justice are nowhere reflected in Joshua," 87. Habel, an Australian, is writing with Aboriginal land rights issues in mind.

18. Ex. 3:8 and vv. 16–17.

19. Gen. 13:14–17; and repeated 15:18–21 and 18, 17:1–21, and 26:3–4.

20. D.W. Davies argues that during the inter-testamental period, "in both Hellenistic and Palestinian sources The Land, became, in some quarters, a symbol for a transcendental order or for the age to come." He cites, among others, Philo's commentary on Genesis 15:7–8 (*et alia*) in which the gift of land becomes a grant of fruitful wisdom; the Mishnah, Sanhedrin 10:1–3, in which it is a share in the world to come; and the pre-Christian Testament of Job in which it seems to be an eternal order beyond this world. See *Territorial Dimension*, 78–9. Davies is concerned with showing that there was flexibility in the interpretation of land, not that the symbolic interpretation carried the day! (cf. op. cit., 14, 142–3). We are interested in noting that Origen and others in the patristic era had a broad platform on which to ground their views.

21. Origen, *Homilia in librum Jesu Nave*, II:2, *PG* 12:835–6. The text is the Latin translation by Rufinus (c. 345–410).
22. "Quam terram? Illam sine dubio de qua dicit dominus. 'Beati mansueti, quia ipsi haereditate possidebunt terram." *PG* 12:835 A.
23. Origen, *In Genesim Homilia IX, PG* 12, 211.
24. *PL* 83:371; *PL* 93:417; *PL* 108:1001; *PL* 113:506; *PL* 167:1004, respectively. Beryl Smalley in *The Study of the Bible in the Middle Ages*, 3rd ed. (London: B. Blackwell, 1983), has shown that Strabo had little to do with the Gloss, which was a compilation of extracts from various sources. Its form owes as much to Anselm of Laon (d. 1117), his brother Ralph, and their pupil Gilbert (c. 1128) as to anyone else. See 46–66, esp. 60–1.
25. *PL* 83:371 A.
26. Pseudo-Bede, *PL* 93:370, 417.
27. *PL* 108:1001
28. *PL* 167:1004–5.
29. *PL* 167:1005.
30. *PL* 198:1259–62.
31. The text suggests that the Egyptians actually made presents of vessels and clothing to the fleeing Israelites. "I will give this people favour in the sight of the Egyptians, and when you go, you shall not go empty. . . . Thus shall you despoil the Egyptians," Ex 3:21–2. The willingness of the Egyptians to give whatever is asked of them is underscored in the Mishnah, *Midrash Rabbah* over Exodus (Bo) XIV:3–4.
32. Glossa Ordinaria, *PL* 113:193 C.
33. *PL* 83:295 B. "Quid ergo haec praefiguraverint nisi . . . quaedam doctrinae quae ex ipsa consuetudine gentilium non inutili studio discuntur?" Verbatim in Pseudo-Bede, *PL* 93:370.
34. *PL* 108:47 C; *PL* 113:193 B.
35. *PL* 167:582–3.
36. Thomas did not comment on the Pentateuch, Josue, or the historical books of the Old Testament. The reference appears in his commentary on the Sent. Bk. III, dist., 37, introductory section. He takes up the doctrine on theft in aa. 3 and 4. Cf. *Summa*, 1–2, q. 94, a. 5, ad 2m. The main issue here is whether "the laws of nature be changed sometimes," since Abraham was told to kill his son Isaac and the Israelites were told to steal from the Egyptians. Thomas's answer is that whatever God commands should be done, and he adds, since whatever God commands is in a certain sense according to nature.
37. *Summa*, 2–2, q. 66, 5 ad 1m and 2m, and q. 94 reference given above.
38. This was also the way Leonard Lessius, the heir to the late medieval doctrine of natural law, writing in the early 1600s, saw it. *Four Books on Justice and Law and Other Cardinal Virtues*, Bk. II, ch. 3, problem 3.
39. In the sixteenth century European theologians did struggle with the problem, and it was of concern to some rulers, such as Francisco de Vitoria at

the court of Philip II of Spain, to cite one example. "De los indios: relecciùn primera," in *Obras de Francisco de Vitoria relecciones teológicas,* ed. T. Urdanoz (Madrid: Le BAC, 1965).

CULTURED NATURE IN CHAUCER'S EARLY DREAM-POEMS

Laura L. Howes

Gardens figure prominently in three of Chaucer's four extant dream-poems as settings through which his dreamers walk, or into which they wake. In the *Book of the Duchess*, Chaucer's narrator enters a well-ordered grove in his dream in which trees, spaced well apart, are kept clean of brush and low-growing branches; in the *Parliament of Fowls*, Chaucer's dreamer enters a walled garden at the urging of his guide, Scipio, where he discovers flowery meadows, an exotic temple, and Nature's own bower; and in the *Legend of Good Women*, written later in Chaucer's career, Chaucer's narrator falls asleep in a small *herber* furnished with new turf benches, before he wakes to a vision of the god of Love himself, and the dream is set, not surprisingly, in a spring meadow reminiscent of medieval tapestry designs. Most Chaucerians tend to read these descriptions as stock medieval *topoi*, which to an extent they clearly are. But these invented gardens also resemble built gardens of the period. New research on the history of gardens suggests that, for many of Chaucer's garden settings, he drew on a pleasure garden aesthetic prevalent in aristocratic culture and evident in built gardens as well as in other literary works. In addition, Chaucer not only uses stock descriptions for these outdoor spaces, but he also combines garden *topoi* in new ways, self-consciously playing on the conventions of nature description. Finally, the placement of these pleasure gardens within their narratives suggests a symbolic role. Themselves well-ordered outdoor spaces, these gardens serve as thresholds into well-ordered narratives, providing a visual and spatial analogue to the construction of a successful story.

Medieval Gardens

Medieval gardens are most commonly thought of as the small, enclosed *herbaria* and cloister gardens represented in numerous manuscript illuminations. Terry Comito, whose remarkable study *The Idea of the Garden in the Renaissance* broadens our area of garden investigation to include cultural and psychological issues, nevertheless wrote in 1978: "The form of the medieval garden, so far as we can reconstruct it, is remarkably fixed,"[1] a notion asserted implicitly or explicitly in most other studies of medieval gardens. Such an idea squares well with the notion that Renaissance gardens differ from their medieval counterparts primarily in their scale, their sense of classical proportion, and in their axial relationship to large Renaissance manor houses.[2]

But thanks in large measure to the archival research of the garden historian John H. Harvey, these rather neat divisions between medieval and Renaissance gardens begin to blur. Harvey has discovered, for example, that "the pleasure grounds of [medieval European] palaces and mansions included not only small herbers but orchards with fish-ponds and other pools, and at times aviaries and menageries."[3] These grounds ranged in size from two acres to over seventy acres, and like their more famous Renaissance offspring, some also included architectural features and automata, as well as roomlike areas—large and small—created by the artful arrangement of trees, shrubs, and flowers.

While France seems to have been at the cutting edge of medieval garden design, the earliest recorded royal gardens in England, according to Harvey's research, belonged to Henry I, who assumed the throne in 1100. His ornamental pleasure park at his manor Kingsbury by Dunstable, less than fifty miles northwest of London, covered nine acres; by the year 1260 the abbey garden at Malmesbury in Gloucestershire, known for the production of grapes and wine during the twelfth and thirteenth centuries, covered forty-three acres and included "streams, pools, fishponds and fruit-trees," and was "kept for the monks to walk in,"[4] thus serving aesthetic and recreational needs as well as agricultural ones. Obviously, a different garden aesthetic from that represented by the small cloister garden is at work in such expansive spaces. In fact, in contrast with the inward-focused cloister gardens, their paths usually arranged in the shape of a cross, these large pleasure parks were often created at some distance from the residence, and are often marked off from the rest of the property by moats, lakes, or high walls. At Peterborough Abbey, about seventy miles north of London, a garden built in 1302 stood approximately 600 feet from the abbot's lodging and church and was separated from them by a large courtyard. A wall built there in 1308 further marked the garden as separate. A century later at Kenilworth Castle, a new pleasure garden was built for Henry V approximately 3,500 feet from the castle, across a large lake.[5] Such distances helped to isolate the pleasure grounds from the other living quarters of a household, providing a measure of privacy unusual in medieval communities, and it is perhaps this distance from the residences that can better distinguish these gardens from Renaissance gardens. In addition, people had to traverse land or water to get to the pleasure grounds; thus, traveling through space into and out of different outdoor realms, as well as the well-orchestrated discovery of new realms with their individual features, must have been integral to the pleasure garden experience. As far as we can determine, from evidence provided by manuscript illuminations as well as textual accounts—including Chaucer's description of January's garden in the *Merchant's Tale*—pleasure grounds were used for outdoor dining, entertainment, and other leisure activities.[6]

Among the most relevant to Chaucer's early poems are records of garden improvements at Clare Castle in Suffolk, the residence of the Lady of Clare, Elizabeth de Burgh, who died in 1360 and who was the grandmother of Chaucer's first royal patron, also named Elizabeth de Burgh, Countess of Ulster. The elder Elizabeth appears to have directed several improvements in her gardens, including the construction of a moat surrounding the garden, a small house in an herber built "for the Lady's deer," a glass chamber inside a pheasant house, and a "tomb" in the herber, whose function is unknown. Mention is also made in the records covering the years 1341–1352 of the purchase of new sand for the paths, new railings, new turf for repairing an area called the "Great Herber," new hedges, a bridge, and a fountain.[7] The younger Elizabeth and her husband Lionel, Duke of Clarence, inherited the castle and grounds from Elizabeth's grandmother in 1361.[8] Another burst of repair activity is recorded for the years 1387–1388 when Roger Mortimer (the grandson of Elizabeth and Lionel by their daughter) was in residence. Gladys Thornton, in her history of Clare, Suffolk, writes of Mortimer's contributions: "the wall round the garden and the hedge round the fish-

pond [were] repaired . . . [and] one great lock and key was bought for
the secret door of the tower."[9] From these partial records, we can form a
general image of a very large area, separated into several outdoor
rooms, both great and small, some housing deer, pheasants, and a fish
pond, some laid with green turf. Buildings, such as the tower with a
secret door, could have been used for solitary pleasures or some form of
courtly dalliance. The entire garden was probably interlaced with
sanded paths, which were possibly edged with railings,[10] and so again,
the experience of walking through such spaces, spotting deer and birds,
watching fish swim in the pond, and sitting—probably on turf
benches—at certain sites all would have contributed to the progressive
enjoyment of these grounds.

Chaucer's employment in the household of the younger
Elizabeth de Burgh began sometime in 1357, and he left the service of
Prince Lionel sometime after October 1360,[11] so he was not part of their
household when they inherited Clare Castle the next year. Still, it seems
possible that Chaucer could have visited the elaborate gardens in
Suffolk during his three-year tenure with Elizabeth and Lionel, and
quite probable that he would have heard of such elaborate arrangements
at the very least.

Equally relevant to Chaucer's early impressions of the royal and
aristocratic garden aesthetic are gardens at royal residences that
Chaucer may have visited as a member of the Countess of Ulster's
household. From June 1356 to April 1359, the countess visited royal
residences at Reading, Stratford, Campsey, London, Windsor,
Woodstock, Doncaster, Hatfield, Anglesey, Bristol, and Liverpool.[12]
We know that the garden at Windsor Castle, for example, was begun as
early as 1110, and under Henry III in 1246 a "beautiful pleasure garden
(*unum pulcrum virgultum*) [was] laid out."[13] In addition, one of the
earliest known master gardeners, John de Wyndewores, was appointed
in January 1336 for work at Windsor Castle, and two years later was
awarded a "grant for life" as gardener there.[14] Other residences Chaucer
visited or heard about almost certainly had pleasure grounds as well,
since gardens increasingly signified wealth and privilege.[15]

Thus, Chaucer may well have visited, glimpsed, or heard
described elaborate pleasure grounds in his early contact with court
culture, and this possibility helps us to consider his gardens as possible
pleasure grounds, and his other outdoor realms as possible gardens and

artfully arranged groves, even though they might not immediately strike modern readers as self-consciously constructed spaces.

Chaucer's Early Gardens

The outdoor areas created by Chaucer in two early dream-poems indeed suggest artfully arranged gardens, and I use the term *garden* here in the broadest sense of the word—as an outdoor area rearranged or replanted by humans. The forest in the *Book of the Duchess*, for example, is far from being the natural wood some critics would have it be.[16] Chaucer's description, in fact, emphasizes its orderliness:

> And every tree stood by hymselve
> Fro other wel ten foot or twelve—
> So grete trees, so huge of strengthe,
> Of fourty or fifty fadme lengthe,
> Clene withoute bowgh or stikke,
> With croppes brode, and eke as thikke—
> They were nat an ynche asonder—
> That hit was shadewe overal under. (419–426)[17]

> [And every tree stood by itself
> From each other a good ten or twelve feet—
> The trees were so great, so powerful,
> Of forty or fifty fathoms tall,
> And clean without boughs or sticks,
> With broad tops and also so thick—
> They were not an inch apart—
> That the earth beneath was completely shaded.]

These trees have been planted—some time before—at regular ten- to twelve-foot intervals so that their leafy canopy shades the entire "floury grene" (flowery meadow) (398) underneath. Also well pruned, they stand forty to fifty fathoms tall, or approximately 80 to 100 yards, and are clean of undergrowth—branches and sticks along their trunks, as well as smaller trees and shrubs in between them. This is a well-maintained grove, an outdoor room with a leafy ceiling, woody pillars, and a soft grassy floor. The grove's connotations thus include wealth

and privilege, since a great deal of dedicated work hours would be
required for the upkeep of such a grove, time that could not be spent in
the production of food or other essentials. In addition, with such large
trees, the passage implies hereditary wealth, reaching back for
generations. Further, the shade of this grove should not, in my opinion,
be interpreted allegorically as some sort of evil shield separating the
man in black from the sunlight of God's grace. Rather, shade figures as
a positive feature in numerous medieval garden descriptions, most
likely due to their Mediterranean lineage.[18]

The small animals Chaucer's narrator then sees in this grove
include an array of deer—fawns, four- and six-year-old bucks, stags,
and does—suggesting that the grove may also be used as the hunting
park for a wealthy household. And perhaps, as with Lady Clare's
garden, which included a special house for deer, the deer should also be
considered part of the overall aesthetic effect. The narrator's pleasure
after entering this space seems to derive in part from his serendipitous
glimpses of various animals. It is here that the narrator also encounters
the mysterious man in black. The grove in the *Book of the Duchess*,
which may or may not belong to the man in black (who most likely
represents John of Gaunt after the death of his first wife Blanche),
would strike medieval audiences who were familiar with gardens like
those of the Lady of Clare as a delightful pleasure park, eminently
suitable for the kind of love-centered dialogue that occurs between
Chaucer's narrator and the man in black.

Along similar lines, the garden in the *Parliament of Fowls* can be
best understood as a large pleasure garden with several separate areas.
The high stone wall that surrounds this garden is reminiscent of that
created by Guillaume de Lorris in his section of the *Roman de la Rose*
and has numerous possible analogues in the world of built gardens. The
fourteenth-century royal garden of the kings of Navarre at Tafalla, for
example, was "surrounded by strong walls plastered over and originally
painted."[19] In February 1366, several years before Chaucer wrote the
Parliament of Fowls, he traveled in Navarre for about twelve weeks,
most likely in some diplomatic capacity.[20] But whether he saw the
garden in Tafalla or not, walled gardens were almost commonplace, the
walls helping to delineate gardens from the surrounding countryside
and cityscapes, further establishing them as preserves of the nobility
and aristocracy.

Once inside the wall, the narrator of the *Parliament* first encounters—again—a grove of trees, this one made up of several different types (a catalogue of trees), which shade another garden "ful of blosmy bowes/ Upon a ryver, in a grene mede" (full of blossoming boughs/ upon a river, in a green meadow) (*PF* 183–184). In the river swim bright red and silver-colored fish (*PF* 188–189). The river is also probably stocked and well tended, since the narrator comments he saw "nothyng dede" (nothing dead) (*PF* 187) floating there, yet another reference to the unnatural state of this seemingly natural space. Birds fill the branches overhead; squirrels, rabbits, and numerous deer again populate the area. The obvious echoes of descriptions of the earthly paradise (echoes that, I believe, are to be found in built gardens as well as literary gardens) soon give way to quite another sort of realm when the narrator spots "under a tre, besyde a welle" (under a tree, beside a well) (*PF* 211) Cupid and a host of allegorical figures, including Lust, Curteysie, Craft, Delyt, and Gentilesse.

In this second part of the *Parliament*'s garden, "upon pilers greete of jasper longe" (on great pillars of long jasper) our narrator sees "a temple of bras ifounded stronge" (a brass temple strongly built) (*PF* 230–231). Dishevelled women dance about the temple; on the roof sit several hundred pairs of white doves. Clearly an exaggerated and dreamlike spectacle, the brass temple with its door and darkened interior houses several additional figures, including Venus, reclining on a "bed of gold" (*PF* 265), and naked from the waist up (*PF* 269). As with the high stone wall, the brass temple has possible, albeit somewhat less definite, analogues in built gardens of the period. For example, I can only speculate about why Roger Mortimer needed a "great lock and key"[21] for the tower in the garden at Clare Castle, but it seems probable that, as suggested before, gardens were used for various forms of courtly dalliance. Manuscript illuminations show numerous couples engaged in the medieval equivalent of "heavy petting," especially when seated, and it seems to me likely that the ubiquitous turf bench—well hidden within walled gardens from the prying eyes of curious onlookers—was the medieval equivalent of the backseat of a Chevrolet. Outdoor structures, such as the tower at Clare Castle, could also have served similar purposes.

From this close, crowded, and highly erotic interior, Chaucer's narrator abruptly—in the space between two stanzas—is again outside the brass temple and seems quite relieved:

When I was come ayeyn into the place
That I of spak, that was so sote and grene,
Forth welk I tho myselven to solace. (295–297)

[When I had come again into the place
That I spoke of, which was so sweet and green,
I walked forth then myself to solace.]

Whether the temple itself sits in a green meadow or sits in another one of the outdoor rooms, perhaps separated from the meadow by hedges or walls, is not clear. The effect of Chaucer's narrator's perambulations, however, is to take him to, into, around, and out of these various areas, as he performs a sort of journey through the garden with its representations of various kinds of human love.

The narrator of the *Parliament* next comes upon the goddess Natura "in a launde, upon an hil of floures" (in a land, upon a hill of flowers) (*PF* 302), and we are told that Nature's rooms—like the orchard in the *Book of the Duchess*—were made of overhead branches designed according to her "mesure," or sense of proportion:

Of braunches were here halles and here boures
Iwrought after here cast and here mesure; (304–305)

[Of branches were her halls and her private rooms
Wrought according to her plan and her measurement.]

This figure of Nature, as David Lawton has written, herself "orders experience and emotion"; she "stands for the kind of order we impose and have to impose on the external world in order to perceive and in order to think."[22] And with this conflation of nature and art, in which nature personified has constructed her own home according to certain aesthetic rules, the apparent dividing line between nature and art disappears. In place of the pleasure garden that seeks to emulate a natural space, made perfect like Eden before the Fall, we find a natural space that emulates pleasure gardens with their series of well proportioned outdoor rooms and adherence to aesthetic principles.[23]

Viewing Chaucer's early dream spaces as self-consciously designed areas augments our reading of these two poems. In the *Book of the Duchess*, the man in black's appearance in an expansive and expensively maintained pleasure park marks him as aristocratic or noble in heritage, further enabling his identification, however symbolic, with John of Gaunt. It also discourages readings that see the park as a "dark wood"[24] or area of chaotic and threatening forces. The man in black may be far from his home or castle, but he is, in my judgment, still very much a part of a well-orchestrated and controlled landscape. In the *Parliament of Fowls*, the outdoor dream-space is widely acknowledged to be a garden, but few view the poem as taking place within a series of outdoor rooms, all artificial and all part of the same extensive and well-planned garden, whether by humans or by nature personified. The narrator's walking in the *Parliament* suggests the ability of each individual to choose his or her own path regarding love. While some dreamers might have chosen to dwell at length in Venus's brass temple, Chaucer's narrator progresses from it into Nature's own bower, indicating in part this narrator's discomfort with French allegorical love discourse and signaling his decision to pursue an alternate poetic route.

Much more, of course, can be made of these and other garden descriptions in Chaucer's work, and I have purposely ignored in this brief discussion most of the literary antecedents upon which Chaucer also drew, and by means of which I believe he sought to establish both his debt to, and his independence from, his literary predecessors.[25] Here I mean to emphasize that his outdoor dream-spaces, which may seem so exotic and foreign to us, were part of Continental and English aristocratic culture of the late Middle Ages, and resemble spaces that Chaucer, his patrons, and his aristocratic acquaintances most probably enjoyed.

Gardens and Narratives

Beyond their roles as markers of social status and wealth, Chaucer's early gardens in the *Book of the Duchess* and the *Parliament of Fowls* serve as thresholds between parts of the narratives through which the dreamers must walk, thus enhancing an analogy between poem and journey. The narrators of these two poems simultaneously travel through created space, since they recount a dream that involved travel, and create a poem. As Michel de Certeau evocatively states in *The Practice of Everyday Life*, "footsteps . . . weave places together,"[26] and as Chaucer's dreamers/narrators walk through their own dreams/poems, their footsteps relate one dream-space and one experience to the next.

The *Book of the Duchess* and the *Parliament of Fowls* follow similar patterns of narrative organization. In both poems the narrator, experiencing some sort of difficulty, reads a book, falls asleep, and begins to dream. The initial dream phases of each poem refer explicitly to the book the narrator has just been reading, but quickly become dreams that show the influence of books not mentioned and of the narrator's waking experiences. In both poems, the narrator enters a garden or grove in his dream and then finds himself in a new and narratively fertile region. What most critics call the "heart" or "core" of each poem occurs in these gardens and is not related in the narrator's voice alone, but includes another voice in dialogue with the narrator (the man in black) or dialogue overheard by the narrator (the conference of birds). Some critics have chosen to identify the difference between these two phases of the dream-poems as that between lyric and narrative modes, arguing that the early phase of each poem is lyric, while the central part of each poem is narrative.[27] But it seems important to me that the narrator asserts his intention to tell a story early in each poem, although in each poem he does not tell a coherent or successful narrative until he has entered the garden.[28] Significantly, narrative coherence emerges in each poem once its narrator has entered an ordered, natural realm, one made coherent by the artistic efforts of humans.

Thus, the narrator's entrance into the garden—produced, of course, by his description of the garden—is also an entrance into a conventional framework that promises to give coherence to his previously unorganized account of his experience. In both poems, this promise is indeed fulfilled, and so the pattern of preliminary narrative, entrance into the garden, and main narrative or coherent story enacts the evolution of the narrator's experience in writing a poem, from preliminary, unorganized string of events to the organization of these events in a conventional manner.[29] The garden, as a natural space that has been organized by human effort, symbolizes the narrator's efforts to control and organize his otherwise unruly experiences. Connecting spaces by walking to, through, and beyond them is, according to de Certeau, an act that organizes that space, an act of signification, since it "implies *relations* among differentiated positions [emphasis added]," and "it is a spatial acting-out of the place."[30]

In an excellent study of how movement through space can produce meaning, Stephen Murray and James Addiss have recently analyzed the experience of walking through Amiens Cathedral, arguing that for a "visitor entering at the west portal and progressing to the east . . . the spaces gradually and progressively reveal themselves as a set of transformations of the initial order." In their concluding remarks on this "processional path," they assert: "The cathedral has created a new kind of reality which obviates for the moment the dictates of a uniform and consistent physical world."[31] The world within the cathedral is continually transformed as one walks through it, and so a visitor and his or her movements participate in the production of meaning in Amiens Cathedral.

When Chaucer's narrators walk into the aristocratic gardens he has evoked for them, their movement into and within these spaces both organizes each space—by making it known to us—and leads to the organization of the narratives he tells. In addition to providing the theoretical basis for the identification of a dream of walking with the act of writing, Chaucer reproduces in these early poems the experience of walking to and within built gardens of the period, an experience most likely common to the majority of his early court audiences. Indeed, the creation of these elaborate and expensive pleasure grounds in his early poems suggests much about his position within aristocratic culture. He does not begin his poems already within these elite spaces, but must enter them by means of a creative act. And despite his extended glimpse of these realms, he remains an outsider: the obtuse and literal-minded narrator in dialogue with the courtly man in black; the narrator eavesdropping on a parliamentary proceeding, albeit avian. His ticket to this world of privilege is his ability to create aristocratic precincts in his poetry by means of his knowledge of conventional *topoi*, by his emulation, however ironic it may be, of courtly poems, and by his knowledge, and perhaps experience, of built gardens at Clare Castle, Windsor, and elsewhere.

NOTES

An earlier version of this paper was presented at the 25th Anniversary Conference of the Medieval Association of the Pacific, held at the University of

California, Davis, on March 1–3, 1991, and has benefitted from the exchange of ideas made possible there. Thanks are also due to Robert W. Hanning and Sandra Pierson Prior, who guided my dissertation research on Chaucer's gardens. A John C. Hodges Summer Research Grant from the University of Tennessee, Knoxville, supported the writing of this article.

1. Terry Comito, *The Idea of the Garden in the Renaissance* (New Brunswick, N.J.: Rutgers University Press, 1978), 25.

2. See Eugenio Battisti, "Natura Artificiosa to Natura Artificialis," in *The Italian Garden* (Washington, D.C.: Dumbarton Oaks, 1972), 14; Claudia Lazzaro, *The Italian Renaissance Garden: From the Conventions of Planting, Designs, and Ornament to the Grand Gardens of Sixteenth-Century Central Italy* (New Haven: Yale University Press, 1990), 70; and Kenneth Woodbridge, *Princely Gardens: The Origin and Development of the French Formal Style* (New York: Rizzoli, 1986), 30.

3. John H. Harvey, *Mediaeval Gardens* (Beaverton, Ore.: Timber Press, 1981), 103.

4. Ibid., 10, 12.

5. Ibid., 85, 107.

6. See Larry D. Benson, ed., *The Riverside Chaucer*, 3d ed. (Boston: Houghton Mifflin Co., 1987), IV (E), ll. 2029–2041.

7. Harvey, *Mediaeval Gardens*, 87–88.

8. Gladys A. Thornton, *A History of Clare, Suffolk* (Cambridge: W. Heffer and Sons, 1928), 38–39.

9. Ibid., 81–82.

10. Harvey reports: "In 1347 sand was taken from the mound next the Lady's Chamber to the garden and two men spent two days sanding, strewing and gathering stones in the garden and walks. The herber was cleaned and railed with rods round the walks" (*Mediaeval Gardens*, 88).

11. Martin M. Crow and Clair C. Olson, *Chaucer Life Records* (Oxford: Clarendon Press, 1966), 20.

12. Ibid., 18.

13. Harvey, *Mediaeval Gardens*, 10–11.

14. John H. Harvey, "The First English Garden Book: Mayster Jon Gardener's Treatise and Its Background," *Garden History* 13 (1985): 86.

15. See Teresa McLean, *Medieval English Gardens* (London: Collins, 1981), 114; and Paul Piehler, *The Visionary Landscape: A Study in Medieval Allegory* (Montreal: McGill-Queen's University Press, 1971), 99.

16. Some critics do recognize the forest as a kind of garden (John Fyler, *Chaucer and Ovid* [New Haven: Yale University Press, 1979], 74–75; Robert W. Hanning, "Chaucer's First Ovid: Metamorphosis and Poetic Tradition in *The Book of the Duchess* and *The House of Fame*," in *Chaucer and the Craft of Fiction*, ed. Leigh A. Arrathoon [Rochester, Mich.: Solaris Press, 1986], 138;

James Wimsatt, *Chaucer and the French Love Poets: The Literary Background of the Book* of the Duchess [Chapel Hill: University of North Carolina Press, 1968], 20–24). But others emphasize its apparently wild aspect. Alfred Kellogg (*Chaucer, Langland, Arthur: Essays in Middle English Literature* [New Brunswick, N.J.: Rutgers University Press, 1972], 86) terms it a "magic forest, in which all manner of beasts . . . live strangely undisturbed"; and R.A. Shoaf ("Stalking the Sorrowful H[e]art: Penitential Lore and the Hunt Scene in Chaucer's *The Book of the Duchess*," *Journal of English and Germanic Philology* 78 [1979]: 319) sees a symbolic "dark wood" analogous to the knight's suffering.

17. Quotations from Chaucer's works are from Larry D. Benson, ed., *The Riverside Chaucer*, 3d ed. (Boston: Houghton Mifflin Co., 1987).

18. Bernard F. Huppé and D.W. Robertson, Jr. (*Fruyt and Chaf: Studies in Chaucer's Allegories* [Princeton: Princeton University Press, 1963], 55) write that these "shadows indicate oblivion" and the loss of eternal life. On shade as a positive feature, see Ernst Robert Curtius, *European Literature and the Latin Middle Ages*, trans. Willard R. Trask (Princeton: Princeton University Press, 1953), 195–200; A. Bartlett Giamatti, *The Earthly Paradise and the Renaissance Epic* (Princeton: Princeton University Press, 1966), 52; A.C. Spearing, *Medieval Dream-Poetry* (Cambridge: Cambridge University Press, 1976), 17–18; and the garden description of Albertus Magnus, which mentions shade as a utilitarian aspect of a pleasure garden, cited and translated by Harvey, *Mediaeval Gardens*, 6.

19. Harvey, *Mediaeval Gardens*, 45.

20. See Donald R. Howard, *Chaucer: His Life, His Works, His World* (New York: E.P. Dutton, 1987), 115. Most scholars date the *Parliament of Fowls* to 1380 or possibly 1381–82 (Benson, *The Riverside Chaucer*, xxix; Howard, *Chaucer*, 307–317).

21. Thornton, *A History*, 82.

22. David Lawton, *Chaucer's Narrators* (Cambridge: D.S. Brewer, 1985), 42, 45.

23. Many critics have written of this garden as a literary *topos*. See, for recent discussions, Kathleen Hewitt, "'Ther It Was First': Dream Poetics in the *Parliament of Fowls*," *Chaucer Review* 24 (1989): 20–28; and Kay Gilliland Stevenson, "Readers, Poets, and Poems Within the Poem," *Chaucer Review* 24 (1989): 1–19.

24. Shoaf, "Stalking the Sorrowful H(e)art," 319.

25. My book in progress on Chaucer's gardens deals in detail with issues of Chaucer's literary indebtedness, especially as expressed by his use of garden *topoi*.

26. Michel de Certeau, *The Practice of Everyday Life*, trans. Steven F. Rendall (Berkeley: University of California Press, 1984), 97.

27. J. Stephen Russell (*The English Dream Vision: Anatomy of a Form* [Columbus, Ohio: Ohio State University Press, 1988], 115–138, 142–159) identifies lyric and narrative modes in the genre of the English dream vision. His structural analysis of such poems finds that they usually start in a lyric mode, proceed into narrative, and then return to lyric at the poem's close. Hanning ("First Ovid," 133) sees the Ceyx and Alcyone story as the "catalyst for getting the poem moving as a narrative."

28. See, for example, lines 44–51 of the *Book of the Duchess* and lines 32–42 of the *Parliament of Fowls*.

29. Others who draw the connection between writing and dreaming include Spearing (*Medieval Dream Poetry*, 6), Hanning ("First Ovid," 126), and Robert R. Edwards, *The Dream of Chaucer: Representation and Reflection in the Early Narratives* (Durham, N.C.: Duke University Press, 1989), 25.

30. de Certeau, *Practice*, 98.

31. Stephen Murray and James Addiss, "Plan and Space at Amiens Cathedral With a New Plan Drawn by James Addiss," *Journal of the Society of Architectural Historians* 49 (1990): 50, 52.

DANTE'S UTOPIAN LANDSCAPE: THE GARDEN OF GOD

Brenda Deen Schildgen

"Vincenti, dabo ei edere de ligno vitae, quod est in paradiso Dei mei."

Apocalypse of John 2:7[1]

The metaphor of the garden of God with God as gardener is one of the many Dante uses to present the utopian vision in the *Divina Commedia*. Offering a view of the universe that is orderly and where transgression is weeded out and salutary action rewarded,[2] the metaphor is a vehicle for some essential Dantean themes. Rich in complex implications, the garden, like the vineyard, both central metaphors in the Judaeo-Christian repertoire of imagery, is cultivated nature, in which order and productivity stem from guidance and care; both the garden and the vineyard remove nature from unguided chaos, but because they are vegetative and subject to the cycles of nature, they both grow and decay. Gardens in the Judaeo-Christian soteriology begin and end in history (Gen. 2–3; Apoc. 2:7), representing a memory of an idyllic utopia before time and history, and forecasting an end of time which will terminate all the contingencies of human activities.

For Dante, the garden metaphor is, in addition to these traditional interpretations of garden typology, one of the primary vehicles for conveying the theological topography of the *Divine Comedy*. "Gardens" as the Church or Empire exist in time as substitute or temporary utopias, with all their illusions of temporal control and their powerful temptations. The "singular" utopian garden exists out of time where God is the gardener, in the poet's vision, standing in opposition to the personal and public forms of violence, desire, and betrayal that characterize history. For Dante, Eden is the locale for mankind's entrance into the scandal of history, and the Church and

Empire—as utopian, human, divinely initiated gardens—are havens
from the scandal, though subject to the same corruptions and
degenerations.[3] God's garden is Dante's and for John the Divine's vision
of the human future which is already present in the divine timeless
topography. The "garden" image for Dante is not a memory of a lost
Golden Age but a projection of an eschatological redeemed history
which is both becoming and already here. It is distinct from the earlier
mythological and pastoral traditions, for it poetically synthesizes a
theology about history, time, and the divine-human relationship.
Through the "garden" metaphor and its topographical opposite, the
wilderness, Dante explores the theology of divine space, the historical
interlude, and the human condition or state of being in relationship to
these.

Dante uses the metaphor of garden (*orto* or *giardino*) and gardener
(*ortolano*) in a few carefully selected locations in the *Commedia*. Just as
in the Bible (John 15:1), Dante uses the God as gardener metaphor only
once ("l'ortolano etterno," *Paradiso*, Canto XXVI, 65) when the pilgrim
happens to be talking to John the evangelist. The garden metaphor,
however, as "orto" occurs twice in *Inferno* (Canto XXIX, 129; Canto
XXXIII, 119), once in *Purgatorio* as "giardino" (Canto VI, 105) where
it refers to the Empire, and seven times in *Paradiso*: three as "orto"
(Canto XII, 72, 104; Canto XXVI, 64) and four as "giardino" (Canto
XXIII, 71; XXVI, 110; XXXI, 97; XXXII, 39). The metaphors in
Inferno are of the "bad garden," the "Church" perverted by clerical
corruption. In *Purgatorio*, Canto VI, 103–105, "il giardino" is the
idealized Empire. In *Paradiso*, the "garden" is the *hortus conclusus* or
the Church (Canto XII), the vineyard where Saint Dominic worked; in
Canto XXVI, the garden Adam identifies as "l'eccelso giardino" (lofty
garden) (110) is Eden, which contrasts with the universal or celestial
garden, the triumphant garden of God of *Paradiso* (Cantos XXIII, 71;
XXVI, 64; XXXI, 97; XXXII, 39).

Dante very specifically restricts his use of the garden metaphor to
the Church, the Empire, and God's celestial garden in contrast to the
classical *locus amoenus* version of the earthly paradise or Garden of
Eden, which Dante calls the "selva antica" (ancient wood) (*Purg.*
XXVIII, 37),[4] language that instantly recalls Virgil's *Aeneid*. In
contrast to the "selva oscura," (dark wood) (*Inf.* I, 2) and "*selva
selvaggia*" (savage forest) (*Inf.* I, 5) of *Inferno* I, Eden is a "compagna
santa," (holy plain) (*Purg.* XXVIII, 118) or "divina foresta" (divine

forest) (*Purg.* XXVIII, 2), Dante here choosing language to sanctify rather than transfigure the *locus amoenus* topos. His description of the "eccelso giardino" (lofty garden), the phrase Adam uses to describe Eden when Dante meets him in heaven (*Par.* XXVI, 110), recalls other ancient versions of the *locus amoenus* topos, which in *Purgatorio* are combined with Edenic and Golden Age innocence:

> Quelli ch'anticamente poetaro
> l'età d l'oro e suo stato felice,
> forse in Parnaso esto loco sognaro.
> Qui fu innocente l'umana radice;
> qui primavera sempre e ogne frutto . . .
>
> (*Purg.* XXVIII, 139–143)[5]

[They who in olden times sang of the Age of Gold and its happy state perhaps in Parnassus dreamed of this place. Here the root of mankind was innocent; here is always spring, and every fruit . . .]

This "garden" motif is not unique to the Greco-Roman and Judaeo-Christian traditions. *Paradisus*, a word of Old Persian derivation (*pairidaëza*) means royal park, enclosure, or orchard.[6] Gardens may indeed have been mankind's first efforts at domesticating nature, and in describing an idyllic natural environment between the divine locale and the wilderness, poets imagine a mythicized version of human space which includes a peaceful and enclosed topographical area between the wilderness and their own domestic living space.[7] This is a pattern one finds as culturally dispersed as West Africa in the *Sundiata* (twelfth century), southern India in the *Manimekalai* (second century C.E.) or northern India in the *Mahabharata* (fourth century B.C.E. to second century C.E.), *Gilgamesh*, Genesis, Enoch, and the *Odyssey*.

Numerous scholars have explored the classical tradition of the *locus amoenus* (found in Ovid, Statius, Virgil, Homer, and Plato,[8] for example), the tradition of which underlies Dante's presentation of Eden in *Purgatorio*, XXVIII–XXXIII. Tracing the sources of Dante's earthly paradise to Latin and Greek descriptions of pastoral settings, these critics show how the classical literary environment synchronizes with the Christian biblical heritage to transform descriptions of Eden. The *locus amoenus* of the pastoral tradition is a domestication of the rawness of the earlier versions of mythical gardens from which man, because of his status as "human" was excluded, just as the pastoral genre is the gentrification of the epic. Dante's "pastoral oasis," the "selva antica" in *Purgatorio*,[9] what Adam calls the "eccelso giardino" (lofty garden), where Beatrice prepared Dante for the "lunga scala" (long stair) (*Par*. XXVI, 110–111), is just such a momentary retreat or stopping place in the arduous journey to the celestial garden of which, beautiful as it is, it remains only a very limited reflection.

Dante's garden imagery follows biblical traditions interpreted by Christian theologians and exegetes[10] and at the same time reaches back to fundamental symbolic traditions that predate Christianity.[11] Literary critics have been attentive to the classical tradition of the *locus amoenus*, the site for retreat, leisure, and love in opposition to the city,[12] or they have sought a Christian morality in medieval *locus amoenus* settings,[13] but I will argue that "gardens" in Dante are the site for theophanic experiences, and therefore qualitatively different to the *locus amoenus* traditions. The celestial garden is a utopian environment outside of time and removed from the forms of violence and division in which history is enacted; its surrogates on earth, Church and Empire, because they are time-bound, human contingencies, fulfill the utopian desire to reform or transform history and also express the temporal potential to decay. All these gardens are distinct from conventional pastoral environments, in which human leisure and lovemaking are frequent activities. In Dante's gardens, humans participate in the utopian opportunity only realized in a universal and timeless future. The metaphor of the celestial "garden" excludes uncultivated nature, usually associated with danger. Uncultivated nature includes the desert, the sea, or the forest, which symbolize wilderness, exile, and lost time—the most bleak human experiences, which in myth often result from violations of nature, internecine disputes, personal crisis, or war. Dante the pilgrim's time in the dark wood of *Inferno* I, Gilgamesh's journey through the forest after the death of his friend, and Odysseus's vexed sea adventures following the Trojan war are examples of how "wild nature" functions figuratively to express such bleak human experiences.

In his use of the garden metaphor and semantically related imagery for Church and divine domain as redeemed nature, Dante echoes Judaeo-Christian texts and their typologies, but he transforms them in a radical synthesis of poetry and theology. In Dante's metaphorical landscape there are temporary gardens existing in history as the Church and the Empire, as well as an eternal timeless garden, both created and guided by God, and into both of these mankind is invited. These places make a theophany possible because the alienation between man and God, matter and spirit, and life and death was harnessed, according to Dante and Christian theology, when the divine Word was made flesh (*Par.*, XXIII, 73).

Though Dante's image finds its source in the Bible, where it is used both in the Old and the New Testaments (Genesis, Ezekiel, Song of Songs, Gospel of John, and Apocalypse), it was broadly circulated in the Middle Ages and is found, for example, in Rabanus Maurus (c. 780–856), who appears in Canto XII, of the *Paradiso*. His encyclopedic *De Universo* (c. 842–846) includes a chapter in the twelfth book entitled "De Paradiso," in which he explains that "paradise" means garden and that there are three gardens: Eden or the *hortus deliciarum*, the Church or the *hortus conclusus*, and Paradise:

> Paradisus, id est hortus deliciarum, mystice aut Ecclesiam praesentem significat, aut terram viventium, ubi illi qui merentur per fidem rectam at bona opera victuri sunt in perpetuum. De quo Dominus ad latronem in cruce confitentem ait: "Amen dico tibi. hodie mecum eris in paradiso" (Luc.XXIII). Aliter autem paradisus (ut diximus) significat sanctam Ecclesiam, de qua in Genesi scriptum est: "Plantaverat Dominus Deus paradisum voluptatis a principio" (Gen.II). Paradisus Ecclesia est: sic de illa legitur in Canticis canticorum: "Hortus conclusus soror mea sponsa" (Cant. IV). A principio autem plantatur paradisus.[14]

> [Paradise is the garden of delights, which means mystically both the present Church and the Church alive on earth, where those who are deserving through correct faith and good deeds are nourished perpetually. For the Lord affirmed to the confessing thief on the cross, "Amen I say to you. Today you will be with me in Paradise" (Luke XXIII). And otherwise, Paradise (as we say) signifies Holy Church, as it is written in Genesis: "In the beginning the Lord God planted a pleasure garden" (Gen. II). Paradise is the Church: as it is recited in the Song of Songs: "The enclosed garden my sister my spouse." In the beginning, thus, the garden was planted.]

Rabanus Maurus's understanding of the metaphor of the garden as taken into Christian typology recalls Genesis, the Song of Songs, and the Gospel of Luke, but shows its wider application to a

soteriological theology of history in which the Church plays the central
role. The metaphor is used similarly in Bede's commentary on the Song
of Songs *Hortus est autem ecclesia*[15] (*The Garden is the Church*),
Honorius of Autun's *Speculum Ecclesiae, "Per Paradysum qui hortus
deliciarum dicitur, Ecclesia accipitur"* ("By Paradise, which is said to be
a garden of delights, we should understand the Church"),[16] as well as in
Thomas Aquinas's commentary on the Gospel of John.[17]

In *Inferno* Dante explores the opposite of the redeemed and
reconciled divine-human potentiality as topographically conveyed by the
"garden" metaphor. "Nature"—and the "natural world" in all its fiercest,
most oppressive, and perverted forms—is a metaphor for the wilderness
of the soul in the first canticle. Like other wilderness topographies in
mythic narratives like the *Odyssey* or *Gilgamesh*, nature in the *Inferno*
is cruel: windy (Canto V, XV), hot, sandy, and desolate (Canto XIV),
dead (Canto XIII), or frozen (Canto XXXIII, XXXIV). The "selva
selvaggia," the anti-Eden of Canto I, *Inferno*, with its fearful and bestial
nature that threatens to destroy the pilgrim; the negative *locus amoenus*
of Canto XIII, "non fronda verde, non rami schietti, non pomi" (no
green leaves, no smooth boughs, no fruit) (4–9); or the anti-garden of
Canto XXXIV—all these images counter the natural world of the *locus
amoenus* topos.

The garden of God stands against the *Inferno* as Dante the
pilgrim moves from this "selva oscura," or desert of failed desire, to the
transcendent "giardino" where grows the rose in "che'l verbo divino
carne si fece" (where the divine word became flesh) (XXIII, 73):

> Perché la faccia mia sì t'innamora,
> che te non ti rivolgi al bel giardino
> che sotto i raggi di Cristo s'infiora?
> Quivi è la rosa in che'l verbo divino
> carne si fece; quivi son li gigli
> al cui odor si prese il buon cammino.
>
> *(Inf. XXIII, 70–75)*

[Why does my face so enamor you that you turn not to the fair garden
that blossoms beneath the rays of Christ? Here is the Rose wherein
the Divine Word became flesh; here are the lilies by whose odor the
good way was taken.]

Here Beatrice draws Dante's attention to the difference between her beauty and the resplendent garden in which the incarnation took place and where the reconciliation between man and God became and becomes possible. Dante uses a similar garden-related redeemed sexual image in the closing canto to the poem when he has St. Bernard say to the Virgin Mary:

> Nel ventre tuo si raccese l'amore,
> per lo cui caldo ne l'etterna pace
> così è germinato questo fiore.
>
> (Inf. XXXIII, 7–9)

[In thy womb was rekindled the Love under whose warmth this flower in the eternal peace has thus germinated.][18]

Culling imagery from long-standing theological and biblical texts, Dante presents a metaphorical understanding of the garden that transfigures the *locus amoenus* topos, which is also a site for lovemaking, for as Beatrice tells us, the incarnation, the transcendent act of love between God and mankind, occurred in God's garden. What Dante has done here is to diminish all the versions of gardens represented in the classical epic tradition and classical pastoral poetry, as well as the secular poetry of the Middle Ages where the *locus amoenus* is featured, and replace them with the eternal garden and the supreme act of love, the result of which was God's birth as man, the act that transformed the human status and made possible "il buon cammino" (the good road), the journey toward a reconciliation between God and man.

The utopian celestial garden first referred to by Beatrice in *Paradiso* XXIII is the focus of *Paradiso* XXVI when Dante must confess his love to the beloved disciple, John, and where he discusses Eden with Adam. In this canto, Dante advances an elaborate commentary on the central scriptural theme of the garden and gardener, connecting it to the organizing themes of his own poem, thus placing his poem in this exalted theological tradition, while presenting his own personal journey in similar semantic terms. The metaphor of "God the Gardener" controls the themes of the canto, and the John-Adam connection draws together the eternal, celestial gardener and the first gardener; the garden at the beginning and end of time; and the unchanging eternity of the eternal celestial garden, which in perpetual motion is the end-point of history, to the fleeting human residence in the Garden of Eden, contrasting the divine Paradise, or "enclosed garden," with the potentially permanent or temporary exilic human condition. The canto also points to three gardens, all of which exist in different times and space: the first is the garden of the eternal gardener, the *hortus conclusus* of Paradise, where space and time are infinite; the second is the *hortus deliciarum*, the natural garden of pleasure, or Eden, which man inhabited for a brief moment in time and where the first transgression took place; and the third is the *hortus conclusus* of the Church, which began with the redemption and exists in historical time only.

In the final flourish of Dante's profession of "Love" in Canto XXVI, the poet deploys the God the Gardener metaphor:

> Le fronde onde s'infronda tutto l'orto
> de l'ortolano etterno, am' io cotanto
> quanto da lui a lor di bene è porto
>
> (*Par.* XXVI, 64–66)

In rephrasing the biblical metaphor from John 15:1, "Ego sum vitis vera, et pater meus agricola est" (I am the true vine and my father is the gardener), Dante's poetic extravagance in these three lines draws attention to the centrality of this sentence. The metaphor and its prominent position in the canto provide the thematic link that unites the two sections of the canto: the interrogation on love (1–66) and the encounter with Adam (79–142).[19]

The motifs—particularly of gardens, gardeners, and love, introduced in lines 64–66—bring the main themes of the canto together. The ostentatious technical display and accumulation of poetic and rhetorical devices show that Dante intended a special place for these lines. Like John, who, more than any of the other evangelists, deploys a range of rhetorical devices in the service of his message, Dante, in the company of the evangelist likewise parades his literary virtuosity in a poetic display that draws attention to its excess. Dante's "eternal gardener" recalls not only John 15:1 and resonances of Apocalypse 2:7, "Vincenti, dabo ei edere de ligno vitae, quod est in Paradiso Dei mei," but also the entire biblical tradition of the garden of God.

The God the Gardener metaphor is unique to John's gospel, and John 15:1–7 is an elaborate expansion of the metaphor, with Jesus as the vine and the Father as the gardener. The "garden" image occurs more frequently in the Bible than the "gardener," and the only use of the gardener metaphor for the divinity is John 15:1. For John, the garden image is a return to established Hebraic imagery, with the vine as Israel and God its husbandman. But John goes further than his sources, because he situates the central events in Jesus' life in a garden ("hortus"), unlike the other gospel versions, making the garden the space where the central events in the human-divine relationship are dramatially enacted. In John, Jesus is arrested in a garden (18:1), he is crucified, buried, and resurrected in a garden (19:41), and Mary Magdalene mistakes him for a gardener when she encounters him after he has risen in a garden: "Illa existimans quia hortulanus esset" (thinking it was the gardener) (20:15).

The garden metaphor in Canto XXVI thus locates the redemption in a garden and the first transgression in Eden, which undoubtedly would have been commonplaces for the medieval imagination. Thomas Aquinas's commentary on the gospel of John, for example, specifically draws attention to the unique character of the Johannine gospel narrative, for he is the only evangelist to locate all the central events in Jesus' life in a garden:

> Ubi notandum, quod Christus in horto captus, et in horto passus, et in horto sepultus fuit: ad designandum quod per suae passionis virtutem liberamur a peccato quod Adam in horto deliciarum commisit, et quod per eum Ecclesia consecratur, quae est sicut hortus conclusus.[20]

> [Where it is noted, that Christ was arrested in a garden, died in a garden, and was buried in a garden: all this designates that through his virtuous passion, we are liberated from the sin which Adam committed in the pleasure garden, and that through him the Church is consecrated, which is an enclosed garden.]

This is actually an expanded commentary on John 19:41, and Thomas includes all of salvation history, from the Garden of Eden to the Garden of the Resurrection: "Erat autem in loco ubi crucifixus est, hortus: et in horto monumentum novum, in quo nondum quisquam positus erat." (Now at the place where he had been crucified there was a garden: and in the garden a new tomb, not yet used for burial.) Thomas rests his expansion of the significance of the garden on references to garden settings found elsewhere in the gospel. These include, as already noted, John 18:1, where Jesus is arrested; John 19:41–42, where he died and was buried; and John 20:1–15, when Mary Magdalene comes to the garden where Jesus was buried and mistakes him for the gardener. Furthermore, the long discourse beginning "Ego sum vitis vera, et Pater meus agricola est" (John 15:1–27), with its elaboration of the metaphor of the vine and its branches, in which the branches bear fruit that will last, clearly is the inspiration for Thomas's idea of the Church as *hortus conclusus*. In Thomas, the garden is the location for the central events in salvation history during which the divisions between man and the divine have been most acute or reconciled. The setting includes the Garden of Eden, the *hortus deliciarum*, where Adam committed the sin; the garden where Jesus was arrested, where he died, where he was buried, where he liberated humans from the sin of Adam, and where God reconciled with man; and the enclosed garden whereby the Church was consecrated.

Dante also connects the redemption and Eden, specifically recalling the redemption in his declaration of love, "la morte ch'el sostenne perch'io viva" (the death that He sustained that I might live) (59), and the first portion of Adam's discussion in part 2 of the canto explaining what brought about his exile from the garden: "non il gustar del legno" (not the tasting of the tree) "ma solamente il trapassar del segno" (but solely the overpassing of the bound) (115, 117). He admits that it was not a sin of greedy pleasure but a violation of boundaries. The "garden" thus defines its boundaries and the redeeming behavior or attitudes that characterize its occupants. Those outside are in the wilderness (desert, forest, or sea) and exiled from its benefits.

The primary source for Dante's *hortus deliciarum*, Adam's "eccelso giardino" is the Judaeo-Christian Golden Age memory, the Garden of Eden, the Earthly Paradise, described in Genesis:

> plantaverat autem Dominus Deus paradisum voluptatis a principio in quo posuit hominem quem formaverat produxitque Dominus Deus de humo omne lignum pulchrum visu et ad vescendum suave lignum etiam vitae in medio paradisi lignumque scientiae boni et mali. (2:8–9)

> [Then the Lord God planted a garden in Eden away in the east, and there he put the man whom he had formed. The Lord God made trees spring from the ground, all trees pleasant to look at and good for food; and in the middle of the garden he set the tree of life and the tree of knowledge of good and evil.]

This garden was also the location of the first transgression (as Adam's speech in XXVI reminds us), the beginning of time, and man's initial alienation from God:

> et ait ecce Adam factus est quasi unus ex nobis sciens bonum
> et malum nunc ergo ne forte mittat manum suam et sumat
> etiam de ligno vitae et comedat et vivat in aeternum emisit
> eum Dominus Deus de paradiso voluptatis ut operaretur terram
> de qua sumptus est eiecitque Adam et conlocavit ante
> paradisum voluptatis cherubim et flammeum gladium atque
> versatilem ad custodiendam viam ligni vitae. (3:22–24)

> [He [God] said, "The man has become like one of us, knowing
> good and evil; what if he now reaches out his hand and takes
> fruit from the tree of life also, eats it and lives forever?" So
> the Lord God drove him out of the garden of Eden to till the
> ground from which he has been taken. He cast him out, and to
> the east of the garden of Eden he stationed the cherubim and a
> sword whirling and flashing to guard the way to the tree of
> life.]

Humans were expelled from this *paradiso voluptatis* into time and history, and from the New Testament on, the garden became not a memory of an uncontaminated divinely ordered past but a projection into an eschatological future, a utopian promise that humans could participate in constructing.

In Canto XXVI, Dante also refers to these becoming and future redeemed gardens. One of these is the *hortus conclusus*, the Church (as implied by John 15:1 f.), with God as the gardener, the vine as Jesus, and the productive branches as his followers. This parable inspired the early model of the Church as a surrogate terrestrial paradise, where the community of disciples were the fruitful branches and the unproductive ones were quickly severed: "Omnem palmitem in me non ferentem fructum, tollet eum: et omnem qui fert fructum, purgabit eum, ut fructum plus adferat" (Every barren branch of mine he cuts away; and every fruiting branch he cleans, to make it more fruitful still") (15:2). In the context of Canto XXVI, the Church as "enclosed" likewise draws boundaries ("si praecepta mea servaveritis") (if you heed my commands) (John 15:10), and violating these results in exile, excision, or exclusion, examples of which appear in *Inferno*. Dante, with images of biting, recalls the transgressive eating of fruit of Genesis 3 and the promised redemptive fruit of Apocalypse 2; he contrasts the love-bite of redemptive love, "sì che tu suone/ con quanti denti questo amor ti morde" (so that you declare with how many teeth this love grips you) (50–51) and "Tutti quei morsi/ che posson far lo cor volgere a Dio" (All those things whose bite can make the heart turn to God) (55–56) with the tasting of transgressive love ("il gustar del legno") (115). Here he distinguishes between the *hortus deliciarum* and the *hortus conclusus*, Eden and the Church, and the Augustinian distinction between "l'amor torto" (wrong love) (62), which occurred first in the pleasure garden, and "l'amor diritto" (right love) (63), which draws one to God, where John promises "Vincenti, dabo ei edere de ligno vitae, quod est in Paradiso dei mei" (Apocalypse 2:7), the promised garden at the end of time where Empire and Church are finally transfigured as a celestial garden.

This theme of Church as *hortus conclusus*, or terrestrial paradise, has roots in early Christianity. Pseudo-Barnabus (6:8–19) identified Christ and the Church with Paradise,[21] and the same idea is repeated by Irenaeus of Lyons, "Plantata est enim Ecclesia paradisus in hoc mundo" (For the Church has been planted as a *paradisus* in this world).[22] The post-Constantinian church tended to neglect the garden typology for Church and God, choosing instead imperial language as, for example, in Eusebius, who preferred the idea of Empire as an image for the celestial kingdom rather than the Church as temporary Paradise.[23]

The Church as garden, defined in *Paradiso* XXVI, is dramatically enacted in *Inferno* and *Paradiso* XII. As a divinely originated institution existing in history, in contrast to the celestial utopia, the garden is subject to cupidity or transcendence and to all the human distortions of time and desire. In *Inferno*, the language of the Church is wrenched from its roots and twisted to express temporal and rapacious personal desires that taint the institution and its soteriological function. For example, in *Inferno* XXIX, the corrupt ecclesiastical garden is dramatized by two leprous inmates condemned to an eternal "gran rabbia del pizzicor" (81) (great fury of the itch). Both attempted to subvert nature, ostensibly by their alchemical work, but their actual violation is revealed incidentally in their speeches. The first speaker boasted he could fly, and like all flights that mechanically emulate a true "ascent," this too, as a twisted desire, was doomed to failure. The other leper who leans on him, like his companion, "di natura buona scimia" (a good ape of nature) (139), takes the agricultural imagery of the Church to agree with Dante the pilgrim about the vanity of the Sienese:

ne l'orto dove tal seme s'appica;
a tra 'ne la brigata in che disperse
Caccia d'Ascian lza vigna e la gran fonda.

(*Inf.* XXIX, 129–131)

[in the garden where such seed takes root; and except for the
company in which Caccia d'Asciano squandered the vineyard and the
great purse.]

Words like *orto* (garden), *seme* (seed), and *vigna* (vineyard)—all with
specific and consistent biblical and ecclesiastical connotations—in the
mouth of a perverter of nature, appropriated to discuss a debased
community of twelve Sienese libertines whose actions and numbers
parody the disciples,[24] counterfeit the garden of the Church. Ironically,
Capocchio, the speaker (136), condemns the prodigality of the Sienese,
but at the same time reveals his own ingenious capacity to distort
words as he had distorted nature. His violence against the nature
language of the Church parallels his attempted violence against nature
itself. As a consequence, Dante shows how the signature of the Church
can be forged by the imitation of its language. The words or metaphors
are not necessarily the reality they pretend to represent.

In Canto XXXIII of the *Inferno*, Dante discloses another example
of the human willingness to corrupt the utopian possibility for which
the "garden" as Church is a metaphor. Here *frate* Alberigo, who is still
alive and a member of the clergy and in hell with other traitors-to-
guests for his murder of Manfred and his son, describes himself as

i' son quel da le frutta del mal orto,
che qui riprendo dattero per figo.

(*Inf.* XXXIII, 119–120)

[I am he of the fruits from the evil garden, and here I am paid date for
fig.]

This is not merely a reference to his signal to the assassins at the
banquet where his guests were murdered,[25] but a specific reference to the
moral failure of the Church which his action confirmed. As the only
still-alive occupant Dante-pilgrim encounters in hell, Friar Alberigo, as
a murderer and violator of table fellowship, as well as a member of the
"Frati Gaudenti," is exemplary of the fruit of the evil garden, the

corrupt Church, and of human action directed against the utopian ideal. He openly declares his moral turpitude, like a devil in a medieval pageant drama, with the same ignorance of the horror of such a blatant communication as he has of the status of his physical body. In his case, like the violent separation of his body and soul, words are also radically separated from the implications of their meaning; "here I receive a date for a fig," he says, almost offhandedly, forgetting that the "fig tree" is the emblem for "Israel" and the "chosen people."

The utopian ideal of the Church, the opposite of this perverted garden and its rotten fruit, unfolds in Canto XII, which is perhaps more specifically than any other in *Paradiso*, the canto of the Church. The canto parades metaphors for the Church—"L'essercito di Cristo," (Christ's army) (37), "la milizia," (soldiery) (41), "sua sposa," (his bride) (43), "l'orto," (72) "la vigna" (vineyard) (86), for example—but when the speaker, an unnamed Franciscan, who later identifies himself as St. Bonaventure (XII, 127), begins to talk about Dominic, he turns to the traditional garden metaphor with its related vineyard, seed, and fruit imagery, all associated with the "Santa Chiesa," (Holy Church) (107) or the "orto catolico" (Catholic garden) (104).

Dante intertwines Dominic's career with images and language that relate him specifically with Christ. (For example, when Dominic is identified, Dante has the speaker use a "Cristo" rhyme, one of four occasions when this happens in the entire poem [71–73].) The child of special circumstances at birth, according to the *Legenda Aurea*, to which the poet turns for Dominic's life, Dominic labored in the vineyard, exemplifying charity and exorcising corruption. Rephrasing John 15:1 ("Ego sum vitis vera et pater meus agricola est"), Dante calls him "l'agricola che Cristo elesse a l'orto suo per aiutarlo" (the husbandman whom Christ chose to help Him in His garden) (71–72). Dominic, the "mirabile frutto" (marvelous fruit) (65), parallels the "frutto della ventre" (fruit of the womb) of the Virgin. In Canto XII the unidentified Franciscan describes Dominic as the husbandman of the vineyard, who rooted out all the "sterpi eretici" (heretical brushwood) (100), examples of whom we saw in "l'orto malo"; and from Dominic sprang the waters by which the "orto catolico" (104) or the Church is made alive. Thus Dante shows the potential of the divinely constituted ecclesiastical garden, which in the absence of Christ and the celestial garden can function as a surrogate on earth, as a *locus amoenus* that is nevertheless active in history, guiding the passageway toward the celestial garden.

For Dante, the Empire as ideal, like the Church, offers the hope for a transformed and divinely guided human history.[26] Dante breaks with biblical tradition when he applies the garden metaphor to the Empire:

> ch'avete tu e 'l tuo padre sofferto
> per cupidigia di costà distretti,
> che 'l giardin de lo 'mperio sia diserto ...
>
> (*Purg.*, VI, 103–105)

[For you and your father, held back yonder by greed, have suffered the garden of the Empire to be laid waste.]

The quote comes from the long invective (VI, 76–151) addressed in the poet's voice, in which Dante denounces Italy's political, moral, and ecclesiastical corruption and decline. In using the garden metaphor for the Empire, Dante reveals the special "religious" status he accords to his ideal of the body politic, and his conviction about the possibility that history could be redeemed. This is in radical contrast with biblical traditions in which the garden of God remained as the idyllic image or shadow over all the human gardens that competed with it. In Ezekiel, for example, in the voice of God the Assyrian Empire, as a great cedar tree, is contrasted with the "Garden of God":

> cedri non fuerunt altiores illo in paradiso Dei abietes non adaequaverunt summitatem eius et platani non fuerunt aecquae frondibus illius omne lignum paradisi Dei non est adsimilatem illi et pulchritudini eius quoniam speciosum feci eum et multis condensisque frondibus et aemulata sunt eum omnia ligna voluptatis quae erant in paradiso Dei. (Ezekiel 31:8–9)

[No cedar in God's garden overshadowed it, no fir could compare with its boughs, and no plane-tree had such branches; not a tree in God's garden could rival its beauty. I, the Lord, gave it beauty with its mass of spreading boughs, and envy of all the trees of Eden, the garden of God.]

Here in Ezekiel, the "garden" image is a synecdoche for God's domain, which, as an ultimate measure of utopian perfection contrasts with all human constructions, whether political, architectural, or social; in this instance the Assyrian Empire, with its universalist claims, posed as an ideological threat to "Israel," a metaphor for binding moral "laws" and for the people of God, and God's truly universal garden. Though the empire emulated God's garden, its idolatrous imitation led to its status as a relic of history, to which all human constructions (in the Hebrew bible, at least), no matter how well they imitated God's garden, were ultimately doomed. For Dante, the Empire as a model of utopian political possibility was initiated by God and only corrupted by man. For Dante, the Empire, like the Church, was the human version of the divine garden, an imagined possibility of a redemptive human institution, in its purest form working against all the political divisiveness of history but anarchically undermined by individual cupidity. In Dante's view, in contrast to the biblical and Augustinian traditions, the earthly form of God's garden besides the Church is the Empire, an ideal that is, nonetheless, just as prone to decay as is the "giardino" of the Church.

Dante's metaphors in the *Divine Comedy* for the divinity and the Church are a compendium of ancient and medieval learning and culture, for his images cross the pagan-Christian boundaries, the urban-rural division, and the imperial and civic political models, and include sources in the whole range of the seven liberal arts. The "God the Gardener" and "God's garden" metaphors are more strictly biblical than others but, nonetheless, poetically represent a synthesis of theological, scriptural, and secular poetic traditions. In the utopian landscape described in the entire poem, Dante brings together the biblical traditions of gardens and wilderness and classical pastoral traditions.

When he uses the "garden" metaphor, Dante refers to the Bible and its commentary tradition to display the topography of heaven and its surrogates on earth, the Church and Empire. The "gardens" are eschatological projections into a redeemed future time, which is already present. But the earthly gardens, confined as they are by time and human susceptibilities to betrayal and desire, remain utopian models that can also be perverted or violated.

The "orto de l'ortolano etterno" (*Par.* XXVI, 64–65), however, is the cosmic garden where the ultimate reconciliation between man and God and the conquest of all that subverts divine principle have taken place and endure. It is not a temporary topography or a waiting place, or a memory of a past utopia. It is not a human replica of the "garden" like the Church or the Empire, but a divinely formed, living, resplendent, and transfigured garden, where Dante "vola con li occhi per questo giardino" (flies with his eyes throughout this garden), which prepares him "al montar per lo raggio divino" (to mount through the divine ray) (XXXI, 97–99), and also where St. Bernard tells him all the heavenly bodies reside and "igualmente empierà questo giardino" (equally shall fill this garden) (XXXII, 39). Unlike all the other authors in the classical, medieval, and even biblical (particularly the *Cantica Canticorum*) literary traditions who describe gardens, portraying their natural wonders in terms of sensual imagery, Dante really provides very little in the way of description. This is because Dante's garden is primarily a metaphorical topography, one that links back, as religious imagery tends to do, to mankind's earliest symbol traditions in an effort to talk about the human-divine relationship. We know about the stars, the lilies, the rose, and finally the light, but these are just hints about the topography of this cosmic garden. We know also that this heavenly garden has made possible the reconciliation between man and God. We know what this "garden" image synthesizes about the human condition, potential, and relationship to the divinity. But unlike all the *locus amoenus* descriptions Dante knew, we don't know what this one looks, smells, or sounds like. Like so much of what Dante tells us about *Paradiso*, this garden eludes representation because

appressando sé al suo disire,
nostro intelletto si profonda tanto
che dietro la memoria non può ire.

(*Par.* I, 7–9)

[As it draws near to its desire, our intellect enters so deep that memory cannot go back.]

NOTES

1. All quotes from the Vulgate are from *Biblia Sacra: Iuxta Valgatem Versionem* (Stuttgart: Württembergische Bibelanstalt, 1969). Translations from the Bible into English are from the *New English Bible with the Apocrypha* (New York: Oxford University Press, 1971). "To him who is victorious I will give the right to eat from the tree of life that stands in the Garden of God." All other translations from Latin are the author's.

2. See Giuseppe Mazzotta, "Order and Transgression in the *Divine Comedy*," in *Ideas of Order in the Middle Ages, Acta*, vol. XV, 1988, 1–21, for a nuanced presentation of order and transgression in Dante.

3. These ideas are developed extensively in Giuseppe Mazzotta, *Dante, Poet of the Desert: History and Allegory in the Divine Comedy* (Princeton, N.J.: Princeton University Press, 1979). See particularly 112–116 and 119–122.

4. See Eugenio Ragni's essay in *Enciclopedia Dantesca V*, Sa–Z (Roma: Istituto Della Enciclopedia Italiana Fondata da Giovanni Treccani, 1976), 137–142, for a full discussion of the word selva in Dante's works.

5. All references to the *Divine Comedy* are to the Charles S. Singleton edition (Italian text, translation, and commentary): *Inferno* (Princeton: Princeton University Press, 1970); *Purgatorio* (Princeton: Princeton University Press, 1973); *Paradiso* (Princeton: Princeton University Press, 1975).

6. A. Bartlett Giamatti, *The Earthly Paradise and the Renaissance Epic* (Princeton: Princeton University Press, 1966), 11. Giamatti gives a summary of the versions of the "garden" in ancient Hebraic, Greek, Roman, and early Christian traditions, tracing the classical pastoral tradition and its overlap into medieval versions of the Garden of Eden.

7. George H. Williams, *Wilderness and Paradise in Christian Thought* (New York: Harper & Brothers, 1962).

8. See Giamatti, *Earthly Paradise*; Derek Pearsall and Elizabeth Salter, *Landscapes and Seasons of the Medieval World* (London: Paul Elek, 1973); Renato Poggioli, *The Oaten Flute* (Cambridge, Mass.: Harvard University Press, 1975).

9. "Pastoral oasis" is Poggioli's term. "Dante 'Poco Tempo Silvano': A Pastoral Oasis in the Commedia," in *Oaten Flute*, 135–152.

10. Pearsall and Salter explore these traditions in the chapter entitled "The Landscape of Paradise," *Landscapes and Seasons in the Medieval World*, 56–75, showing the range of descriptions of Paradise by theologians, poets, artists, and travel writers in the Middle Ages.

11. Paul Ricoeur, "Metaphor and Symbol," in *Interpretation Theory: Discourse and the Surplus of Meaning* (Fort Worth, Tex.: The Texas Christian University Press, 1976), discusses the sources and nature of these fundamental symbols.

12. Hymn to Demeter, Homer, Horace, Ovid, Virgil, for example. See Giamatti, "Classical Gardens," in *Earthly Paradise*, 33–47, for an overview.

13. D.W. Robertson, "The Doctrine of Charity in Medieval Literary Gardens," *Speculum* (1951): 24–49, explores a number of versions of medieval gardens from *Beowulf* to Andreas Capellanus's *De Amore* to Chaucer's "The Merchant's Tale," arguing that they all reinforce the same lesson, the repudiation of cupidity and embrace of charity.

14. Rabanus Maurus, *De Universo, PL* CXI, col. 334–335.

15. Bedae Vernerabilis, *Opera, In Cantica Canticorum, Corpus Christianorum* CXIXB (Turnholti: Typographi Brepols Editores Pontificii. 1983), 263.

16. *PL* 172, col. 833.

17. S. Thomae Aquinatis, *Super Evangeluim S. Ioannis Lectura*, ed. P. Raphaelis Cai (Taurini and Romae: Marietti, 1952).

18. Singleton translates "germinato" as "unfolded," which modifies the word's generative connotations.

19. For other commentaries on Canto XXVI, see Joseph Cremona, *"Paradiso* XXVI," in *Cambridge Readings in Dante's Comedy*, ed. Kenelm Foster and Patrick Boyde (Cambridge: Cambridge University Press, 1981), 174–190; Pier Vincenzo Mengaldo, "Appunti sul Canto XXVI del *Paradiso*," in *Linguistica e retorica di Dante* (Pisa: Nistri-Lischi, 1978), 223–246; Giovanni Getto, "Il Canto XXVI del *Paradiso*," *Lectura Dantis Scaligera* (Florence: Le Monnier, 1966), 26; Fernando Figurelli, "Il Canto XXVI del *Paradiso*," *Nuove Letture Dantesche*, VII (Florence: Le Monnier, 1974), 127–150; and Kevin Brownlee, "Language and Desire in Paradiso XXVI," *Lectura Dantis* 6 (1990), 46–59.

20. S. Thomae Aquinatis, *Super Evangelium S. Ioannis Lectura*, 457.

21. Williams, *Wilderness and Paradise* , 28.

22. Irénée de Lyon, *Contre les Hérésies*, Livre V, xx, 2, ed. Adelin Rousseau, Tome II, texte et traduction (Paris: Éditions du Cerf, 1969); Irenaeus, *Against Hersesies*, in *The Ante-Nicene Fathers* (Buffalo, 1924), I, 548.

23. *Ecclesiastical History* (I, iv, 5–15) and Williams, *Wilderness and Paradise in Christian Thought*, 35.

24. Singleton notes that Dante names five of this crew, called the Brigata Spendereccia of Siena. *Inferno*, 539.

25. According to Singleton, citing the commentary of Benvenuto, Friar Alberigo is said to have signalled the invitation to the assassins with the phrase, "Bring the fruit." *Inferno*, 621.

26. Dante develops and explains his political philosophy in *De Monarchia*, ed. Federico Sanguineti (Italy: Garzanti, 1985).

FATHER GOD AND MOTHER EARTH: NATURE-MYSTICISM IN THE ANGLO-SAXON WORLD

Karen Jolly

FIELD CEREMONIES

Here is the remedy by which you can improve your fields, if they will not grow properly, or if any harm has been done to them by sorcery or witchcraft.

Take then at night before daybreak four sods from four sides of the land and mark how they stood before.

Then take oil and honey and yeast and milk of all the cattle that are on the land, and part of every kind of tree growing on the land, except hard trees, and part of every well-known herb, except burdock only, and pour holy water on them, and then let it drip three times on the bottom of the sods.

And then say these words:

Crescite, grow, *et multiplicamini*, and multiply, *et replete*, and fill, *terram*, the earth. *In nomine patris et filii et spiritus sancti sitis benedicti.*

And Our Father as often as the other.

And afterwards carry the sods to church and have a priest sing four Masses over the sods, and turn the green sides to the altar. And afterwards take the sods back to where they stood before, before the setting of the sun.

And he must have four crosses made of 'quickbeam' [aspenwood] and let him write on the end of each: Mattheus and Marcus, Lucas and Johannes. Lay the cross at the bottom of the pit (made by cutting away the sods).

Say then:

Crux Mattheus. Crux Marcus. Crux Lucas. Crux Sanctus Johannes.

Then take the sods and lay them on the crosses. And say then nine times these words: *Crescite* and as often the Our Father.

And then turn to the east and bow humbly nine times, and say then these words:

Eastwards I stand, for favors I pray.
I pray the great Lord, I pray the mighty prince,
I pray the holy Guardian of the heavenly kingdom.
Earth I pray and sky,
and the true holy Mary,
and heaven's might and high hall,
that by the grace of the Lord
I may pronounce this charm, by my firm will,
raise up these crops to our worldly benefit,
fill this earth by firm faith,
make beautiful these grasslands; as the prophet said
that he would have favors on earth
who dealt out alms judicially,
according to the will of the Lord.

Then turn three times with the course of the sun, then stretch yourself along the ground and say the litany there. And say then *Sanctus Sanctus Sanctus* to the end. Sing then *Benedicite* with arms outstretched and *Magnificat* and Our Father three times. And commend it (the land) to Christ and Holy Mary, and to the Holy Rood in praise and worship, and to the benefit of the owner of the land and all those who are subject to him.

When all this is done, then take unknown seed from beggars and give them twice as much as you take from them. And collect all the plowing implements together, bore a hole in the plow-tail and put incense and fennel and hallowed soap and hallowed salt in it.

Then take the seed and place it on the body of the plow. Say then:

Erce, Erce, Erce, mother of earth,
may the omnipotent eternal Lord grant you
fields growing and thriving,

flourishing and bountiful,
bright shafts of millet-crops,
and of broad barley-crops,
and of white wheat-crops,
and of all the crops of the earth.
May the eternal Lord grant him,
and his saints who are in heaven,
that his produce may be safe against every foe,
and secure against every harm
from witchcraft sown throughout the land.
Now I pray the Sovereign Who created this world
that no woman may be so eloquent, and no man so powerful,
that they can upset the words thus spoken.

When you drive forth the plow and cut the first furrow, say
then:

Hail to thee, earth, mother of men,
may you be fruitful under God's protection,
filled with food for the benefit of men.

Then take flour of every kind and have a loaf baked as big as
the palm of your hand, and knead it with milk and with holy
water, and lay it under the first furrow.
Say then:

Field full of food for the race of man
brightly blooming, be thou blessed
in the holy name of Him Who created heaven
and the earth on which we live.
The God Who made this earth
grant us the gift of fertility
that each grain may by profitable to us.

Then say three times: *Crescite. In nomine patris sitis
benedicti, Amen.* And Our Father three times.
MS Cotton Caligula A vii, fol.171a (twelfth century)[1]

This ceremony for healing the land calls on both God the Father and
Mother Earth, and expresses a mystical view of nature produced by the
early medieval synthesis between Germanic and Christian culture

(roughly 600–1100); it also stands on the brink of a radical change in European thought that arose in the twelfth century. The oddness of the pre-twelfth-century view from the standpoint of later European or "Western" thought forces us to reassess the twelfth-century premises on which these modern scientific views were founded, in order to properly understand the earlier views from which they emerged.

This "nature mysticism" of the early medieval period reveals the existence of holistic worldviews lacking the fundamental distinctions of natural-supernatural and reason-revelation taken for granted in modern Western culture. People *experienced* and *knew* this unified reality through their senses and interior reflection on what they perceived. The framework of meaning governing this perception was the result of the Germanic-Christian synthesis, creating a worldview in which microcosm and macrocosm were interconnected through God, and everything was alive with the presence of God and other spiritual beings.

On the other hand, the modern Western perception of nature is rooted in a post-twelfth-century worldview that has developed rigidly defined categories that separate things that can be observed and tested with the senses as "rational" and "natural" from the supernatural, things that by definition cannot be investigated because they don't follow the "laws" of nature this mode of rationality has discovered or devised. Western culture has placed a premium on a certain kind of logical order in things, with certain tests ("empirical evidence," "repeatability") that now set the standard for what is real or true. Wrapped up in this separation process is the related evolution of the concepts of nature and mysticism: mysticism becomes a distinct way of relating to supernature when "science" isolates nature as a "rationally" understood phenomenon.[2]

A worldview is the way a culture, or an individual, perceives its relationship to the divine or supernatural, the physical realm, and other people.[3] Despite the modern division of these three into distinct categories, they are clearly inseparable: beliefs about nature and divinity are interdependent, and social relations obviously reflect religious beliefs as well as affect the human relationship to the environment. However, the modern Western system of thought makes a distinction between them, based on whether there is sufficient *proof* to accept a particular phenomena as *fact*, using scientifically verifiable *evidence*. For example, when someone explains a natural phenomenon such as an earthquake as a sign from God, the reaction of many a modern Westerner would be "That's too mystical an explanation" or "How can you know that?" Or if someone argued that a traffic fatality was the work of demons, the modern Western line of thinking would reject this explanation as the least likely because it needs more proof; other, more impersonal, explanations (such as coincidence or human error) require less evidence and are hence more likely. This type of thinking assumes that spiritual entities are non-existent or less real than natural forces measurable by human observation.

The critical phase for the development of this mode of rationality about human beings in relation to nature and the supernatural occurred in the twelfth century, when some fundamental concepts about knowledge developed, a product of a synthesis of classical Christian thinking. By looking at what views were like before this twelfth-century revolution in epistemology, we can see all the better how radically things developed in the direction of distinguishing the supernatural and mysticism as nonrational ways of knowing. Nature emerges out of supernature only when this system of rationality is developed; earlier views of nature therefore appear "mystical" because nature and supernature were not differentiated. They were perceived as one, both experienced simultaneously through one another, using the senses as well as the imagination.

This early medieval holistic view is more than just perception; it is also action: humans interact with nature as a channel to the spiritual. The natural or physical affects human life materially and spiritually, and humans tap the spiritual through the physical. While modern Western culture has developed an affective view of nature to counterbalance the technological and scientific, early medieval culture saw nature from an effective perspective: changes in the microcosm are produced by changes in the macrocosm and vice-versa, and humans can mediate that interaction. There was, then, a very concrete, pragmatic application of nature mysticism in the early medieval period.

In this exploration of early medieval views of nature as mystical, I will first examine the question of mysticism as a construct and offer some suggestions for approaching it in its historical context. Second, I will address the evidence that early medieval worldviews were founded on an essentially mystical understanding of nature. Last, I will use the Anglo-Saxon tradition as an example of these emerging views.

Ways Of Knowing: Mysticism

Two fundamental and inter-related questions arise whenever medieval mysticism is discussed: what *is* mysticism and why were there so many mystics writing in the High Middle Ages? I am reversing this second question in order to better understand mysticism as a phenomenon: why weren't there any mystical writings in the *Early Middle Ages*? A cursory glance at any anthology or study of European mysticism usually shows a gap at roughly 600–1100. Prior to 600, classical Christian mysticism was grounded in Neoplatonic thought, most prominently in the author known as Pseudo-Dionysus; after 1100, both philosophical and descriptive treatises by mystics flourished, particularly in the thirteenth and fourteenth centuries. The explanation for this gap is obviously complex; nonetheless, we can only take one piece at a time.

The piece on which I would like to focus, which made the difference between virtually no mysticism in 950, and lots in 1350, is their view of the natural world and the relationship of humans to it. While recognizing that social, economic, and political factors had a role in the differences between the two time periods, my argument is this: Locating mysticism in the earlier medieval period is hard because of a lack of distinction between reason and revelation, nature and supernature; the development of that distinction caused mysticism to be set aside as a separate kind of knowledge from the rationality established in the twelfth-century renaissance. If we define mysticism from within its historical context, we see that European worldviews shifted significantly so that mysticism emerged as a distinct category only after 1100.

Let us start with the generic concepts of mysticism used commonly today. A mystic is a person who has experienced a life-transformation through direct contact with something "Other" in the spiritual dimension (called God or Divinity or Reality); usually this experience is the result of intense meditation, and is not subject to rational or material explanations or descriptions. A mystic is someone for whom God is more real than the sensory world, and thus, for mystics, the life of this material world is less important to who they are than the experience of God; this view causes the mystic to see all of the natural world in terms of the spiritual dimension so real to him or her.

We only know about such people because occasionally they may choose to do the impossible, that is, write or tell about their indescribable experience.[4] More so than with any other writings, language itself is insufficient because it is based on the sensory world, while the mystical experience is of a totally other world. To describe it is in many ways to deny it, to place it in a foreign context. The antithesis between the experience and the telling means that many who had such experiences never talked or wrote about them.

Nonetheless, two traditions of mystical writing emerged in the High Middle Ages: philosophically argued treatises about the mystical experience, picking up on the Pseudo-Dionysian tradition of Late Antiquity (like the Cloud of Unknowing); and descriptive autobiographies detailing, usually through physical analogies, the mystical experience (like Julian of Norwich).[5]

Mysticism, therefore, is the product of the study of the people we know about who talked about their experiences in some fashion. As an ism, it is a construct used to cluster together a group of individuals, based on their records, who seem to have had a similar experience, and we then call these collective experiences a phenomenon, labeled mysticism.

Thus our first problem is that we need to distinguish between the mystical experience, to which we have no direct access ourselves, the individual mystic, and the writings by such individuals about their experience. Although we create the construct "mysticism" based on these mystical experiences, we cannot know any of these experiences directly, but only through the mystic's writings, which are framed within the individual mystic's worldview. There is a gap, then, between the experience and the writing, mediated by the individual mystic, who is a part of, and a product of, his or her own cultural environment.

Apart from this set of ideas, however, the modern usage of the adjective *mystical* is less strict, and vaguely describes anything that has to do with the supernatural—experiences perceived to be outside of the natural, scientifically explained material realm assumed by the modern worldview to be "real." Likewise, the related word *mystery* usually means today something that cannot be explained (yet) within Western terms of the rational. The use of these common terms reveals to us how much the Western notion of mysticism is colored by the prevailing scientific worldview.

In reaction to the lack of spirituality in the Western mode of rationality and in response to cross-cultural contacts, some scholars have attempted to develop this universal or generic definition of mysticism as a basis of study. This approach is problematic because it assumes that all "mystics" in all religions have had the same essential experience but just described it differently, according to their own religious traditions. However, by what mode of rationality can we penetrate into these mystics' experiences and know them to be the same? The evidence of mysticism, the writings of mystics, shows that mystics are inextricably intertwined with their own culture, so that, as Steven Katz has said, "there are no pure (i.e., unmediated) experiences."[6] I am reminded of T. S. Eliot's poem "Four Quartets," the part sung by Old Deuteronomy in the musical *Cats*:

> The moments of happiness . . .
> We had the experience but missed the meaning,
> And approach to the meaning restores the experience
> In a different form, beyond any meaning
> We can assign to happiness. I have said before
> That the past experience revived in the meaning
> Is not the experience of one life only
> But of many generations—not forgetting
> Something that is probably quite ineffable . . .[7]

Culture-specific language plays an even greater role in limiting mysticism because of mysticism's essentially indescribable nature, increasing the distance between the experience and the description even further than is found in ordinary discourse.

The desire to find a generic mysticism cross-culturally is a product of modern syncretism; those who seek it are consciously avoiding the differences between religions, searching for a single universal truth. They assume, unlike the usual Western mode of rationality, that the experiences are real and true and that the real and true bits of any mystics' description are the same parts as for other mystics—which ends up being very circular. As a result, I have to agree with Hans Penner that mysticism as a universal concept is an illusion, potentially distorting the religious system being examined.[8]

My rules, then, for using this term *mysticism* are as follows. First, mysticism must be seen in its historical context. If a generic mysticism exists, it is an outsider's construct, useful only for comparison purposes because it can help focus discussion. The danger of a generic definition of mysticism is that it is product of the most common—*but not necessarily the most important*—denominators. The common features found in many mystics' writings are not necessarily the definitive ones, and the unique factors we exclude may be essential components from their perspective, and thus significant to our understanding of their culture. The problem with comparative history is that the least important factors may end up dominating more important ones. *Universality* is not in itself the only or best measure of significance; it must be balanced with diversity.

Second, what constitutes mysticism must be *defined* only by and within the historical context. To do otherwise (i.e., from an outsider's definition) is to invoke parameters foreign to that culture. In practice, we should allow the culture being studied to define what is essential to their mysticism (if the concept exists), within their worldview's parameters.

Since our notions of what is mystical about a mystic are very much a product of post-twelfth-century thought, they bear examining in relation to this question of why we don't find mysticism in the early Middle Ages. In terms of the reversed question I am asking about medieval mysticism, or the lack of it, in the early Middle Ages, the contextual approach is much more appropriate than the generic. Most of all, this approach allows us to examine the way in which the development of medieval mysticism is intertwined with changing views of the natural world.

Views of Nature: The Early Middle Ages

Because early medieval worldviews are, from a modern standpoint, mystical, it is hard to then separate a group of phenomena that pre-twelfth-century Christians would perceive as other than the ordinary experience of reality. The distinctions that the modern mind might make between different experiences of reality are different from the early medieval; or if the terminology is similar, the meanings are distinguished for different reasons. Caroline Walker Bynum stated the difference between pre-and post-twelfth-century thought very clearly in her book *Jesus as Mother*:

From the world of the early Middle Ages, in which the
supernatural may break into everyday life at any moment and
anything may be a sign or "sacrament" of the holy, we move in
the twelfth century into a world in which what we today call the
material or secular is increasingly seen as having its own laws
and operations, as other than the spiritual and perhaps even
corrupting to it. To ninth-century theologians, for example, the
problem in dealing with the Eucharist was really the problem of
explaining how it could be of special import when in fact any
object or event might suddenly reveal God; by the thirteenth
century the problem was to explain how bread and wine, which
looked like bread and wine, could be anything else.[9]

This early medieval worldview, prevalent from the late seventh
century through the twelfth, is actually a complex mixture of different
traditions, which are better served by using the plural, *worldviews*.
However, scholars have accustomed themselves to talking about the
early medieval perspective as "Augustinian," a somewhat misleading
term, in that the great fourth-century Church Father is only remotely
responsible for some of the ideas, and inaccurate because it implies a
single, coherent system of thought that is shared, at most, by only a
small group of intellectuals in the early Middle Ages. Nonetheless, it is
a good place to begin, because the notions attributed to this worldview
lead us into posing some important questions about the relationships
between Christian thought and the Germanic animism surviving in
popular folklore. There is something very mystical about both of them
that pulls them together into a mixture that appears strange to the
modern mind. The familiar dichotomies of natural-supernatural,
rational-emotional, reason-revelation, and affective-effective are inter-
related in a different way than is common in post-twelfth-century
thought. An examination of a variety of early medieval sources reveals
a great deal of coalescence between these oppositions: from Gregory
the Great in the late sixth century to Ælfric in the eleventh, there is an
emerging tradition of a Christian nature-mysticism.

Early medieval views appear mystical to us because they did not
separate natural from supernatural in the rigid way that modern (or even
post-twelfth-century) thought does. The twelfth-century distinction
between supernatural and natural was based on two realms: the natural
one was material, observable, and transitory; the spiritual was above
and beyond the natural in its immutability. In this view the spiritual

occasionally impinged on the natural, but they were perceived as fundamentally different in their essence. On the other hand, early medieval writings tended to differentiate along the lines of visible and invisible, a basic distinction using sight that was not concerned with origins; rather, such views assumed that there were invisible things just as real as visible things, and that these things you could not see were *always* present in the things you could see.

For example, the animism of pre-Christian Germanic culture surviving through folklore believed that the material realm was infused with spiritual entities, and that people had coercive power over them: the Æsir, elves, dwarves, and spirits inhabiting trees, stones, and wells, as well as worms and invisible flying poisons, could be propitiated or counteracted through human action and word.[10] For example, medical remedies assumed the existence of unseen and hence spiritual entities resident in plants, as shown in the popular lay *The Nine Herbs Charm*:

Remember, Mugwort, what you made known,
what you arranged at the Great Proclamation.
You were called Una, the oldest of herbs,
you have power against three and against thirty,
you have power against poison and against infection,
you have power against the loathsome foe roving through the land.

And you, Plantain, mother of herbs,
open from the east, mighty inside.
Over you chariots creaked, over you queens rode,
over you brides cried out, over you bulls snorted.
You withstood all of them, you dashed against them.
May you likewise withstand poison and infection,
and the loathsome foe roving through the land.

Stune is the name of this herb, it grew on a stone,
it stands up against poison, it dashes against pain.
Unyielding it is called, it dashes against poison,
it drives out the hostile one, it casts out poison.
This is the herb that fought against the snake,
it has power against poison, it has power against infection,
it has power against the loathsome foe roving through the land.

Put to flight now, Venom-Loather, the greater poisons, though you are

the lesser,
you the mightier, conquer the lesser poisons, until he is cured of both.
Remember, Camomile, what you made known,
what you accomplished at Alorford,
that never a man should lose his life from infection,
after Camomile was prepared for his food.

This is the herb that is called Wergulu.'
A seal sent it across the sea ridge
a vexation to poison, a help to others.
It stands against pain, it dashes against poison,
it has power against three and against thirty,
against the hand of a fiend and against mighty devices,
against the spell of mean creatures.

There the Apple accomplished it against poison
that she (the loathsome serpent) would never dwell in the house.

Chervil and Fennel, two very mighty ones.
They were created by the wise Lord,
holy in heaven as He hung [on the cross];
He set and sent them to the seven worlds,
to the wretched and the fortunate, as a help to all.

These nine have power against nine poisons.
A worm came crawling, it killed nothing.
For Woden took nine glory-twigs,
he smote then the adder that it flew apart into nine parts.

Now these nine herbs have power against nine evil spirits,
against nine poisons and against nine infections:
Against the red poison, against the foul poison,
against the white poison, against the purple poison,
against the yellow poison, against the green poison,
against the black poison, against the blue poison,
against the brown poison, against the crimson poison.
Against worm-blister, against water-blister,
against thorn-blister, against thistle-blister,
against ice-blister, against poison-blister.

If any poison comes flying from the east,
or any from the north, [or any from the south],
or any from the west among the people.
Christ stood over diseases of every kind. [cross drawing]
I alone know a running stream
and the nine adders beware of it.
May all the weeds spring up from their roots,
the seas slip apart, all salt water,
when I blow this poison from you.

Mugwort, plantain open from the east, lamb's cress, venom-loather, camomile, nettle, crabapple, chervil and fennel, old soap; pound the herbs to a powder, mix them with the soap and the juice of the apple. Then prepare a paste of water and of ashes, take fennel, boil it with the paste and wash it with a beaten egg when you apply the salve, both before and after.

Sing this charm three times on each of the herbs before you prepare them, and likewise on the apple. And sing the same charm into the mouth of the man and into both his ears, and on the wound, before you apply the salve.[11]

Although this text uses herbs and salves, it does so with what we would consider "unscientific" means: spells, prayers, and ritual actions, done by someone with the ability to call upon that power, in order to bring out the essential virtue of these natural objects. We see here a convergence of physical and spiritual causes and cures of illness: bodily symptoms and interior problems, such as temptations from devils or attacks by spirits, are both lumped together and cured with physical (plants) and spiritual (prayers, charms) ingredients.

But even more important than these vestiges of pre-Christian religion is the fact that early Christianity fostered this same notion of the overlap of spiritual and material, thus fusing very nicely with the aforementioned Germanic notions. A commonplace found throughout Christian literature is the notion of "spiritual medicine," using the concept of healing as a metaphor for salvation. But it is much more than a metaphor in the early Middle Ages; the overlap of Christian ritual and physical healing can be located in four major components of Christian practice:

1. Exorcisms, in which the devil is driven out through the power
   of the liturgy; these exorcisms are also found in medical
   manuscripts as cures for illnesses with physical symptoms;
2. Liturgical rituals for the sick and dying that use blessings of
   oil and last rites to bring spiritual healing to someone who is
   suffering physically; these rituals are also incorporated into
   medical manuscripts;
3. The tradition of miracles and the cult of the saints, in which
   there is a power resident in the relics of the holy dead; and
4. The Eucharist itself, in which the transformation of bread and
   wine into the body and blood of Christ is able to accomplish a
   spiritual reconciliation between God and humans.

Baptismal and Eucharistic theology and ritual, central to the
belief and practice of Christianity, demonstrate this interconnectedness
in which visible and invisible, body and soul, mirror each other, as in
this explanation from the eleventh-century abbot and homilist Ælfric:

> But the might of the Holy Ghost approaches the corruptible
> water through the blessing of the priests, and it can afterwards
> wash body and soul from all sins through ghostly might. Lo we
> see two things in this one creature. According to true nature the
> water is a corruptible fluid, and according to a ghostly mystery
> has salutary power; in like manner, if we behold the holy housel
> in a bodily sense, then we see that it is a corruptible and
> changeable creature. But if we distinguish the spiritual might
> therein, then understand we that there is life in it, and that it
> gives immortality to those who partake of it with belief. Great is
> the difference between the invisible might of the holy housel and
> the visible appearance of its own nature.[12]

This text has been associated with the Eucharistic views of Ratramnus,
later condemned as heresy. That is not to say that Ælfric was a heretic;
rather, the distinctions that led to this view being heretical arose after
his time. Ælfric exhibits greater clarity on the visible-invisible
distinction, and is less clear on the spiritual nature *because* he has no
reason to perceive the natural and supernatural as so distinct as to
require explanation of how one could be in the other. Consequently,
from a post-twelfth-century view in which the material is wholly

distinct from the spiritual, this passage could look mildly heretical because it appears to suggest that the Eucharist is corruptible.[13]

Because the early medieval Christian view of nature as spiritual is so close to Germanic animism, the latter survives in part through the former. The combination of the pagan and the Christian view of the interconnectedness of nature and supernature, microcosm and macrocosm, can be found in both liturgical and medical manuscripts, in which Christian ritual and prayer are used as an effective way of tapping spiritual power to cure. For example, the tenth-century *Leofric Missal* included exorcisms and blessings of oil and salt that were themselves exorcised from liturgical practice after the twelfth century; meanwhile the popular tenth-century medical manuscript *Lacnunga* had similar Latin blessings for the same objects as part of its set of charm-remedies.[14]

The "Field Ceremonies" quoted at the beginning is the most famous example of this mixture of liturgy and charm-remedy, calling on both Father God and a subordinate Mother Earth.[15] This is a world in which earth can be anthropomorphized and addressed as a principle created by God, and with no sense of contradiction with the Christian cosmology. To say that these self-proclaimed Christians were ignorant of monotheism and not fully Christian avoids the issue of how they perceived their reality as God created it. These ceremonies indicate a strong Christian sense of God's presence governing over the natural world: they have incorporated their folk sense of nature into the Christian cosmology quite neatly, in a holistic view of the world that is both metaphysically and personally satisfying. What a comforting ritual this must have been in light of the insecurities of agricultural life in the early Middle Ages: to be able to call upon the God who made it all, to make physical contact with the elements themselves and make them right with the larger cosmic forces, and to both appeal and command, with the voice of God, quoted straight from Genesis 1, "*Crescite*, grow, *et multiplicamini*, and multiply," thus invoking the creative power present in the very beginning of nature.

These views of nature were a product of the Germanic-Christian cultural synthesis and can be traced back to at least 600 and Pope Gregory the Great (590–604), who stands at the crossroads between Late Antiquity and the early Middle Ages. He still retained some sense of the Pseudo-Dionysian mystical distinctions in which interior spiritual experiences were differentiated from rational orders of thought;

nonetheless, the majority of his work that had an impact on succeeding generations was much more down to earth, concerned more with physical manifestations of spirituality rather than interior experience as a separate phenomena.

In one instance in Gregory's biography of St. Benedict, Gregory used terminology reminiscent of the Pseudo-Dionysian mystical tradition: when Peter questioned Gregory about Benedict abandoning his wayward monks and going off to "live with himself," Gregory explained that Benedict was withdrawing in such a way as to be both outside himself and inside himself "in a state of ecstasy," a Pseudo-Dionysian explanation of a mystical state.[16] However, the majority of the biography is taken up with recounting stories of Benedict's saintly character, especially through miraculous occurances. For example, when the earth refused to accept the dead body of a young monk who was guilty of loving his parents too much, Benedict gave the monk's friends a consecrated wafer to put on his breast, and the earth received him. This miracle demonstrated, according to Gregory, "how much merit Benedict had in the eyes of the Lord Jesus Christ, since even the earth cast out the body of the monk who lacked his blessing."[17]

It is this kind of Late Antique spirituality that continued into the early medieval period, rather than the more intellectualized philosophy of the Pseudo-Dionysian mystical tradition.[18] The hagiographical tradition of the early Middle Ages followed this pattern of miraculous proof established by Pope Gregory, and, along with the developing cult of the saints, carried on this spiritual-physical connection. Intimate contact between the saint and God was presumed, rather than made explicit as in Late Antique or high medieval mystical writing; proof of sanctity lay not in the recounting of a mystical experience but in the miracles accomplished as a *result* of the saint's intimate contact with God.

Spiritual understanding and change could be accomplished and manifested in and through the physical realm, which helps explain the simplistic and seemingly barbaric view of conversion in sixth-century historians like Gregory of Tours. Conversion by the sword and by the spirit, success in one demonstrating the other, is evidence of a lack of distinction between spiritual and physical changes. Therefore, it was not paradoxical for them to conquer a pagan people, their success being evidence of God's favor, and then demand conversion as a condition of the peace settlement.

Similarly, Gregory of Tours does not distinguish natural from supernatural agencies: human situations (political in particular) were affected by spiritual realities manifested in the physical world. For example, after recounting how an army burned the church containing the relics of St. Martin, he explained that the invaders decided to back down when they saw the miraculous power of the saint manifested in the survival of the altar cloths and some herbs also placed on the altar.[19] Giselle de Nies argues in her book on Gregory of Tours that there is a logical coherence in his apparent ramblings, located in his use of God's design in nature, including the miraculous. God is always speaking through the natural realm; He raises His voice when using miracles.[20]

Both Pope Gregory I and Gregory of Tours consistently used the natural world as interactive with humans: nature communicated God's messages to humans, and humans had the ability to command nature. Gregory of Tours was convinced that natural phenomena in the skies were portents, usually a warning of some great political change. Even when he wasn't sure what the message was, he nonetheless believed they should be read as from God: "Portents appeared. Rays of light were seen in the northern sky, although, indeed, this happens often."[21] Saints, by virtue of their spirituality, demonstrated an Adam-like power over the natural world: a raven fed by Benedict obeyed the saint's command to throw away some poisoned bread given to him by an enemy.[22] Likewise, the natural world served as a necessary corrective to the spiritual life: Benedict cured his lustful temptation (a physical/spiritual battle) by throwing himself into a nettle bush: "So through the wounds of the skin he drew out from his body the wound of the mind by changing his lust to pain."[23] There was a *physicality*, then, about their spirituality that the modern mind finds disconcerting.

The link between spiritual/moral character and power or success in the natural or political realm is very strong in early medieval hagiography. Physical events of any kind could be read as signs or messages from God, usually used to substantiate the power of God resident in a saint. This belief is evident in the eighth century, in which Bede establishes an Anglo-Saxon tradition of saint's lives, particularly the power of pious saint-kings. The stories he tells link physical actions and rewards with spiritual qualities and rewards. For example, King Oswald was pious because of his humility, kindness, and generosity, for which God rewarded him with a great earthly kingdom, as well as eternal rewards. In one episode, Bede describes how Oswald gave up his own feast at Easter to the crowd of needy people at his door. Bishop and Saint Aidan then declared that the king's right hand would never perish, a prophecy fulfilled when the severed arm and hand of Oswald were kept, uncorrupted, as a venerated relic.[24] The lack of corruption in the body proved the piety of the soul; and the physical remains continued to serve as a spiritual gateway.[25]

Physical manifestations of power in relics and saints were a kind of "divine medicine," a favorite term that not only evokes healing as an analogy, but is also manifested literally: the physical healing is frequently the manifestation of the spiritual healing (conversion, confession, or overcoming sin). The Gospels in the New Testament set the precedent for this when Jesus said to the paralyzed man, "Take heart, son; your sins are forgiven." His explanation was to ask: "Which is easier: to say, 'Your sins are forgiven,' or to say, 'Get up and walk'? But so that you may know that the Son of Man has authority on earth to forgive sins . . . ," he then healed the man.[26] Paradoxically, the New Testament established another tradition of miracles, which also followed in the medieval hagiography: when asked about a man blind from birth ("Who sinned, this man or his parents?"), Jesus replied: "Neither . . . but this happened so that the work of God might be displayed in his life."[27] Consequently, miracles in the natural realm, particularly healing, can serve either to induce or manifest a spiritual change in the person, or simply to prove God's power and His authority resident in a holy person.

Such imitation of Christ by saints sets up a system of veneration that counteracts pagan idols but is not to be confused with them. The presence of a monotheistic deity at the center of the cult of the saints preserves it from theological error; however, in the *popular practice* of the cult of the saints, the focus on the more human and accessible saint as a channel for God does leave it open to accusations of idol worship. Bernard of Angers, in the late tenth century, defended relics and the cult of the saints as not idol worship or paganism, but as "revering the memory of a martyr in honor of the highest God," proven by such miracles as the healing of a boy born blind, lame, deaf, and mute who merited "divine medicine."[28] Miracles and healing are seen as manifestations of the supreme deity, through whatever natural or human channels.

In this context of physical expressions of spirituality, the relationship of body to soul, seen to unseen, was a complex one, whose mystery was not unraveled by separating them but in understanding how one speaks of the other—the physical is always a spiritual message. The life of this world was a mysterious business, a mystery to be resolved through spiritual understanding. The modern Western world has lost, to a large degree, that sense of mystery in everyday life, only reclaiming it when something extraordinary (i.e., beyond human control) occurs (which we like to think doesn't happen very often). The modern cosmology is constituted on laws of nature based on observation; early medieval worldviews constructed a spiritual realm based on Scripture, tradition, authority, and experience.

Consequently, in early medieval worldviews, almost everything that happened was inexplicable from human sense observation and human reason: in other words, humans by themselves cannot explain the world they see around them without reference to concepts outside human understanding, concepts revealed through revelation. The world was then made explicable by invoking a cosmology inhabited largely by unseen agencies (God, angels, demons, spirits); knowledge of this unseen realm was therefore based not on external senses but on interior understanding granted from divine authority outside an individual (revelation, Scripture, the teachings of the church): it was an "imaginative" endeavor.

As a result of this epistemology, the questions asked about observed phenomena were not of the "how" kind, but of the "who," not how did the lightening happen and why, but who made the lightening and why—a very different kind of question based on an animate, purposeful creation. When Ælfric tried to explain the mystery of man's creation out of dust, he likened it to the equally mysterious growth of trees from seeds: God accomplished both in His own mysterious way; humans should not be so concerned with how He did it, but with who He is who did it.

> Now we cannot investigate how of that dirt he [God] made flesh and blood, bones and skin, hair and nails. Men often see that of one little seed comes a great tree, but in the seed we can see neither root, nor rind, nor boughs, nor leaves: but the same God who draws forth from the seed tree, and fruits, and leaves, may from dust raise flesh and bones, sinews and hair.[29]

Similarly, in explaining Christ's miracle of the loaves and fishes, he emphasized that this was no more astounding than the multiplication of seed in the harvest: whether it was an ordinary event like plants growing or an unusual event like a miracle, it was the same power in the hands of Christ doing both. Therefore, there was no reason to distinguish the supernatural from the natural:

> God has done many *wonders* and daily works; but those *wonders* are much weakened in the sight of men, because they are so usual. It is a greater *wonder* that God Almighty every day feeds all the world, and directs the good, than that *wonder* was that he filled five thousand men with five loaves: but men wondered at that, not because it was a greater *wonder*, but because it was unusual. Who now gives fruit to our fields, and multiplies the harvest from a few grains of corn, but he who multiplied the five loaves? The might was there in Christ's hands, and the five loaves were, as it were, seed, not sown in the earth, but multiplied by him who created the earth.[30]

Ælfric made some attempt, here and elsewhere, to distinguish between the ordinary and the unusual, but the natural or supernatural origins of a phenomenon were not significant. What was important was the spiritual source: God or possibly the Devil or other spiritual entities. Since God is the origin of both the natural and the supernatural, and is equally present in both, the distinction between them is unimportant. Any phenomena that cannot be explained as consistent with the revealed character of God must be the trick or illusion of the Devil, whose purposes are very different from God's.[31]

    This type of explanation had the added benefit of giving meaning to everything, and was thus eminently logical. It is just that the criteria for accepting evidence was different: in the early medieval use of the Latin word *scientia* (knowledge), there was no distinction between knowledge by revelation or knowledge through human reason: it either was of God or was not. The post-twelfth-century view of this term, as science, has evolved to the point today of eliminating revelation altogether, relying entirely on human reason. The whole faith-reason debate, and its consequences in Western history, was a product of the intellectual climate of the twelfth century; prior to that, knowledge was explored within a different framework, in which knowing was based on an authoritative, revealed cosmology governed by spiritual entities not directly perceived by the senses but understood through the imagination.

To understand how this spiritualized nature functioned, we need
to realize how Christianity established itself in Europe between the
seventh and eleventh centuries: the religion transformed the animistic
view of the Germanic peoples by providing it with a new system of
interpretation or perception for the human experience. The sensory
reality was unchanged, the belief in an animated nature was retained,
but how an individual reconciled himself to that reality was clarified by
Christian doctrine. The Germanic perceptions of nature as alive with
spirits slid over into the Christian ones of a God-inhabited nature with a
great deal of ease, as seen in the medical remedies; early medieval
Christian literature sought to impose a value system on this experience
of nature: nature as a moral tale, as a revelation or message from God,
revealing good and evil.

One example that shows this spiritualized view of nature
emphasizes as well the revelatory message of both miraculous and
natural events. Bernard of Angers tells the story of Vuitbert, a priest
whose eyes were maliciously torn out by his godfather, the evil priest
Gerald. St. Foy eventually restored Vuitbert's sight, which is the main
point of the story, but Bernard made some interesting comments about
the gruesome scene of Gerald ripping out Vuitbert's eyes "with the
same fingers which were consecrated to holding the body of Christ." In
such a horrific act, one may ask, where is the grace of God? Bernard
seems to answer that question in the next section:

> These things did not happen without the presence of the
> heavenly power, which does not abandon men who call upon
> divine assistance and is always near those calling on it in truth
> and which passes judgment for those enduring injury. Those who
> were present immediately saw a snow white dove, or as the doer
> of this evil deed claimed, a magpie. This magpie or dove took up
> the bloody eyes of the poor unfortunate and rising high above
> the earth carried them toward Conques.[32]

There follows an explanation by Bernard as to why the evil Gerald saw
the bird as black rather than white: his perception of reality was literally
colored by his evil conscience. Sensory experience of the natural world
is bound up with the inner man; consequently, the inner man achieves
spiritual enlightenment through reflection on the natural world. This
accords well both with the Christian tradition (as Paul in Romans 1:20
says, "For since the creation of the world God's invisible qualities—his

eternal power and divine nature—have been clearly seen, being understood from what has been made") and with the Germanic traditions of a living nature manifesting a spiritual reality.

Anglo-Saxon Examples of Nature Mysticism

The large body of vernacular literature in Anglo-Saxon England affords us a unique view of this nature-mysticism blending Germanic traditions into Christian ones. Between the eighth and the eleventh centuries, a surprising abundance of literature of various types was written in the Anglo-Saxon language rather than Latin. The native language reveals more of the conceptual worldview operating in these centuries. Two types of sources are particularly enlightening for the study of nature-mysticism: the Venerable Bede (673–735), who in many ways lays the foundation for later Anglo-Saxon homiletic and hagiographical writing, reveals the basic Anglo-Saxon view of the environment as it was Christianized; and the meditative poems of the tenth century—*The Wanderer, The Seafarer*, and *The Dream of the Rood*—demonstrate nature as a means of spiritual experience through a physical or vicarious pilgrimage or conversion.

Meditation is of course frequently a prelude to a mystical experience; and the Pseudo-Dionysian tradition of the previous period (Late Antiquity) and the subsequent period (the High Middle Ages) discusses the philosophical stages of meditation extensively. Closely related is the dream-state, seen as a deathlike experience, and hence spiritually revealing. Even though writers in this in-between period, the Early Middle Ages, do not analyze philosophically these states of being, they nonetheless employ them as a means of expressing spiritual ideas. In the Late Antique and High Medieval periods, these stages of meditation were made explicit in the analysis of the mystical experience. In the early medieval period, meditation and dreaming are there in the literature without any explicit discussion of mystical states.

What has happened is that the classical philosophical underpinnings of mysticism, as in the cosmological tradition of Pseudo-Dionysus, receded into the background, and the Gregorian tradition of nature as miraculous prevailed, infused with a more naturalistic, holistic view of spirituality from Germanic animism. Literally, everything is alive with God. In worldviews in which the fundamental dichotomies of natural-supernatural and reason-revelation were meaningless, what sorts of experiences, beliefs, and practices of individuals could then be categorized as mysticism? The term *mysticism*, defined in the earlier and later periods as a unique, transformative, otherworldly experience becomes very diffuse in this context because it is hard to find any direct reference to, or analysis of, such a mystical experience. Rather, there are stories that describe dreams or experiences in nature that reveal a spiritual truth. These stories are either exemplary or meditative, but not otherworldly; they are very much caught up in the natural world as a spiritual experience, and are unable to imagine a spiritual experience or state of being apart from this world.

Bede's story in his *Ecclesiastical History* about Caedmon's gift of song is an example of a life-changing experience of a mystical type. Caedmon, so incapable of song that he slunk out of the mead hall whenever there was singing, was given by God in a dream the miraculous ability to sing poetic praise to God. The gift was maintained by meditation on God's revelation. It is significant also that Caedmon's hymns were mainly about the Creation: this was a very experiential spirituality, located in the physical world. "Let us sing how the eternal God, the Author of all marvels, first created the heavens for the sons of men as a roof to cover them, and how their almighty Protector gave them the earth for their dwelling place."[33] Humans related to God primarily as the Creator of all that they experienced around them; and conversely, humans related to the natural world as God's creation, a revealed message of spiritual truth.

The Anglo-Saxon experience and perception of the environment therefore contributed to their spiritual understanding. Bede, like Gregory before him, taught Christian truth by explaining God's actions in the world, primarily miracles. What comes through in Bede's account of how God revealed Himself to the English is the particularly Anglo-Saxon view of nature, used as an analogy to explain conversion. In one of the most beautiful passages frequently quoted from Bede, one of King Edwin's chief men responded to Paulinus's presentation of the Christian message with this argument:

> Your Majesty, when we compare the present life of man with that time of which we have no knowledge, it seems to me like the swift flight of a lone sparrow through the banqueting hall where you sit in the winter months to dine with your thanes and counsellors. Inside there is a comforting fire to warm the room;

outside, the wintry storms of snow and rain are raging. This
sparrow flies swiftly in through one door of the hall, and out
through another. While he is inside, he is safe from the winter
storms; but after a few moments of comfort, he vanishes from
sight into the darkness whence he came. Similarly, man appears
on earth for a little while, but we know nothing of what went
before this life, and what follows. Therefore if this new teaching
can reveal any more certain knowledge, it seems only right that
we should follow it.[34]

This passage demonstrates a principle found throughout Anglo-Saxon
writing: the contrast of the civility and safety of the hall and the world
of men (kin, comitatus) versus the insecurity and harshness of the
wilderness or outside world. But it also shows how this concept of the
natural world was spiritualized: it was more than allegory, it was the
human experience itself. Soul and body came to know God through this
earthly existence. What is natural is also spiritual by definition.

The early eleventh-century poems *The Wanderer* and *The
Seafarer* demonstrate this tradition of nature-mysticism or spiritualized
nature. Both of these poems are soul-searching meditations very much
set in the natural world; their self-reflective aspects focus on the
physical rather than the spiritual. The theology was expressed not
through the language of philosophy but through rich imagery. There
was no Pseudo-Dionysian analysis of the mystical state; rather, the
meditation was expressed entirely through the physical experience of
separation, which includes loss and desire. Anne Savage, in an article
on the Old English meditative tradition, notes that there was no clear
distinction between meditation and mystical experience, no separation
of reason and emotion, or any such boundaries in these meditative
poems.[35]

The Christian theme of life as pilgrimage was presented in very
literal, physical terms by the mind of the wanderer. The exile dreamed
of what he had lost, awakening to a barren, friendless environment:

Often, when grief and sleep combined together enchain the
wretched solitary man, it seems to him in his imagination that he
is embracing and kissing his lord and laying hands and head on
his knee, just as at times previously in days of old he enjoyed the
gift-throne. Then the friendless man awakes again and sees
before him tawny waves, sea-birds bathing, spreading their
wings, rime falling and snow, mingled with hail.[36]

The wanderer's experiences caused him to reflect on the transitoriness of earthly existence, in the famous "ubi sunt" (where are . . . ?) passage; the concluding wisdom earned by this experience is to seek consolation from the immutable heavenly realm. The majority of the poem, then, is a reflective description of the earthly experience that leads to this wisdom, not a meditation on the joys of the spiritual kingdom to come: the only spiritual experience the wanderer has was through the physical journey of this world.

The Seafarer also uses the contrast of the safe life with men versus the traumatic experience of a traveler; but the seafarer feels compelled to choose the way of alienation, if only to know that truth, that this world is transitory:

> Now, therefore, my thought roams beyond the confines of my heart; my mind roams widely with the ocean tide over the whale's home, over earth's expanses, and comes back to me avid and covetous; the lone flier calls and urges the spirit irresistibly along the whale-path over the waters of oceans, because for me the pleasures of the Lord are more enkindling than this dead life, this ephemeral life on land.[37]

Seeking out the direct experience of the natural world in all its wildness is here part of a planned spiritual journey, in the tradition of monasticism. John Shields, in analyzing *The Seafarer*, sees the poem as a spiritual exercise for someone aiming for perfection of the soul, and yet the poem is not in itself a mystical revelatory experience such as we find in later periods.[38]

In both *The Wanderer* and *The Seafarer*, the transitoriness of the physical world is contrasted with the eternal, in a melancholy way, without any sense of an experience of the other world—just a longing for it and its permanence. Meditation is a process of the mind and imagination in relation to the sensory experience of life; there is no interior spiritual revelation separate from the insight gained from this sensory experience.

The Dream of the Rood most clearly represents a life-transforming experience in the vision of the cross as a means of conversion. This is the closest to a "mystical" experience, mediated through not just a vision but also a physical object: the tree from which the cross was made was endowed with a heroic personality and great transformative power. This poem, even more than the other two,

emphasizes the difference between this material, transitory world and
the eternal realm, in this case by meditating on the spiritual meaning of
a physical object in the tradition of relics.

Interiority is established through the dream mode: "Lo, I will tell
of a wonderful dream which came to me in the middle of the night,
when speech-bearers are asleep."[39] The vision is therefore not part of
the daily life of men or subject to their analysis, and yet it is very
sensory on a visual level. The dreamer's perception of the cross on two
levels simultaneously, as blood-stained and bejeweled, invokes this
contrast of two realities intertwined. The cross's experience of life on
earth is similar to the wanderer's and the seafarer's: pain and exile must
be endured to reach glory. The anthropomorphized tree is part of God's
creation, serving and glorifying Him just as human beings should. This
particular tree has been singled out, like Mary or one of the other saints,
for a miraculous role in God's plan; and like the saints and their relics,
this tree functions as an exemplar and as an intermediary: the dreamer
and the reader experience a vicarious conversion.

Spirituality, then, in the Anglo-Saxon meditative tradition, is
expressed and experienced through the world God made. Going even
further, Steven Glosecki (*Shamanism and Old English Poetry*), in a
daring and yet convincing analysis, sees all of these meditative poems
as containing a shamanistic type of ecstasy, an animistic form of
mysticism that has effective power in nature. The poem does more than
create an emotional mood; the words themselves in their poetic,
chanted form have the power to change lives. Glosecki, therefore, does
not see that much distance between charm remedies and poems such as
The Dream of the Rood, *The Wanderer*, and *The Seafarer*. Rather, we
have read these latter poems as affective poetry, according to our
modern poetic traditions, rather than as effective, manipulating the
connection between natural and supernatural power.[40] Implicit in this
view of reality is the inseparability of physical and spiritual strength,
evident in hagiography, medical remedies, sermons, and poetry.

Conclusions

We have a tendency to make distinctions based on post-twelfth-
century thought between such things as natural-supernatural, reason-
revelation, affective-effective, and emotional-rational that have no

applicability in this earlier period. Using these pairs of opposites only helps us see how they were, in fact, part of a whole and not even intertwined, since a real separation only becomes apparent later.

Mystics and mysticism flourished in the High Middle Ages because the twelfth-century renaissance intellectuals began invoking this distinction between natural and supernatural, reason and revelation, and began rejecting the popular, more holistic views (which nonetheless continued in mystical writing). Hence mystics form a separate phenomena, as they are today—something quite unusual. In fact, that is one reason why thirteenth- and fourteenth-century mystics wrote: to show the difference between their experience and the intellectual tradition that had separated itself from experiential understandings of reality.[41]

On the other hand, the contrast between the early Middle Ages and post-twelfth-century thought shouldn't obscure the essential connection between the two periods: later mysticism is hanging on to a sense of connectedness with nature, in opposition to the coldness and separation from nature emerging from scholasticism. When Julian of Norwich in the fourteenth century sees the meaning of the universe revealed in a little hazel nut, she has much in common with Ælfric: the sense of mystery, of powerful meaningfulness in each bit of God's creation, the macrocosm revealed in the microcosm.[42] This "non-rational" meaning is not new but old; now it is uncommon, but once it was common.

Since our notion of the mystical is a product of twelfth-century thought that began a separation between different human experiences of reality, we see that mysticism as a concept is the product of a particularly Western development of thought and calls into question its applicability to other cultures standing outside of that development. For example, what foreign baggage is attached to the word when it is imported into studies of Buddhist or Islamic mysticism?[43] Much of our notions of mysticism as a phenomenon are linked to a particular mode of rationality developed only in Western culture.

The modern Western approach to nature is nonmystical: it is either cold science or the affective approach to nature found in poetry. Lost is the sense of microcosm and macrocosm, the interconnectedness, the power of and in nature, the sense of personal meaning in nature.

I have a cartoon I use in classes to explain different modes of rationality and perceptions of reality: A son asks, "Father, tell me about the stars." The father replies, "My child, the stars are the toys of the cherubim and the beacons of the departed, they are the music of our eyes, the chimes of exultation and the sparks or our aspiration. They have lit our long journey from the swamp to this day when we stare back, reflecting their images like tears of love in a silver mirror." The son responds, "Father, I fear yours is not a scientific mind," while another character comments, "Twinkle, twinkle little star, I don't wonder what you are: you're the cooling down of gases forming into solid masses."[44] Giving this same scientific answer is the pragmatic Eustace of C.S. Lewis's Narnia tales, who is then told by a living star, "Even in your world, my son, that is not what a star is but only what it is made of."[45] Truly, the modern scientific view frequently cuts off the sense of wonder, and is only countered by the affective view of poetry. But in going back to the early medieval period, we find a total sense of awe and wonder, coupled with an effective use of nature devoid of any "scientific" investigation.

The larger picture is this: Christianity as a religion has an orderly component and a spiritual one: the spiritual manifests itself in various ways (for example, monasticism, mendicants, heresy, and mysticism) in a creative tension with the intellectual and hierarchical orderliness of the Church. Mysticism thus plays a role in balancing the Christian tradition. But the nature of this balance has changed over time: with the increasing secularization of Western society, the mystical balance provided by religion declined, while the scientific rationality followed its own secular course, with the results seen all around us. Our views of nature—affective, effective, manipulative, spiritual, scientific—are a product of this development.

NOTES

1. Godfrid Storms, trans., *Anglo-Saxon Magic* (The Hague: Martinus Nijhoff), 1948), 172–77.
2. On what the twelfth-century renaissance means as an important intellectual and cultural transition, see Robert L. Benson and Giles Constable, eds., *Renaissance and Renewal in the Twelfth Century* (Cambridge, Mass.: Harvard Univ. Press, 1982), and Benedicta Ward, *Miracles and the Medieval Mind* (Philadelphia, 1982).

3. Ninian Smart, *Worldviews: Crosscultural Explorations of Human Beliefs* (New York: Charles Scribner's Sons, 1983), 6–8.

4. See Geza von Molnar, "Aspects of Western Mystical Tradition and the Concept of 'Education' (Bildung) in German Literature," *Studia Mystica* I (1979): 5, and Michael N. Nagler, "Mysticism: A Hardheaded Definition for a Romantic Age," *Studia Mystica* I (1979): 39; also, F.C. Happold, *Mysticism: A Study and an Anthology* (London: Penguin, 1970), 16–17, 20–21, 24–25.

5. There are combinations of the two as well. The Pseudo-Dionysian tradition used a Neoplatonic notion of ideas and language that relied on a kind of correspondence between the ideal realm and human thought that allowed for some kind of theoretical explanation of the mystical experience. Most of these are manuals detailing the steps to perfection or union with God (one cannot, however, aim to have a mystical experience, since you would be focusing on self rather than God, essentially going the opposite direction). Descriptive writings explained the mystical experience by personal example, setting up in some cases a role model for others; these descriptions are consequently culture-specific.

6. Steven T. Katz, "The 'Conservative' Character of Mystical Experience," in *Mysticism and Religious Traditions*, ed. Steven T. Katz (Oxford: Oxford University Press, 1983), 4–6.

7. T.S. Eliot, "Four Quartets: The Dry Salvages" in *The Complete Poems and Plays* (New York: Harcourt, Brace & World, Inc., 1971), 133.

8. Hans Penner, "The Mystical Illusion," in *Mysticism and Religious Traditions*, 89–116; on the same issue in that volume of essays, see Robert Gimello, "Mysticism in its Contexts," 61–88, and H.P. Owen, "Experience and Dogma in the English Mystics," 148–56. See also Peter Moore, "Christian Mysticism and Interpretation: Some Philosophical Issues Illustrated in the Study of the Medieval English Mystics," *The Medieval Mystical Tradition in England: Exeter Symposium IV* (Cambridge: D.S. Brewer, 1987), 154–176.

9. Caroline Walker Bynum, *Jesus as Mother: Studies in the Spirituality of the of the High Middle Ages* (Berkeley: University of California Press, 1982), 12.

10. For discussion of Germanic beliefs, see: J.H.G. Grattan and Charles Singer, *Anglo-Saxon Magic and Medicine* (London: Oxford University Press, 1952), 52–62; Stephen Glosecki, *Shamanism and Old English Poetry* (New York: Garland, 1989), chapter 2, "Vestiges of Animism"; Gale R. Owen, *Rites and Religions of the Anglo-Saxons* (Totowa, N.J.: Barnes & Noble, 1981); H.R. Ellis Davidson, *Myths and Symbols in Pagan Europe: Early Scandinavian and Celtic Religious* (Syracuse, N.Y.: Syracuse University Press, 1988).

11. *Lacnunga*, MS. Harley 585, ff. 160a–163a, trans. Storms, *Anglo-Saxon Magic*, 186–191. As two separate charms (LXXIX b and LXXX b), see translation by Grattan and Singer, *Magic and Medicine*, 151–157.

12. Ælfric, A Sermon on the Sacrifice of Easter-Day, Benjamin Thorpe, ed. & trans., *The Homilies of the Anglo-Saxon Church: the first part containing the Sermones Cahtolici or Homilies of Ælfric in the original Anglo-Saxon, with an English version*, 2 (London: Aelfric Society, 1846; repr. New York: Johnson Reprint Corp., 1971), 271.

13. Numerous articles have been written about Ælfric's position, some seeing him as a proto-Protestant, an anachronism that distorts his views: see Luke M. Reinsma, *Ælfric: An Annotated Bibliography* (New York: Garland, 1987), entries 631–774. On Rantramnus, see discussion by Brian Stock, "The Eucharist and Nature," in *The Implications of Literacy: Written Language and Models of Interpretation in the Eleventh and Twelfth Centuries* (Princeton, N.J.: Princeton University Press, 1983), 241–277.

14. F.E. Warren, *The Leofric Missal* (Oxford: Clarendon Press, 1883; repr. 1968), 223, 249–257; *Lacnunga* ff. 192b–193a, Grattan and Singer, *Magic and Medicine*, 202–205.

15. For studies of this remedy, see John D. Niles, "The AEcerbot Ritual in Context," *Old English Literature in Context*, ed. John D. Niles (Totowa, N.J.: Rowman & Littlefield, 1980), 44–56, and Thomas D. Hill, "The Averbot Charm and Its Christian User," *Anglo-Saxon England* 6 (1977): 213–221.

16. Book 2:III, in *The Dialogues of Gregory the Great, Book Two: Saint Benedict*, trans. Myra L. Uhlfelder (Indianapolis: Bobbs-Merrill, 1967), 10.

17. Book 2:XXIV, Gregory, *Dialogues* (Uhlfelder, 34–35).

18. On Late Antique spirituality, see Peter Brown, *The Cult of the Saints: Its Rise and Function in Latin Christianity* (Chicago: University of Chicago Press, 1981). These miracle stories have baffled some scholars because they appear inconsistent and irrational from our post-twelfth century view. In fact, they were very rational within an early medieval mode of rationality, as William McCready, in *Signs and Sanctity: Miracles in the Thought of Gregory the Great* (Toronto: Pontifical Institute of Medieval Studies, 1989), as well as others, has demonstrated.

19. Book VII:12, in *Gregory of Tours: The History of the Franks*, trans. Lewis Thorpe (New York: Penguin, 1974), 395–96.

20. Giselle de Nies, *Views from a Many Windowed Tower: Studies of Imagination in the Works of Gregory of Tours* (Amsterdam: Rodopi, 1987), 123.

21. Books VIII:8 and VII:11, *Gregory of Tours*, 439–40, 395.

22. Book 2:VIII, Gregory, *Dialogues* (Uhlfelder, 15–16).

23. Book 2:II, Gregory, *Dialogues* (Uhlfelder, 7).

24. Book III:6, in Bede, *A History of the English Church and People*, trans. Leo Sherley-Price (Baltimore: Penguin), 147.

25. See Charles G. Loomis, "Folklore of the Uncorrupted Body," *Journal of American Folklore* 48 (1935): 374–78.

26. Matthew 9:1–8, *New International Version*.

27. John 9:1–3, *New International Version*.

28. Miracles of Saint Foy, XII, XXVIII, trans. in Patrick Geary, ed., *Readings in Medieval History* (Peterborough, Ont.: Broadview Press, 1989), 352.

29. Ælfric, The First Sunday after Easter, ed. and trans. Benjamin Thorpe, *The Homilies of the Anglo-Saxon Church: The Sermones Catholici or Homilies of Ælfric*, 1 (London: Aelfric Society, 1844; repr. New York: Johnson Reprint Corp, 1971), 236–37.

30. Ælfric, Midlent Sunday, Thorpe, *Homilies* 1, 184–87.

31. See, for example, the story of Benedict and the imaginary kitchen fire in Gregory's *Dialogues*, Book II:IX–X (Uhlfelder, pp. 18–19); or the story of a girl turned into a mare revealed to be an illusion by St. Macarius, told by Ælfric in *Ælfric's Lives of the Saints*, Volume 1, ed. Walter W. Skeat Early English Text Society vols. 76, 82 (London: Oxford University Press, 1881, 1885; repr. as one volume 1966), 471–73. The Devil cannot change the natural world, only create deceptive illusions.

32. Miracles of St. Foy, in Geary, *Readings*, 347.

33. Book IV:24, in Bede, *History* (Sherley-Price, 245–247).

34. Book II:13, in Bede, *History* (Sherley-Price, 124–25).

35. Anne Savage, "The Place of Old English Poetry in the English Meditative Tradition," in *Medieval Mystical Tradition in England*, 93.

36. *The Wanderer*, ll. 39–48, trans. S.A.J. Bradley, *Anglo-Saxon Poetry* (London: Dent, 1982), 323.

37. *The Seafarer*, ll. 58–66, trans. Bradley, *Anglo-Saxon Poetry*, 333.

38. John C. Sheilds, "The Seafarer as a Meditation," *Studia Mystica* III (1980): 29–41.

39. *The Dream of the Rood*, ll. 1–3, own translation (also available in Bradley, *Anglo-Saxon Poetry*, 160–63).

40. Glosecki, *Shamanism*, 137–38.

41. Peter Dinzelbacher, "The Beginnings of Mysticism Experienced in Twelfth-Century England" in *Medieval Mystical Tradition in England*, 111–131.

42. *Julian of Norwich, Showings*, trans. Edmund Colledge, O.S.A. and James Walsh, S.J. (New York: Paulist Press, 1978), 130–31.

43. Andrew Louth, *The Origins of the Christian Mystical Tradition From Plato to Denys* (Oxford: Clarendon Press, 1981), xiv, sees mysticism and theology as twin traditions in Western Christianity as Neo-Platonism and Christianity were linked in mysticism. See also Katz, "The 'Conservative' Character of Mystical Experience," in *Mysticism and Religious Traditions*, 3–60.

44. Wallace Tripp, illus., *Marquerite, Go Wash Your Feet* (Boston: Boston, Little & Co., 1985), 25.

45. C.S. Lewis, *The Voyage of the Dawn Treader* (New York: Macmillan, 1952), 180.

INDEX

For Product Safety Concerns and Information please contact our EU
representative GPSR@taylorandfrancis.com
Taylor & Francis Verlag GmbH, Kaufingerstraße 24, 80331 München, Germany